NEW YORK

CITY and STATE

First Edition
1993

TABLE OF CONTENTS

NEW YORK STATE

GUIDELINES

MAP LIST

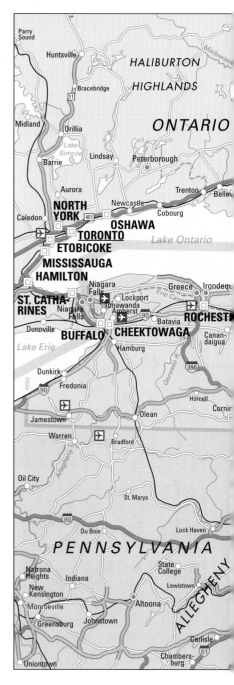

NEW YORK STATE

0	50	100 km

0   50 miles

NEW YORK – City and State

©Nelles Verlag GmbH, 80935 München
All rights reserved
ISBN 3-88618-390-4

First Edition 1993

Publisher:	Günter Nelles
Chief Editor:	Dr. Heinz Vestner
Project Editors:	Steve Cohen Anne Midgette Marton Radkai
Cartography:	Nelles Verlag GmbH Dipl. Ing. S. Stetter
DTP-Exposure:	Printshop Schimann, Brautlach
Color Separation:	Priegnitz, Gräfelfing
Printed by:	Gorenjski Tisk, Kranj Slovenia

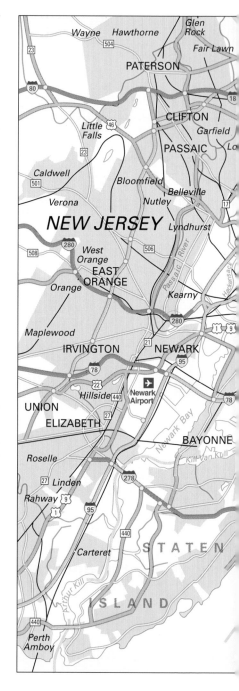

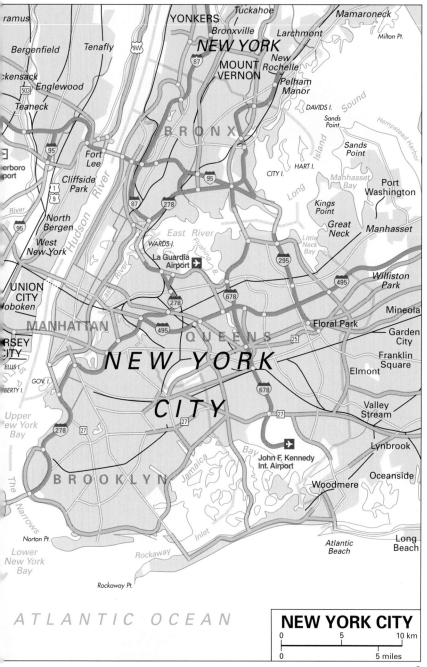

ramus
YONKERS Tuckahoe Mamaroneck
Bronxville Larchmont Milton Pt.
Bergenfield Tenafly **NEW YORK**
9W
kensack Englewood MOUNT New Rochelle
503 VERNON Pelham Manor
Teaneck DAVIDS I. Sound
Sands Point Hempstead Harbor
B R O N X
Sands Point
rboro 95 Fort Lee HART I. Port Washington
port CITY I. Manhasset Bay
Cliffside Park 95 Kings Point
9 87 278 Great Neck Manhasset
River
95 North Bergen East River
West New York WARDS I. Little Neck Bay
La Guardia Airport 295
UNION CITY Williston Park
oboken 278 678 495
MANHATTAN Mineola
RSEY 495 Q U E E N S Floral Park Garden City
CITY Franklin Square
LLIS I. **N E W Y O R K** 25 Elmont
GOV. I. 678
BERTY I. **C I T Y** Valley Stream
Upper ew York Bay 278 27 27 27 Lynbrook
B R O O K L Y N Jamaica Bay Oceanside
John F. Kennedy Int. Airport Woodmere
Norton Pt. Atlantic Beach Long Beach
The Narrows
Lower New York Bay Rockaway Inlet
Rockaway Pt.

A T L A N T I C   O C E A N

NEW YORK CITY

0   5   10 km

0   5 miles

HISTORY

New York's first inhabitants were tribes of Indians who found everything they needed to live comfortably in the area. The New York of those days was comprised of barren salt marshes in the area south of today's Wall Street, and hilly forests bisected by life-giving streams in the midtown area, opening into broad peaceful meadows and fertile farming lands in Harlem and the Bronx. The Algonquin-speaking Indians gradually abandoned their nomadic lifestyle, built villages of bark huts, grew maize and beans, smoked home-grown tobacco and hunted or trapped beavers, deer and wild turkeys. They were gradually absorbed into the Five Nations, a loose confederation of Iroquois tribes called to life by a Mohawk chief named Hiawatha. It was a rudimentary Indian political system that might have successfully resisted the white man had it come later and been better organized.

Europeans

Though there is little evidence to support it, the first European to discover the North American continent is alleged to have been a Viking named Leiv Eiriksson (11th century). The much-hailed Columbus never set foot on the present official territory of the USA. The Venetian Giovanni Caboto, or John Cabot, as he was better known to his British employers in 1497, and later the Florentine Giovanni da Verrazano, flying the French

Preceding pages: Lady Liberty, the symbol of New York. Pantomime art on the streets of the city. Skyscraper jungle. On location in Central Park. Left: The marriage of Hiawatha, leader of the Five Nations.

flag, actually cruised along the North American coast. Verrazano, in search of the Northwest Passage to the Pacific, made a forced landing on Long Island and reported his findings to his employer François I of France.

Nearly 100 years later, in 1609, the British explorer Henry Hudson, sailing in the *Half Moon* for the Dutch East India Company, discovered the convenient depths of New York Harbor for shipping traffic. He also found hospitable Indians who called their land *Mannahattanink*, a word probably meaning "island." Hudson continued up the river that now bears his name, in search of that still elusive Northwest Passage, and discovered Hudson Bay. The combination of navigable waterways and friendly Indians willing to trade in furs (mink, otter and beaver) led to the establishment of trading posts, among them Fort Nassau, near present-day Albany.

Dutch settlers began arriving in 1619 and in 1624 a small party of eight families stayed downriver at Nut Island (now known as Governor's Island), while others marched on to the Fort Nassau settlement. The Dutch called their colony Nieuw Nederland. The earliest Manhattan residents were settlers working for the Dutch West India Company who landed in 1625. They founded a colony south of today's Wall Street to avoid overcrowding on Nut Island. In 1626, Peter Minuit, a businessman who ran the trading company and served as governor of the new Dutch colony, bought Manhattan for 60 guilders' (the equivalent of $24) worth of baubles from Indians who happened to be passing through, and who therefore thought they were getting a great deal. New Amsterdam, the down-river capital of Dutch commerce, which would later become New York City, was modeled after the settlers' motherland, with tulip-filled gardens, a windmill, a canal and houses built in the typical Dutch style. Under Governor William Kieft a defen-

sive wall was built around the city, hence the name Wall Street, which traces one section of the old fortification.

An International City

Nieuw Nederland (New Netherland) extended from about Virginia in the south to the New England states in the north. The rest of eastern continental America was occupied by the British, French and Spanish. By the early 1640s, New Amsterdam had started opening its doors to traders other than the Dutch.

The governor of New Amsterdam as of 1646 – and indeed the last Dutch governor of New Netherland – was Peter Stuyvesant, an austere and tough captain who had lost a leg to a Portuguese cannon ball in a sea battle near Curaçao. He hobbled around his little overseas fief on a wooden peg decorated with silver studs.

Above: Henry Hudson explored the river named after him. Right: Manhattan in the days when it was called Nieuw Amsterdam.

During his tenure the colony doubled its land-holdings and population. Stuyvesant ruled the colony for seventeen prosperous but troubled years, exacting various taxes from his increasing number of subjects, persecuting Jews and Quakers, and limiting the consumption of alcohol, which came as quite a shock to the community, which drew considerable comfort economic and otherwise from its many grog shops.

There were some improvements in the political administration under Stuyvesant, however. By 1653, the city had its first representative government modeled after the common council of the Hague. Religious tolerance was officially instituted, and new laws further opened up trade barriers and eased the way to private ownership of land. Nearby English settlers from New England started coming in larger numbers to the city, followed by other Europeans, including Germans, Swedes, Italians, Finns, French, Spaniards and the Irish. New Amsterdam was already a fairly significant center of inter-

t' Fort nieuw Amsterdam op de Manhatans

national commerce. No less than eighteen languages were spoken here, and its population mix included an enclave of freed African slaves, who lived in the area where SoHo is today.

In 1664, a British naval force led by Colonel Richard Nicholls landed at Nut and Long Islands, and staked a British claim for the territory of New Netherland. King Charles II had granted these lands to his brother, the Duke of York, under claims dating back to John Cabot's explorations in 1498. Stuyvesant, whose tyrannical rule had earned him few friends, found little support for defense among his fellow Dutch. He resisted a British blockade of the harbor for eleven days. The city was subsequently rechristened New York in honor of the Duke. In fact, the entire colony was called New York for a while, until it was broken up into smaller units to ease administration. As for Stuyvesant, he retired to his farm where he died in 1672. In 1673, the Dutch were temporarily put back in power and New York was re-

named New Orange. By 1674, the British were in control again.

For the first few decades the British let their colony take care of itself. As the 17th century wore on, however, the Crown sought to increase its control over its distant subjects. The administrative reforms bunching New York and New Jersey together with New England and a tighter regulation of trade gradually created bad feelings between the Americans and the British. Among the reactions against royal iniquity was a short-lived revolt instigated by James Leisler, a German resident, in 1689. He seized the fort below Wall Street, and even managed to govern the city for almost two years. The rebellion was ultimately quashed and Mr Leisler was hanged for treason.

In 1712, a group of slaves revolted without any success. Though not specifically anti-British, this was a cry against the establishment and could thus be considered as part of New York's heritage of being cantankerous. Other avenues of dissent developed during the 1734 trial of

publisher Peter Zenger. The city's first newspaper, The New York *Gazette,* had been established in 1725 essentially as a mouthpiece for the British governors. Zenger decided to offer the public a different point of view and established the independent New York *Weekly Journal.* It printed a variety of pointed satirical cartoons lambasting the British overlords and articles exposing poverty, corruption and injustice.

The British decided to muzzle Zenger with a libel charge, but surprisingly, he was acquitted by the courts, setting a precedent for freedom of speech and the press that would later become a basic pillar of the American Constitution.

The Revolution

The war that led to the founding of the USA was based on certain political and

Above: The spirit of '76 is in their eyes.
Right: George Washington takes the oath of office on Wall Street, April 30, 1789.

social ideals, which in turn were based on hard currency. As the British hold on North America grew in scope and in strength, the colonials felt their rights were equally being infringed upon. After the Seven Years' War (1756-63) between the British and the French, much of the territories beyond the Appalachian Range were placed under military control, which put them out of reach of willing settlers. But more significantly, in order to cover the costs of the war, the British decided to saddle the colony with taxes. Parliament passed the Revenue Act, the Sugar Act and finally the Stamp Act, all in 1764. Of course, the colonies were not represented in the said parliament. In 1765, American delegates gathered in New York and unilaterally revoked the parliamentary right to taxation. British tax collectors were attacked and British goods boycotted.

The Stamp Act was finally repealed, but Americans had smelled victory and independence. The British, for their part, sensed that colonial discipline could be restored by greater use of the stick. The Townshend Act, taxation of various colonial imports, brought about the first major confrontations, notably the Boston Massacre on March 5, 1770, which escalated over the next five years into a full-fledged war.

The British, under the able command of Lord Howe, maintained control of New York throughout the revolution. Their strong military presence in the city attracted loyalists from the areas stricken by the revolutionary virus. They enjoyed a relatively comfortable lifestyle, with theaters, balls and the usual amenities. As the war itself became acute, however, New York took on the character of a beleaguered garrison town.

On July 9, 1776, George Washington stood south of today's City Hall, and had the Declaration of Independence read to his assembled soldiers. His attempt to take the city, however, failed miserably.

Washington himself barely avoided capture. There were several skirmishes at McGown's Pass (107th Street today) and on Harlem Heights, and another resounding defeat for the Americans in the Battle of White Plains north of the city.

The cause of independence, however, was attracting the undecided sections of the colonial population. Furthermore, while Howe conquered Philadelphia in 1777, a large British force under John Burgoyne was forced to surrender at Saratoga. In 1778, France started supporting the American cause as revenge for its defeat by the British in the Seven Years' War. Washington's army recovered rapidly from a devastating winter at Valley Forge, and Captain John Paul Jones raided British supply ships.

The First National Capital

The peace process began around 1779 and ended with a treaty on September 3, 1783. The British, still stationed in New York at the end of the war of Independence, left at about the same time George Washington led his soldiers in a triumphal parade from Harlem to Canal Street on November 25, 1783. Two weeks later, at the Fraunces Tavern, which still stands today at Pearl and Broad Streets, George Washington bade farewell to his officers and resigned his commission.

His retirement was short-lived, however: On April 30, 1789, Washington took the oath of office as the first President of the United States at Federal Hall on Wall Street. He first lived at 1 Cherry Street, then at 39 Fifth Avenue, in a large red brick house with white steps.

New York, the capital of New York State from 1784-96, had also been the home of Congress since 1785 and became the first capital of the United States in 1789. Congressional meetings were held in the old City Hall. A year later the government was moved to Philadelphia, in part due to the distracting clatter of horse carts and carriages outside the meeting hall. In spite of its demotion, however, New York continued to grow. By the early 1790s, it numbered about 60,000, being the largest city in the new-born nation.

Influential New York residents began to fashion the framework for New York's preeminence as the nation's business center. Among its most illustrious residents was Alexander Hamilton, who helped frame the United States Constitution and became the first Treasury Secretary (he is portrayed on the ten-dollar bill). His Federalist political philosophy called for close cooperation between the government and the private sector, including agriculture, manufacturing, business and trade. The opposition was led by Thomas Jefferson, president from 1801 to 1809, whose first vice-president, Aaron Burr, killed Hamilton in a duel in 1804. The dual nature of American politics was already taking shape. Burr was the dynamic leader of Tammany, a partly philanthropic, partly political organization that was to play a long role and not always the cleanest one in New York City's Democratic politics.

Hamilton's foresight helped establish New York as the country's financial hub. In 1784, he founded the First Bank of the United States modeled on the Bank of England. (It was closed in 1811 by an act of Congress.) In 1791, he opened a factory in Paterson, New Jersey, and followed that up in 1792 with a stock exchange that met under a tree on Wall Street. Hamilton opened his own newspaper in 1801, the New York *Post,* which is still going strong.

Not so coincidentally perhaps, Jefferson had won the election in 1800, and freedom of the press had been written into the Constitution, giving Hamilton the gun to fire his verbal ammunition.

The 19th century opened brilliantly for New York city. The cornerstone for a new

Right: New York in the mid-19th century was one of the most important trade centers.

City Hall, still in use today, was laid on May 26, 1803. In 1807, entrepreneur Robert Fulton opened a shipping line connecting Albany and New York using steam-powered ships. In 1811, City Hall was completed and the island of Manhattan was divided into a rectangular grid above 14th Street, where previous development had been concentrated. Twelve north-south avenues were designated, numbered from east to west, each 100 feet wide. East-west streets linked the piers on the East and Hudson rivers, creating the country's largest seaport. This was the era of Jeffersonian democracy, characterized by free-wheeling trade; opening the country's western frontier (thereby beginning the slow genocide of the American Indians); industrial experimentation, the heart beat of New York City; and unlimited social and economic opportunities.

The War of 1812 with the British only temporarily cramped New York's business growth. By 1813, Fulton had already established a regular ferry link with Brooklyn. By 1818, scheduled shipping services from New York to other American ports and Europe began to move goods and passengers with reliability that encouraged more trade.

It was Governor De Witt Clinton who came up with the tax dollars to sponsor the Erie Canal, which opened in 1825 and gave trade with the interior an enormous boost. It linked Albany with Buffalo and the Great Lakes. Grain was milled and shipped to the rest of the country. Ships loaded with cotton stopped off in New York on their way to New England textile mills and returned with cloth for the city's budding clothing businesses.

Immigration Commences

Even a recession in the 1830s could not stop the nation's physical growth, which in turn also created a need for labor. This was filled by waves of immi-

grants from Europe, who began arriving as early as 1819, many, if not most, arriving by way of New York.

The U.S. was an attractive place to come to, a little wild and exotic, certainly with enough space. Besides work, there was also social and political freedoms, and the dream of instant wealth, be it the Gold Rush of 1848 or the thought of oil in the bathtub in Texas later in the century. The first migratory peaks came in the late 1840s with shiploads of Irish families escaping the devastating Potato Blight of 1846, and Germans leaving their homeland after the failed revolution of 1848. The city could hardly keep up with these surges in the population, and the failure of housing and transportation to accommodate the new and usually poor arrivals became a perennial problem. The city water supplies were frequently inadequate. A proper sewer system was non-existent and garbage collection consisted mainly of pigs eating trash tossed into the streets. Typhoid and cholera were rampant.

New York's politicians quickly recognized the power of the immigrant vote, primarily the Irish, who comprised a third of the electorate. Tammany Hall responded to the situation by wooing the flotsam and jetsam of Europe for its own political ascent.

Still, business prospered as long as the supply of cheap and desperate labor did not dwindle. The rich became richer, and the poor poorer and more numerous.

And the city grew and grew. The first freight elevator was installed at 201-3 Cherry Street in 1850, a portent of heights to be scaled in the near future. Construction of Central Park began in 1858 to create some restful greenery in the midst of a city beset by perpetual growing pains.

The Civil War and its Aftermath

New York, which had already abolished slavery in the late 18th century, officially supported the the Union against the secessionists during the Civil War.

21

Abraham Lincoln, then a provincial dark horse leading a strange new political party, called the Republicans, descended from the Hamiltonian Whigs, had given his famous "Might makes right" speech condemning slavery at Cooper Union in 1860, a year before his inauguration as the 16th president of the USA. While the war raged on in the south, New York contributed economically, and intellectually, perhaps, to the war effort. The most damaging violence the city experienced during the war was four days of draft riots in July 1863, when a law was passed requiring compulsory military service, yet allowing the wealthy to finance a substitute for their service for a fee of $300. More than 1000 rioters were killed. More than 50 buildings, including the enlistment office at 677 Third Avenue, were looted and burned. Financial markets quivered and New York's population

Above: A photograph of Abraham Lincoln in 1863 reveals the strain of the Civil War.
Right: The Brooklyn Bridge in 1875.

diminished for the first time since the beginning of the Revolutionary War.

With the reopening of the Southern markets in 1865 and the united effort to reconstruct the country after four grueling years of war, New York recovered quickly. As more people moved westward, new immigrants came to take their place. The country's rapid expansion after the war required money and strong arms for construction of railroads, telegraph lines and factories. The Stock Exchange became one of the nation's vital nerve centers, where companies were created, dissolved, traded or swallowed up. Commodity exchanges were established for sales and purchases of cotton, metals, coffee, cocoa and sugar. The buccaneers of Big Business, J. P. Morgan, Cornelius Vanderbilt, Andrew Carnegie, Gould and "Bet-a-million" Gates, set to work in New York rearranging the nation's financial physiognomy, building railroads, giant corporations, banks and palaces. They worked together in cartels, and against each other when it came to profit. They were the urbane versions of Billy-the-Kid or Dillinger, ruthless and tough and yet philanthropic enough to clear their names for posterity.

When John D. Rockefeller created the Standard Oil Company in 1892, which produced, distributed and sold oil, he also created the kind of trust that was finally to shock lawmakers into passing antitrust legislation to curb the excesses of laissez-faire economy. The great financial turnover created the myth of ubiquitous money. Corporations wanting to be near the pot of gold established headquarters in New York, creating the need for more labor. New service industries evolved to cater to business in lines such as insurance, advertising, printing and publishing. Newspapers were founded by Horace Greeley and William Cullen Bryant, attracting writers such as Washington Irving and James Fenimore Cooper, Walt Whitman and many more.

New York was already the garish, noisy, bustling town it is today, a nation in its own right. In 1879, Walt Whitman gave a description in his inimitable style of "that area comprising Fourteenth Street (especially the short range between Broadway and Fifth Avenue) with Union Square, its adjacencies, and so retro-stretching down Broadway for half a mile. All the walks here are ample and free.... The whole area at 5 o'clock, the days of my observations, must have contain'd from thirty to forty thousand finely-dress'd people, all in motion, plenty of them good-looking, many beautiful women." As for Broadway, it was the city's social strip, with hotels, shops and restaurants.

William Marcy Tweed, known as "Boss Tweed," was equally a product of these wild and woolly days. Tweed, who shot up the ladder of success in New York's political establishment, was corrupt on a legendary scale. He established a powerful political machine, buying votes for favors and filling his and his cronies' pockets with bribe money. In the six years following the Civil War, Tweed and Co. are estimated to have collected some $100 million worth of golden grease. As the Commissioner of Public Works, Tweed "sold" contracts, then encouraged padded bills from the contractors and split the difference. Tweed was eventually brought down by articles in the *New York Times* and Thomas Nast's explicit cartoons in *Harper's Weekly*. Tweed ultimately and ironically died in Ludlow jail, which had been one of "his" projects, and was buried in Greenwood Cemetery in Brooklyn. Though corrupt, his lavish spending and taking of city tax money did leave an indelible architectural mark: see, for example, the Tweed Courthouse on Chambers Street and the Brooklyn Bridge, which the Tweed ring initiated in 1870.

Liberty Beckons

Meanwhile the flood of immigrants continued unabated. They came from

23

France, from Italy, from China; they set up neighborhoods with shops, theaters, temples or churches and kept their native culture alive as well as they could. Chinatown, for example, began in the 1870s, and, barring growth, has remained pretty much the same since. The Chinese influx also led to the Exclusion Act of 1882, slamming the door on further Far Eastern immigration. The new immigrants also brought ideas, not all of which were considered healthy by American standards. Indeed, the Paris Commune in 1871, duly reported on by the New York *Times,* and the unsettling effects of an economic crisis in the mid-1870s gave rise to the first tentative steps of an organized labor movement and to the first Red Scares. A railroad strike in 1877 spread to the entire country before being brutally suppressed.

Meanwhile the city was evolving into a modern industrial metropolis. Street cars

Above: Liberty beckons the huddled masses to the land of milk and honey. Right: Those who have made it enjoy the benefits.

and elevated railways improved transportation through the city. In 1882 Thomas Alva Edison after inventing the light bulb also had a powerplant built on Pearl Street, and gas lighting gradually became a romantic memory. The Metropolitan Museum of Art (1870) and the New York Public Library (1877) joined the roster of New York's great buildings. Fifth Avenue consisted of a line of pompous mansions. A telegraph cable connected New York with Europe. The Statue of Liberty arrived as a gift from France in 1886.

The incorporation of neighboring independent townships followed: The Bronx was slowly colonized, while the Brooklyn Bridge made incorporation of that hitherto independent township an inevitability by 1898. The counties of Queens and Richmond (known since the mid-1960s as Staten Island) were also tied to Manhattan.

The contradictions in this new society were mind-boggling. Feudalism had been recycled, given a constitution, an election every now and then, and the modern

serfs, who arrived voluntarily in droves, were allowed to rise through the ranks if they had the acumen, or if it happened to be their manifest destiny. On the one hand wealth was promoted and protected from above. The Republican presidents who succeeded Lincoln were by and large puppets of the industry's managerial profit margin, and did what the lobbies wanted (the McKinley Tariff of 1890 is an example). And the book of the 1890s was Carnegie's *Gospel of Wealth.* On the other hand, the rank and file of the USA, the blue-collar workers who kept the engine running day in, day out lived in ghastly, unsanitary conditions, underpaid, without job security, with dangerous working conditions, without health insurance, without proper education for their children.

Photographer Jacob Riis had been the first to capture the cruelty and inhumanity of working conditions in his book, *How The Other Half Lives,* in 1890. Ten years later Theodore Dreiser published *Sister Carrie,* which took a hard look at the hypocricy of the Gilded Age and was promptly suppressed.

Under the circumstances, the growth of a labor movement with political clout was inevitable. It began with the National Labor Union, founded in 1866, was followed by the Order of the Knights of Labor, which, after considerable success in member-gathering, gave way to the American Federation of Labor (AFL) in 1886. It was well organized, excluded non-skilled workers and was essentially pro-establishment, making it partly acceptable to the industrial upper crust, which used every means at its disposal, including murder, to break unions. A vigorous world-wide economic crisis in the 1890s exacerbated the conditions of the working man and further promoted progressive movements. In 1905, the International Workers of the World (IWW), with headquarters on Cooper Square, was founded. African-Americans had also flocked north to escape violent discrimination in the South in the late 19th century. In the city, they formed their own

New York had the world's highest population and theater density. And there were other records being made and broken: Morgan became a billionaire in 1900, Orville Wright flew over Manhattan in 1909 as part of the 300th anniversary celebration of Henry Hudson's voyage in 1609. The IRT subway opened 84 miles of track in 1904, and the entire New York City Transit System was essentially completed by 1918. The first skyscraper, the Flatiron Building, was built in 1902 using the new technology for the mass production of cast iron. In 1913 Frank Woolworth paid 13 million dollars for the world's tallest skyscraper, money scraped together from his chain of five-and-dime stores.

The cultural scene in those days was as lively as ever, with Greenwich Village at the center of things. Complacency gave way to the exploring spirit of young, radical writers like John Reed (buried in the Kremlin wall), Eugene O'Neill, Dreiser, looking for new meaning in life, new metaphors, new and controversial subjects.

neighborhoods. Discrimination on the part of employers and unions lead to the foundation of the NAACP in 1909.

If anything improved workers' conditions, however, it was such tragic events as the Triangle Shirtwaist Factory fire in 1911, in which 145 workers were killed, combined with a new journalistic spirit that gave these stories publicity. Conservatives did not like this new school of reporting – President Theodore Roosevelt, a native New Yorker, coined the term *muckrakers* but by the same token his adherents were not prepared to compromise or make amends.

Reaching for the Sky

Automobiles had started appearing on New York streets in 1899. Edison had started projecting movies in New York that seemed to keep people distracted.

Above: New York's streets were crowded even at the turn of the century. Right: A depiction of the flip side of Prohibition.

World War One and Beyond

Theodore Roosevelt, whose presidency lasted for the first decade of the 20th century, broke with America's traditional isolationism. Woodrow Wilson, who also believed in America's world mission, though elected on a non-interventionist ticket in 1915, dragged the U.S. into World War One in 1917. New York played only an administrative role in the war as the embarcation point of thousands of doughboys. The mood in the city, however, was not good, with fear of spies and war hysteria causing violent outbreaks of anti-Germanism.

Postwar economic troubles, a renewed influx of immigrants fleeing war-ruined Europe and the Russian Revolution, the sense that the world beyond the Eden of the U.S.A. was a sinful place and its denizens equally wicked creatures, gave

rise to a strong nativist movement. Add to this the unsettling effect of inflation and a spate of strikes, and the result was the imposition of immigration quotas. Indirectly, these times of troubles also gave rise to some curious legislation, such as the Volstead Act, which prohibited the sale of alcoholic beverages in the USA from 1919 until its repeal in 1933.

Prohibition was a kind of civil war on an ideological level, pitting the inevitability of a modern world against an atavistic fear of novelty. Writer Henry Mencken saw the period as a struggle between America's backwoods, Baptist bigotry and the civilized world of the cities, at the forefront of which stood New York. "There, where the cows low through the still night, and the jug of peruna stands behind the stove," he ranted in *Prejudices*, "there is the reservoir of all nonsensical legislation which now makes the United States a buffoon among great nations. Prohibition was invented to the damage of our bank accounts, our dignity, our ease." His barbs were echoed in the cynicism that wafted through the works by what came to be known as the Lost Generation, the writers Sinclair Lewis, F. Scott Fitzgerald, Sherwood Anderson, John Dos Passos and a little later Ernest Hemingway.

Still, in spite of, or because of, the pall of dour Republicanism held over the nation by Presidents Harding (corrupt), Coolidge (aloof) and Hoover (incompetent), the twenties earned the epithet "Roaring." New York was alive with speakeasies that kept society lubricated using imported and home-brewed concoctions. Running liquor, though illegal, seemed to have replaced the six-shooting heroics of the Wild West, and it was extremely lucrative for those who dared.

The cocktail of the age was a mix of gangsterism, sentimentality, Charleston, money and nonchalance, and one of its finest literary exponents was F. Scott Fitzgerald, whose *Great Gatsby* appeared in New York in 1925. In the same year a Tammany Hall graduate, Jimmy Walker, became Mayor of New York. Like

27

Gatsby, he epitomized his times. He was an ex-singer, a high-lifer, a womanizer, a fancy dresser (with a huge wardrobe), an extrovert who threw lavish parties, and was most comfortable in New York's nightclubs. He legalized boxing matches in the city and when Charles Lindbergh returned from Europe after his pioneering solo flight, he organized an equally pioneering ticker tape parade. New York was also a regular stop for touring jazz musicians. For them, every city or town was an "apple" on the "tree" of a tour; New York, the most desirable of all, was the "Big Apple."

Building in New York continued at a hectic pace, with mammoth hotels, office and apartment buildings replacing the mansions on Fifth and Park Avenues. The Chrysler Building reached the 1049-foot mark in 1929, but was surpassed in 1931 by the Empire State Building, which measures 1250 feet.

Above: Crowds gathering in the financial district after the Wall Street Crash.

The Stock Market, meanwhile, had become the world's largest gambling hall. Hundreds of thousands of Americans, from street-sweepers to bankers, invested their savings in the hopes of magic growth. Businesses opened on the basis of cheap paper loans, and the few voices advocating caution were dismissed as crackpots until October 24, 1929, when the market simply crashed.

The Depression

As an effect of the crash, unemployment reached about 30 percent by 1933. President Hoover thrashed about for solutions as the homeless set up shanty towns they called Hoovervilles. In 1932, troups were used to disband a demonstration in Washington. It was an election year, and even the desperate cries of "Prosperity is just around the corner" could not save the Republicans from resounding defeat at the hands of the Democrat from Hyde Park, N.Y., Franklin Roosevelt.

The Roaring Twenties had proven vacuous and frothy. The 1930s were sober, in spite of the repeal of the ridiculous Volstead Act. New York, which had suffered as much as any place after the Crash, also produced one of its most interesting mayors. Fiorello LaGuardia, born into an Italian-Jewish family, had command of six languages and the wherewithall to make it from a processing job to the city's highest office in 1933. He was popular with the townees for his wit, vim and city-wise ways. But he was also a Liberal bent on saving his city after the double impact of the Depression and the corrupt rule of his predecessor, Jimmy Walker. He used the police force to combat crime in all forms, he had welfare housing built, and he kept an eye on the city's overall image.

LaGuardia extracted a $1 billion loan from the Roosevelt administration and he let New York become a testing ground for a variety of FDR's New Deal programs. Federal relief was funneled through the Works Project Administration (WPA) into construction, service trades and arts projects that employed thousands. The Triboro Bridge connected the Bronx and Queens with Manhattan in 1936. The Rockefeller Center project, which had started in 1929 and been delayed by the crash, was resumed. The Rockefellers leased the property through 2015 and poured $100 million into the construction of 14 buildings on 17 acres.

LaGuardia hired Parks Commissioner Robert Moses, who outlasted several mayors and is credited with creating the city as we see it today during nearly four decades of city service. He was responsible for the construction of 627 miles of roads, seven bridges, Lincoln Center, the United Nations Building, the World Trade Center, extending the subway and laying out 5000 acres of parks and beaches. By 1942, New York had two airports: LaGuardia (now used for inland flights exclusively), and Idlewild, later renamed John F. Kennedy. New York also hosted two world fairs: the one in Flushing Meadows in 1939 called the "World of Tomorrow" even demonstrated television for the first time.

Increasingly, New York was asserting its position as a world capital with a genuine international flair. Refugees from Fascism in Europe were settling in the city, turning it into an intellectual and artistic beehive: The New School of Social Research was originally the *Institut für Sozialforschung* in Frankfurt, and its most important teachers, Max Horkheimer and Theodor Adorno, came with it. They were to influence several generations of American students and thinkers. And there were many more, from Hannah Arendt, Béla Bartók, Bertold Brecht, and Kurt Weill, to Enrico Fermi and Leo Szilard, whose work at Columbia University on splitting the atom ultimately led to the the Manhattan Project and the atomic bomb. Talk of this was already in the air in August 1939, a few weeks before the outbreak of World War Two.

The Capital of the World

During the war New York became a kind of surrogate capital for all of Europe's extinguished capitals, Berlin, Vienna, Paris, Rome, Budapest. After the war it once again became a funnel for returning soldiers and fresh waves of huddled masses, especially refugees from Eastern Europe where the double invasion of the Nazis and later the Red Army had caused massive emigration. The fear of social decline, the first diplomatic skirmishes of the Cold War and the "loss" of China to the Communists gave rise to another Red Scare. The scandalous inquisition led by Senator McCarthy put a damper on spirits for a while. Besides ruining careers, it severely damaged America's cultural life by constantly associating artistic and intellectual pursuits with "redness."

If McCarthy and his supporters were hoping to change America's political direction, they failed. Truman advocated greater foreign policy involvement for the USA, and he offered the nation a "Fair Deal," meaning more social programs. This has been the norm for most presidents, however often reluctant, until Ronald Reagan.

For New York it meant a renewed period of investments. Several housing projects appeared in the late forties, notably the Peter Stuyvesant project on the Lower East Side and the Park West Village on the Upper West Side. The latter failed in financial scandal, a chronic illness in the New York building industry. The mammoth Port Authority Bus Terminal, bounded by Eighth and Ninth Avenues and 40th and 41st Streets, was completed in 1950. As if to seal its international role in the world, New York appropriated a few plots along the East River for the United Nations building, which was constructed between 1948 and 1953. The property, extending from 42nd to 48th Streets and valued at the time at about $8.5 million, was donated by John D. Rockefeller. Other developments, too, lifted the face of the city in the downtown area: in 1952, the Lever House, with its modern landscaped plaza, set the architectonic tone for the rest of Park Avenue from 59th Street to Grand Central Station. The Seagram Building, designed by Ludwig Mies van der Rohe and Philip Johnson, was another milestone in New York construction history. Ground was broken for the Lincoln Center for the Performing Arts in 1959. Today it covers four square city blocks between Columbus and Amsterdam Avenues, from 62nd to 66th Streets, and includes Avery Fisher Hall, opened in 1962, the Vivian Beaumont Theater (1965), The Metropolitan Opera House (1966), The Juilliard School of Music (1968), and Alice Tully Hall (1969).

Above: The UN settled in New York making the city the world's capital. Right: John F. Kennedy raised the hopes of the youth.

Rise and Fall

The conservative look of the 1950s was deceptive. McCarthyism had left a shadow, the Korean War and the emergence of the USSR and China as superpowers had an unsettling effect on society. Anti-conformism seeped in, judging from the writings of the Beatniks Jack Kerouac and Allen Ginsberg. The economy seemed sound enough, but it had mostly benefited the middle class and polarized society.

In New York, as in many other cities, the newest waves of immigrants were Hispanic, mainly Puerto-Rican, and they took over their own neighborhoods: East Harlem, the South Bronx, the Lower East Side and Brooklyn's Williamsburg. Harlem, which had already become the physical and cultural capital of black America in the twenties and thirties, continued to attract African-Americans from the South who were in search of jobs and fleeing segregation and discrimination. This in turn resulted in what has come to be known as "white flight," the white middle class leaving the city to form its own sterile enclaves in the suburbs. Rural Long Island and Westchester benefited, of course, and later New Jersey

A combination of factors led to the decade of revolution that swept across the USA, affecting the inner cities in particular. First, there was the increasing push for civil rights for African-Americans under the leadership of Dr. Martin Luther King. Secondly, the Democrat John F. Kennedy, elected president in 1960, seemed genuinely interested in including all Americans irrespective of age or color in his pursuit of New Frontiers. His assassination on November 22, 1963, shook America to its roots.

New York in the sixties was one of the major theaters of events: It had riots, sit-ins, love-ins, teach-ins. Once again, as earlier in the century, the village became the magnet for new, emancipated artists,

their fans and imitators. These were the years of Andy Warhol proving Pop Art could be lucrative and anti-establishment at the same time. It was home to the underground culture of Jerry Rubin proclaiming drugs and sex, to Lou Reed singing *Venus in Furs* and *Waiting for the Man*, to happenings in dilapidated lofts in Chelsea and SoHo, to Abbie Hoffmann and the revolutionary Weathermen. New York was dynamic and corrupt, the place to be if you were a banker, a stockbroker or an aspiring poet or musician.

As the decade wore on the turbulence grew, especially with deepening American involvement in the hopeless Vietnam War, and with the assassinations of Martin Luther King and New York Senator and Democratic candidate Robert F. Kennedy (brother of JFK) in 1968. The civil rights movement had already sprouted more radical and violent forms under Malcolm X, the Black Muslims, and the Black Panthers, and America's New Left (Marcuse's lore) had also developed a violent streak in the Weathermen.

31

Racial violence affected most American cities, Los Angeles, Detroit, Newark, Cleveland, Atlanta, but New York was by and large spared. Still, general disillusionment, a weakening economy, and a drastic drug problem (New York is the main entry point and market for illegal drugs) that had always existed but now hit the middle class, were pushing up the crime rate. Muggings, burglaries, murder became the order of the day, and corporate America was opting out, further exacerbating the social tensions by increasing unemployment.

The federal government, now under Nixon backed by the middleclass "silent majority," appeared unwilling to address the problem except to rant against the permissive society and lawlessness. Mayor Lindsay, in an attempt to defuse the situation, increased New York's wel-

Above: Martin Luther King strove for non-violence but died by the sword. Right: The Stock Market, an international symbol of good and evil both.

fare rolls, effectively pushing the city to the brink of bankruptcy by the mid-seventies. Higher taxes drained businesses from the city. In October 1975 New York was saved by a last-minute bail-out through loans from union coffers of sanitation workers and teachers.

The Municipal Assistance Corporation (MAC), founded by New York's state governor Hugh Carey, and the Emergency Financial Control Board oversaw city spending. Loans were negotiated from the federal government and private industry. Municipal services were cut back ever further, with thousands of jobs lost and wage and hiring freezes affecting teachers, police and fire fighters. Welfare programs were scaled down, exacerbating the frustrations of the city's poor.

Rescuing the Big Apple

The end of the Vietnam War in January 1973, and the resignation of Nixon in April 1974, also signaled the end of the protest movement. Barring a few resilient enclaves, the long-haired rebels of the sixties suddenly discovered the pleasures of affluence and the three-piece suit. A new fashion evolved for white man's New York, involving the discothèque, the psychiatrist and the fitness center. The new New York was for the likes of John Travolta, discoing his way from icky Brooklyn to the gold-paved sidewalks of Manhattan.

The nickname "Big Apple" was dug out of the archives, Bobby Short made *I love New York* a city anthem, and how many Midwesterners arrived at La Guardia airport whispering the immortal line crooned by Sinatra "I wanna be a part of it." Cocaine was domesticized for the upwardly mobile who could afford it without mugging (though the white-collar crime rate increase should not be underestimated).

In 1978, Mayor Abraham Beame lost the election to the irreverent and cunning

mayor-you-love-to-hate-but-always-re-elect: "Ed" Koch. He made New York attractive to big business again, thanks to tax incentives, belt-tightening measures, a tough stance with unions and an attempt at battling crime. He nagged the state for more funds. Even the federal government under Carter, who once visited and deplored South Bronx, chipped in. By 1985, New York had repaid its loans and was reporting a surplus.

The dynamic seventies and early eighties spurred a new spate of building, for example the World Trade Center, the Trump Tower, the Citicorp Center and a new AT&T Building. Battery Park was built on the site of the earliest Dutch Manhattan settlements, giving busy Wall Street brokers a place to relax during breaks. The move to Manhattan created a social problem as solvent professionals began moving into neighborhoods where the rents were lower. An apartment on the Lower East Side costing $125 a month in 1977 could only be had for over $700 ten years later. Speculation and overcrowding pushed the prices of real estate beyond any reasonable measure, but still more people arrived.

The Reagan years divided society again into the haves and have nots. Under the banner of "family values" and "morality," the rich got richer, and the trickle-down theory dried up. Millions of jobs had indeed been created, but mostly in the low-paid service industry. But the Reaganauts, still whistling *Happy days are here again,* ignored the newest plagues: homelessness, overcrowded jails, AIDS and crack. Racial tensions increased, epitomized by a 1991 stand-off between Orthodox Jews and African-Americans in the neighborhood of Crown Heights. On the other hand, the violence that hit Los Angeles and other cities in May 1992 did not affect New York. Locals credited the city's first African-American mayor David Dinkins with responsibility for this and his approval rating rose accordingly. Nevertheless, as the city ploughs into the 1990s, it has to come to grips with increased crime and fiscal insolvency.

33

MELTING POT

One of the most enduring images in American history is of immigrants entering the New World at the turn of the century huddled on overcrowded ships, bent on reaching the Promised Land, achieving the ephemeral American Dream. For many of them, their first image of America was New York and the proud beacon of the Statue of Liberty. Some of those who made it through Ellis Island, a difficult exam, continued on south and west. Many, however, opted to stay in New York, which offered an array of opportunities. The notion of New York as a city of immigrants began in the early 1800s. German immigrants began to pour in during the 1820s, followed 20 years later by a wave of Irish immigrants, escaping famine in their country. Asians, that is Chinese, came in the 1880s followed by

Above: Some of the many cultures that live side-by-side in New York. Right: Maintaining traditions in the melting pot.

Southern Europeans, mainly Italians. Jewish immigrants from Eastern Europe began arriving in the 1890s, fleeing the pogroms in Russia.

A century later, although Ellis Island has become a museum of its past as a processing center, immigrants are still on their way. Kennedy airport has become the official entry. Thousands, mostly from Latin America, travel to *El Norte* illegally and often in life-threatening conditions. New York is one place they can disappear into, find illegal employment, risk being caught by immigration officers and thrown out of the country. The magic appeal of the city nevertheless keeps the people coming year in year out.

All these groups arriving in the city have left their mark in some way. The most obvious is the variety in "skin color," and the number of accents or even languages spoken. The French film director Louis Malle, a New York resident, once said that the reason he felt so at home in New York is because he felt that he could be anyplace in the world. And when a friend complained to the Hungarian playwright Ferenc Molnàr that Americans were linguistic morons, Molnàr proved him wrong by addressing the nearest policeman in Hungarian, and being answered in Hungarian.

Each group has settled a particular area of the city where shop signs, sometimes street signs and even architecture reveal who is living there. Manhattan's Lower East Side has always been the domain of Jewish immigrants from Eastern Europe and Russia; today, some may no longer live there but they still have their shops there. In Brooklyn's Brighton Beach, Russian immigrants have practically set up a separate community. So have Greek residents in Astoria, in Queens. Perhaps the most famous ethnic enclave visited by tourists is Chinatown, in lower Manhattan, a constantly growing destination for emigrés from Hong Kong and China. In spite of its international renown, Chinatown is a secret to outsiders. It is a community with its own rules and regulations, with its own banking and welfare systems. Its growth, however, is impinging on its northern neighbor, which is almost equally famous: Little Italy. Around East 86th Street are the Germans, the Hungarians have their place a few blocks to the south.

The "melting pot" can quite literally be tasted. The French have expensive restaurants and Americans have taken to opening "bistros" because they are indeed *très chics!* No block in New York seems to lack a pizza parlor, although pizza in that form was allegedly born in New Haven, Connecticut. Ubiquitous *felafel* sandwiches have given fast foods an exotic Middle Eastern flavor. And whenever New Yorkers get tired of cooking, there is always the local Chinese take-away or a corner deli with pastrami and coleslaw, bagels and other delicious Yiddish specialties.

With all these cultures living cheek-by-jowl, it might appear astonishing to the

casual visitor that there is not a perpetual state of civil war raging in the city streets. All has not been peaceful, of course. As the African Americans began moving into Harlem, they had trouble with the local Irish population.

In *West Side Story*, a rewrite of *Romeo and Juliet*, Leonard Bernstein depicted the violent clash between rival white and Puerto-Rican gangs. Gang fighting has also erupted between Chinese and Italians. And more recently there have been clashes between various ethnic groups, including African-Americans, Jews, Italians and Koreans. Still, overall, relations have been peaceful. That is the essence of New York's melting pot. Everyone has a little space and is accepted for what he or she is. When wars break out in the home countries, it's their problem. In New York everyone is an American, and many fought hard enough to get there, to leave the murderous squabblings in Europe, Latin America and Asia behind. So there is no point in starting it all over again in Eden.

COLLAPSING METROPOLIS

Brochures and books offer one picture: Shiny skyscrapers, interesting if at times eccentric people, the mighty Statue of Liberty, the ethnic mix, the vim and vigor of youth. But after getting involved in city life, some may discover a very different New York. The first ride from the airports to Manhattan reveals that something is amiss. New York, flaunted as a universal megalopolis, is criss-crossed with tortuous streets, full of pot holes and peppered with hub caps and less identifiable refuse. The city's famous yellow cabs bounce about on this surface with menacing groans and thumps. Stray a little from the quiet rows of brownstones or the spectacular skyscrapers of the midtown area, and you arrive in dingy neighborhoods with burnt-out houses, car wrecks, and shuttered storefronts.

Above: Home sweet home behind the ruined face of a highrise. Right: Business as usual, the rich get richer....

There can be no doubt about it: New York is collapsing. There are blatant signs, such as the run-down neighborhoods and the homeless people who are scattered all over the city. They sleep in doorways, panhandle among the Fifth Avenue crowds, sprawl on the sidewalks of the Bowery.

There is crime, the daily bread of local tabloids. Crime in New York has reached such proportions that the 1991 fall clothing collection included bullet-proof vests for school children. An average of six homicides a day take place. City Hall is quick to place the blame on rampamt drug addiction, a problem aggravated by the appearance of the highly addictive crack, a cocaine derivative.

The voices suggesting that the drug problem itself is a symptom of a greater evil, of the wide gap between rich and poor, of racial inequality in an egalitarian society, of frustration and disillusionment, are far too weak to prevail. Recently, gangs have widened their horizon to include the general public, and their crimes are sometimes not even drug-related: Take the case where a group of middle-class kids raped a woman jogging in Central Park "just for fun."

AIDS is another of the city's nemeses, filling the hospitals, insidiously spreading and decimating the arts scene. Pundits like to compare New York to other towns with a shabby reputation such as Calcutta. It has been said, however, that the misery in New York is in fact greater.

In the old days, veterans reflect, New Yorkers would have worked together to overcome these problems. They wistfully recall the days when one could sleep out in Central Park. These days, however, people generally tend to look out for themselves. This self-centeredness has also spread to entire communities, that are increasingly clashing with each other. Director Spike Lee has chronicled racial tensions within New York in films like *Jungle Fever* and *Do The Right Thing*.

Politicians, one saying has it, approach problems with an open mouth, and for New York it is probably the only way. The Reagan years, with their massive cuts in anything resembling a social program, cost the city a lot of jobs and money. The Stock Market Crash of October 1987, left the city shivering, and the deepening recession since has pushed up unemployment.

In 1991, all Mayor Dinkins could do was offer a 28 billion-dollar budget with a built-in deficit and cuts in services ranging from the clean-up teams to the Public Library. The people demonstrated but to no avail. Dinkins pointed his finger at the state government in Albany, accusing them of not providing enough support for the city, but Albany has a deficit of its own. Fortunately, the old Municipal Assistance Corporation sold a billion dollar worth of bonds to help out for the year. But the city will have to pay it back at some time.

The Association for a Better New York, which came up with the "I love New York" campaign in the 1970s, is also working hard again at reshaping the city's image. It published a book titled *This Really is a Great City (I Don't Care What Anybody Says)*, attempting to revamp the bad publicity.

New Yorkers have by and large become used to living with the city as it is, for it does have a special charm, as long as one averts one's eyes from the ubiquitous filth. During the day the entire city seems to be a single blaring horn. At night ambulances and police sirens give invisible tragedies a macabre accompaniment. In the wee hours it's the garbage trucks clanking along the streets. Indeed, New York never sleeps. Like the resilient cockroach, who fearlessly crawls up to the top of even the highest highrises to investigate New Yorkers' kitchens, New Yorkers tend single-mindedly to go about their business without looking left or right. They know when to go out and get back home, when to leave a subway car, which neighborhoods to stay out of, how to avoid the weirdos of everyday life.

37

LOWER
MANHATTAN

NEW YORK BAY
FINANCIAL DISTRICT
LOWER EAST SIDE
CHINATOWN
LITTLE ITALY
SOHO AND TRIBECA
GREENWICH VILLAGE

New York, like many other large cities, has often sacrificed historic buildings and neighborhoods to the needs of the business community. In **Lower Manhattan**, however, business and history live on side by side: The past is alive in these narrow streets and landmarked federal buildings, standing in the shadow of a forest of modern skyscrapers.

NEW YORK BAY

The appropriate place to start any tour of New York is the place where the earliest European settlers, the Dutch, first settled. In 1626, the same year that Peter Minuit did the first big New York deal by buying the entire island for $24-worth of trinkets, a Dutch group established a fortified settlement, Fort Amsterdam, most likely on the location now occupied by the **United States Customs House**, at Broadway and Bowling Green. Needless to say, today's Customs House, a magnificent structure with Ionic columns and ornate friezes, is not the original. The British had a fort here named Fort George after the king. After the American Revo-

Preceding pages: The friendly face of New York law. The sun does set on the city. Left: Skyscrapers literally reach for the clouds in New York's Financial District.

lution, the fort was torn down to make way for Government House, intended as the residence of the nation's first president. In those days, New York, and not Washington D. C., served as the nation's capital. George Washington took the oath of office nearby. The Parthenon-like **Federal Hall National Memorial**, at 26 Wall Street, was the location of the swearing in, commemorated by the statue of Washington in front.

New York did not remain the U.S. capital for long. So rather than waste a good building, the New Yorkers turned Government House into the residence of the state's governor. When Albany became the state capital in 1796, the building again lost its purpose. It became the rather elegant Elysian Boarding House, and then a customs house. Gutted by fire in 1815, it was replaced by a row of handsome brick houses, which served as offices for the shipping companies that were flourishing in the area. The customs house, meanwhile, moved to **Wall Street**, first to Federal Hall, and then to the building currently occupied by Citibank. In 1892, however, the Treasury Department bought this land and announced a competition to design a new building. Cass Gilbert won and completed his pompous, neoclassical structure in 1907. The building was abandoned when the

43

Customs Service moved to the World Trade Center in 1973. There is a happy ending: The **Museum of the American Indian** is expected to move into the building in 1992, bringing the ownership of the site full circle.

Just north of the Customs House is **Bowling Green**, New York City's first park. During the Dutch days, it was a cattle market and, later, a parade ground. In 1733, a group of citizens leased it as a bowling green, for the exorbitant rent of a single peppercorn a year. Later, an equestrian statue of King George III was placed in the park. On July 9, 1776 a crowd gathered here to listen to a reading of the Declaration of Independence and in a frenzy of patriotism, destroyed the statue.

Near Bowling Green are the vestiges of the great shipping companies that once operated here. Number **1 Broadway**, stands on the site of the former Archibald

Above: The Unknown Soldier in Battery Park, a phantom in time and space.

Kennedy House. George Washington did actually sleep here during his stay in New York during the Revolutionary War. The house served as the United States Lines headquarters during the 1800s; note the tridents, fish, shells and other marine motifs in the building's façade. The **U.S. Post Office** at 25 Broadway is the former headquarters of Cunard Lines and features one of the most impressive interiors in the city, which reportedly was inspired by Raphael's *Villa Madama* in Rome. Across the street at **26 Broadway** is one of the most venerable business addresses in the world. Behind these walls, John D. Rockefeller founded Standard Oil and one of the great fortunes of all time.

Battery Park

At the lower end of Broadway is **Battery Park**, New York's first landfill. The Dutch rearranged the land in earnest. They leveled hills and dug canals, dumping dirt and rocks into the bay. In three centuries, more than 21 acres were added to the tip of the island. The park is named for the line of cannons that once overlooked the harbor, but those military days are long over: On hot summer days, New Yorkers come down here to stroll, take in the sea breezes, which turn icy in the winter, and to admire the unobstructed views of the Statue of Liberty.

Within the park are a few notable sites. To the north is a picturesque **fireboat station**, moored to one of the oldest piers on the Hudson River. The tower, once used as a lookout, bears a clock honoring servicemen killed in World War One. The pier was headquarters of the harbor police. It now houses the Marine Division of the Fire Department. Another is the **Netherlands Memorial Monument**, given to the people of New York by the Dutch in 1926. On it is a map of Manhattan in Dutch times and an Indian receiving a 24-dollar gift. On a path off to the right is a statue of the engineer John Ericsson, who

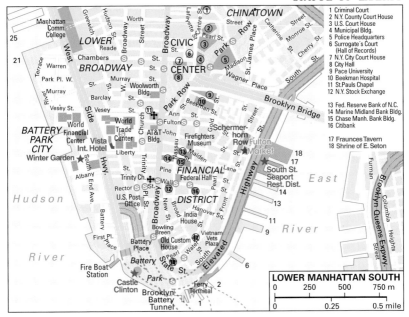

Map labels:
CHINATOWN
LOWER BROADWAY
CIVIC CENTER
BATTERY PARK CITY
FINANCIAL DISTRICT
Hudson River
East River
LOWER MANHATTAN SOUTH
0   250   500   750 m
0   0.25   0.5 mile

1 Criminal Court
2 N.Y. County Court House
3 U.S. Court House
4 Municipal Bldg.
5 Police Headquarters
6 Surrogate's Court (Hall of Records)
7 N.Y. City Court House
8 City Hall
9 Pace University
10 Beekman Hospital
11 St.Pauls Chapel
12 N.Y. Stock Exchange
13 Fed. Reserve Bank of N.C.
14 Marine Midland Bank Bldg.
15 Chase Manh. Bank Bldg.
16 Citibank
17 Fraunces Tavern
18 Shrine of E. Seton

designed one of the earliest ironclad warships, the *Monitor*. The **Verrazano Memorial** recalls the man who first sighted the area of metropolitan New York. And, most prominently, there is **Castle Clinton**, a squat red sandstone structure that was built to protect the harbor in the tense years preceding the Britain-U.S. War of 1812. At the time it was called the West Battery. After the war, the fort was renamed Castle Clinton, after De Witt Clinton, mayor of New York City and governor of New York State. When the purpose of the building changed in 1824, though, so did the name: Castle Garden, as it was called, hosted entertainment events, fireworks, scientific demonstrations, like S.F.B. Morse's "wireless telegraph," and famous people, like the Marquis de Lafayette. In 1845, a roof was added and it became a serious theater, most famous for the 1850 evening when it hosted the American debut of "Swedish Nightingale" Jenny Lind. By 1855, though, things were changing again and the building served as an immigrant depot.

Approximately eight million people were processed here in the years 1855-89. In 1896, the building was remodeled again to serve as the New York Aquarium but despite its popularity it was almost razed in the 1940s by Parks Commissioner Robert Moses.

The building was spared thanks to concerned citizens and to the distraction of World War Two. In 1946, it was declared a national monument and now serves as a mini-history center for the waterfront. Most important, it is where tickets are bought for the ferries to Ellis Island and the Statue of Liberty.

The **Statue of Liberty**, a symbol of the United States throughout the world, was a gift from the French in 1886. It was sculpted in copper plates by the Alsacian Auguste Bartholdi, the ribbing is by Gustave Eiffel (whose name was immortalized in the great Eiffel Tower in Paris). At 151 feet, it is one of the world's tallest statues. It was restored for its 100th anniversary, which was celebrated with July 4 Independence Day fireworks of such in-

tensity that many wondered if they might scar the new exterior.

Residents and visitors never seem to tire of looking at her: Ms. Liberty is also visible from a number of standpoints, whereby passing her on a ship gives the impression she is striding forward. A trip inside her body is possible, but remember, on crowded summer afternoons lines may stretch so long that it is impossible to get out to the island after 2 p.m. Go in the morning, preferably during the week, off-season. Those who do make it out to the island, should prepare for a steep climb to the top. An elevator transports sightseers up ten stories but there are 171 steps to climb after that. Should the crowds be too dense and time too short, the statue of Liberty can be seen from a distance from the **Staten Island Ferry** which leaves the Municipal Ferry Terminal to the east of Battery Park. The ride costs only a quarter.

Above: Lady Liberty, looking out over New York Bay, greeted millions of immigrants.

Ellis Island, named after Samuel Ellis, the merchant who owned the island during the American Revolution, replaced Castle Clinton as an immigration valve in 1892. It lies north of the Statue of Liberty. Before the immigration complex was shut down in 1932, 17 million (poor, not rich) immigrants had gone through it, 1.25 million alone in the peak year 1907. For many a long journey ended happily here, with a ticket to the New World. Others who were considered unfit, usually because they had some communicable disease, were sent back. Others waited weeks and months here before a decision was made.

Ellis Island served as a detention center for German immigrants during World War Two. By the time it was closed in 1954 the buildings had decayed. Nearly 30 years later, descendants of immigrants, led by Chrysler Chairman Lee Iacocca, organized an eight-year, $156-million restoration project, which was completed in 1990. Today, visitors can retrace the steps of those millions of haggard immigrants. The tour begins in the **Baggage Room**, where many left nearly all of their belongings. It proceeds to the **Registry Room**, where they were given a medical examination and their papers and motives were checked. The **Stairway of Separation** was next, leading to the ferryboats that would take those admitted, approximately 98 percent, to Manhattan or New Jersey. Those not admitted were put on outgoing boats.

In these halls are exhibitions portraying the immigrant experience, personal property brought here by those travellers, and the **American Immigrant Hall of Honor**, specifically listing the names of 200,000 immigrants who passed through here. An **Oral History Studio** allows visitors to hear immigrants recounting their experiences. The **Ellis Island Family History Center** provides computerized records of 17 million immigrants who landed at New York's ports. Because of the popularity of these exhibits, crowds in Battery Park waiting for ferries may outdo those for the Statue of Liberty.

Manhattan's Southern Tip

To the east of Battery Park is an exit leading out to **State Street**, a former upper class residential street whose sole representative today is the **Rectory of the Shrine of the Blessed Elizabeth Bayley Seton** at number 7. This elegant Federal-style house, built in 1793 and enlarged in 1806, served as command post for the Union army during the Civil War. After the war an Irish immigrant, Charlotte Grace O'Brien, bought the house and created a home for immigrant Irish girls. It is now a shrine to Elizabeth Seton, the first American-born saint.

The little triangular park named after Peter Minuit, New York's first governor, has a memorial to the first Jewish immigrants to arrive in New York in 1654. The **Battery Maritime Building** at 11 South Street, was built at the turn of the century

on the spot where people used to catch the ferry to Brooklyn before the Brooklyn Bridge was inaugurated in 1898. The terminal, in typical Beaux-Arts style, was painted green to simulate the color of oxidized copper. Ferries servicing **Governor's Island**, site of the earliest Dutch settlement, depart from this terminal.

This part of New York is ancient in New World terms, but little has survived the great building boom of the 1950s and 1960s. Sheer glass, concrete and steel towers have replaced the old houses and imbued the area with a depressing, monotonous modernism.

Broad Street, which crosses Water Street, was once a canal that served shipping and sewerage interests during the Dutch days. The City Hall of those days stood here in the middle of what was known as New Amsterdam. The British filled up the canal and made the new street into a strip of warehouses. At number 85 is a small sub-sidewalk level display of 17th-century artifacts dug up during the recent construction boom. **Pearl Street**, which runs from State Street to the Brooklyn Bridge, was once the waterfront of southern Manhattan and was named after the shells found on its beach.

Where Pearl and Broad meet stands **Fraunces Tavern**, a turn-of-the-century reconstruction of an 18th-century house. The original edifice dates back to 1719. It belonged to a powerful New York dynasty, the De Lanceys, who were later forced to leave the New World for overtly supporting the British King, George III, during the Revolution. The house became a warehouse and then a tavern owned by Samuel Fraunces, a cook well known for his desserts. George Washington, whose famous wooden teeth perhaps belie an excessive fondness for sweets, chose Fraunces's as the place to bid farewell to his officers in 1783 when he briefly retired. Later, Fraunces served as chief steward to President Washington.

The building was leased to various government agencies, then sold to a Brooklyn butcher. By the mid-1800s, the entire neighborhood was in a state of decay. After being burned several times, Fraunces Tavern was abandoned until purchased by the Sons of the Revolution, who restored it to its present condition. Above a ground floor restaurant are two floors containing period rooms and early American exhibits.

Pearl Street leads north to **Coenties Alley**, a slight variation of the Dutch *Coentje,* a combination of names of two citizens who lived on the street. This newly restored street, with pretty cobblestones and quaint little shops contrasts with the entire neighborhood. A little beyond Coenties Alley is the **Vietnam Veterans Plaza**. Centuries ago, this was a park where sailors used to hang out between journeys. In 1985, it was designated as the site of the memorial. The

Above: Manhattan's old port is a major attraction for tourists and New Yorkers alike.

sculpture itself consists of a wall into which excerpts from letters sent home by soldiers in that war have been etched. It is a rallying point for citizens on Memorial Day, in late May, and Veterans Day, in mid-November.

To the west, Coenties Alley ends at **Stone Street**, the first paved street in the city. Its original name was Brouwers Street in the 1600s, after the brewery owned by Stephanus Van Cortlandt. Carriages and carts rolling by caused a great deal of dust, and Mr. Van Cortlandt's wife, who tried to keep her house clean, urged her husband to pave the street.

At the northeast end of Stone Street is a vestige, at least in name, of the former British colony's last reigning king, **Hanover Square**. Formerly the center of a plush residential neighborhood, it was modeled after a typical London park. One of its more notorious residents was Captain William Kidd, pillar of the community, contributor to the Trinity Church (see below), and according to the British, one of the most vicious pirates in history.

He was sent to the gallows in 1701 for his crimes. He is alleged to have buried his booty somewhere, and to this day, every now and then, hopefuls will dig into area beaches looking for instant wealth. Also on the square was a somewhat more respectable enterprise, New York's first newspaper, *The New York Daily Gazette*, established in 1725. Unfortunately, this building and many others of that era were destroyed in an 1835 fire. The venerable **India House**, at 1 Hanover Square, was built after the fire, in 1854. A grand Italianate brownstone, it served as the model for the other, distinctive brownstones built around the city, and as the first home of the Hanover Bank. Later, the New York Cotton Exchange and the shipping firm W.R. Grace were located here. It is now a private men's club.

Fires were not infrequent in New York of old. On **Maiden Lane**, a cross street on Pearl Street, there is a small museum (at No. 59, near William Street) displaying the paraphernalia of the firefighting trade. In the days of New Amsterdam, Maiden Lane was the place where women used to come to wash the laundry, hence the name. Seeing the slick greenish glassy towers that grace it today, it is hard to imagine those idyllic times.

On The Waterfront

Further north, on the east side of John Street is the **South Street Seaport Restoration District**, a tribute to the days when these piers handled commercial traffic, before the onset of steamships and the move to the deeper piers of the Hudson. Concerned citizens started the drive to restore the area in 1967, and it opened in the early 1980s, as a mixture of restored veteran buildings and new ones made to look old. Some complain the area is just another shopping center: It boasts well over 100 shops and restaurants. Others applaud it as the revitalization of an area previously in serious de-

cline. It is also New York's only successful waterfront development, and an area where New Yorkers and tourists alike can stroll and enjoy a pleasant mixture of thrills, from shopping to museum-browsing. Of special interest is **Schermerhorn Row**, a rehabilitated group of early 19th-century warehouses and offices once belonging to one Peter Schermerhorn. On the second floor of one of them is the restaurant, **Sweets**, opened in 1842, and still going strong

Across Fulton Street is **Fulton Market**, a re-creation of an 1882 building that housed a meat and produce market. The current edifice houses bustling shops and restaurants, some selling fast food, others selling produce, meat, fish and spices for the do-it-yourself cooks. But the name Fulton Street is perhaps best associated with the old **fish market** at the end of the street out on pier 18. It was established in 1821, when fishing boats could pull up on the dock and unload their catch. Today much of that catch is brought in in refrigerated trucks. Privateers and restaurateurs jostle for the best cuts, but not during the day: The Fulton Street fish market really gets going during the graveyard shift. There are occasional 6 a.m. guided tours for curious early risers.

South of the market are **Piers 15**, **16** and **17**, along with their resident ships, several permanent members of the Seaport collection and a couple of visitors. *The Peking*, a steel-hulled, four-masted barquentine built in 1911, is always on view, as is the *Wavertree,* a full-rigged ship built in 1885 and recently restored. The *Ambrose,* a lightship that marked the harbor until a tower replaced her in 1963, is also at the pier. Tugboats, a sidewheeler that does harbor cruises, ferryboats and schooners also rest at anchor here. Besides the ships surrounding Pier 17, the renovated dock has become a vast mall of ships and restaurants, as well as a viewing area for the **Brooklyn Bridge**

towering overhead. On a summer day, it is one of the most crowded places in New York. On any evening in the South Street Seaport, the development's bars and restaurants are also crowded.

FINANCIAL DISTRICT

Coming north from Battery Park, one hardly notices the narrow cross street that has become a symbol for financial wheeling and dealing all over the world. This deep canyon, whose walls consist of stark skyscrapers, hardly evokes the image of sweating stockbrokers losing millions and making billions by the minute. How could such a place bring about a worldwide depression? Are those anonymous corporate types walking along the street truly the same people who have their finger on the international fiscal pulse? And yet, **Wall Street**, the lifeline into the **Fi-**

Above: South Street Seaport Restoration never looked quite as prim. Right: The sober exterior of the frenzied Stock Exchange.

nancial District, has for long lived up to its reputation.

Number **74 Wall Street** was the original home of the Seamen's Bank for Savings, a connection recalled by nautical touches in entry archways. The bank was chartered in 1829 and was one of the first stops for sailors, who accumulated considerable fees during their long, expense-paid trips at sea. A peculiar note is the address, which is not original. The real number is 76, but as the two digits add up to 13, superstitious would-be depositors refused to leave money. (The same peculiar note applies to many New York skyscrapers and highrises: They are missing a 13th floor, something one would hardly expect from the hard-boiled New Yorkers!) **55 Wall Street** is one of the area's most impressive buildings and one of the first built after the great fire of 1835. The first section, started in 1842, is an broad three-story construction, shaped like a Greek temple, with a domed central hall intended to be a trading hall for the Merchants' Exchange. Around the turn of

the century, its space was doubled and 16 Corinthian columns were added. First the First National City Bank moved in, then Citibank took over.

Another Greek-revival building is on the corner of Wall and Pine Streets, the **Federal Hall National Memorial**, mentioned earlier as the site where George Washington took the presidential oath of office. The current building was erected in 1842. The statue of Washington, however, is fairly close to the hallowed spot where he was administered the oath.

Across the street is a building that embodies the big money power of the street. The Morgan Guarantee Trust Company at **23 Wall** was the creation of the financier J. Pierpont Morgan, whose wealth was such that he was able to buy up his colleagues and rivals Frick and Vanderbuilt. On the other hand, at the Corner of Wall and Broad stands the building mentioned every day at least once all over the world: The **New York Stock Exchange**. From the outside it looks solid, even grand. The neoclassical entrance speaks

in solemn tones. Tours inside, however, reveal something close to frenzy.

The materialism of the Stock Exchange contrasts sharply with the peaceful spirit of **Trinity Church** at Wall Street and Broadway. It was built on the cemetery that still surrounds it. Some famous men are buried here, Alexander Hamilton, one of the framers of the Constitution, and steamship inventor Robert Fulton. The church was a dark, somewhat dingy building until a good cleaning job once again revealed the pink sandstone of its walls. It is the third church on the site. The first was built of wood in 1698, paid for by the taxes of all of the colony's citizens, regardless of faith, because the Church of England was the colony's official religion. It burned down in 1776. A second church was built in 1790, but its roof caved in in 1834. The present church, built in 1846 in the Gothic Revival style, has doors modeled after the famous Ghiberti doors of the Baptistry in Florence. They were donated by tycoon William Waldorf Astor in 1894. The little

chapel is also a later addition, having been built in 1913.

Heading uptown on Broadway from Trinity Church is an area of more banks, the sleek, modern colossi of Chase Manhattan and Marine Midland headquarters. On the cross street, **Liberty Street**, is a megabank, the **Federal Reserve Bank of New York**. Filling a block, this powerful institution was designed by architect Philip Sawyer after the Strozzi Palace in Florence. Much attention was paid to detail, right down to the handiwork of the wrought iron lanterns lighting the doorway. The outside and inside of the bank, including five floors of underground vaults, can be visited, though it is wise to reserve a tour in advance.

The **World Trade Center**, on the northern edge of Liberty Street, has been controversial since opening in 1970. It is

Above: The World Trade Center, two exclamation marks at the end of the island. Right: You can't beat City Hall, but there's no harm trying.

also known as the Twin Towers, owing to the pair of plain, 1350-foot towers that stick out of it, and have become a hallmark of New York's skyline. 50,000 people work here and another 80,000 visit in a normal workday. Some complain about its blandness and outrageous height. None complain about the view. The **Observation Deck** on the 107th floor has a spectacular, panoramic, 360 degree view.

For years, the World Trade Center held the position of number one downtown business complex to itself. Lately that position has been threatened by a more stylish development. Across **West Street**, bordering the Hudson River is the **World Financial Center**, located in the new neighborhood of **Battery Park City**. The Financial Center is composed of four soaring glass towers, but in contrast to the monochord simplicity of the Twin Towers, these buildings are covered in granite and reflecting glass, and each has a different height and silhouette. It also houses a popular glassed-in atrium, the **Winter Garden**, featuring 45-foot Californian palm and convenient benches. South, in Battery Park City proper, is a **Japanese rock garden**. With its violet lights and sounds of gently lapping waves from the Hudson, this garden is popular with residents and visitors on summer nights.

Civic Center east of Battery Park City and the World Trade Center is another historical landmark, and a good antidote to the concentrated business ambience in the two latter venues. **St. Paul's Chapel** on Broadway, between Church and Fulton Streets, is the only extant pre-Revolutionary church in the city, built in 1766. It is the place George Washington came to pray during the time of his presidency in New York. The interior is lit by Waterford crystal chandeliers. The church offers music concerts in the afternoons.

North of the chapel at **233 Broadway** is a prominent skyscraper in this city

known for its skyscrapers. The **Woolworth Building**, designed by Cass Gilbert (of, for instance, Customs House fame) and completed in 1913, is no longer New York's tallest building, a distinction it held for 17 years. But it remains one of its most original owing to its mass of wild, gothic details. The entrance foyer boasts an elaborate glass mosaic ceiling and a number of bronze ornamentations on granite walls, including a portrait of Mr. Woolworth himself.

In spite of the appearances, and in spite of what many disgruntled New Yorkers might say, the city *does* have a government. It has ruled from **City Hall** since 1811. This French Renaissance palace combined with a number of Federal elements stands in a little park northeast of the Woolworth Building. Its steps are a stage for city politics: Visiting dignitaries are greeted here, the Mayor tries to explain the latest budget to journalists here, and New Yorkers who strongly disagree with those budgets tend to gather in the park to express (loudly) their displeasure.

The **New York City Courthouse** at 52 Chambers Street on the northern edge of the park is a building born in scandal: It was built during the rule of Boss Tweed, and cost 52 times its allotted budget. Much of the surplus filtered back into Tweed's pocket. Across Chambers Street is a delightful Baroque gem, the **Hall of Records** housing the Surrogate Court, at 31 Chambers Street, has often been compared to the Paris Opera. And straddling the eastern end of the street is the massive, **Municipal Building**, decorated with rows of columns and statues. The modern edifice behind it is the NY Police Department Headquarters.

The heavy hand of the law continues up Center Street: The **United States Courthouse** and **New York County Courthouse** are in the usual neoclassical style. Farther up Center Street the **Criminal Courts Building** recalls the punitive side of American law. This dark yellow Art-Deco building was once the Manhattan Detention Center for Men, familiarly known as the Tombs.

LOWER EAST SIDE

In the 18th century, the Lower East Side was a rural area divided up by the two great landowning families, the De Lanceys and the Rutgers. In the early 1800s, it became the residential choice of prosperous sea captains and merchants, whose trade depended on the turnover of the South Street docks. They built elegant rowhouses in the Federal style.

The immigrant wave that changed the face of the neighborhood began in the mid-19th century with the arrival of the Irish. Jewish immigration began in the 1880s mainly with the arrival of Russian Jews, who were fleeing the murderous pogroms of Czarist Russia. By World War One two million had arrived in the US, and many had settled in the Lower East Side. Working and living conditions in the New World were abysmal; tuberculosis was so common that it was known as the "Jews' disease."

In spite of these difficult conditions, the neighborhood quickly developed a strong social infrastructure, which included the settlement house movement, theaters, music schools, reading rooms, clubs and various social organizations. The area also became an important cradle of and a fertile ground for reformist and radical thought in America.

The quadrangular section formed by Canal, Essex, Delancey Streets and the Bowery does often look and sound as one might imagine one of the former Galician or Ukrainian *Shtetts* did: numerous discount shops, kosher groceries, linen and apparel stores, a variegated, noisy crowd grave Hasidic Jews, the sing-song of Yiddish, the ubiquitous yarmulka. Of course, Saturday is the Sabbath; the shops are closed. The quintessence of Jewish life in the Lower East Side is the **Essex Street Market** (between Stanton and Broome

Left: Lower East Side has become a peaceful home to Jews from all over the world.

Streets), though these days Spanish and Chinese are also becoming part of the local linguistic and ethnic make-up. The Lower East Side is in fact only 35 percent Jewish: It is also 35 percent Puerto Rican, 17 percent Chinese, eight percent African-American and five percent "other," as a recent census showed.

Seward Park, which graces the southern end of Essex Street, was previously a gathering place for immigrants looking for work and is now the site of a Sunday **flea market**, is one of the genuine Lower East Side landmarks. The **Henry Street Settlement Houses** stand on Henry Street between Montgomery and Grand Streets. The modest late-19th century Federal-style townhouses offer a number of period decorative details. Above all, they have earned a lasting neighborhood reputation for having helped thousands of people get a good start.

Essex Street crosses **Hester Street**, which became synonymous with the Lower East Side during the heyday of Jewish immigration. It was the site of the busiest street market, jammed with peddlers and their pushcarts. It was also the the embodiment of a ghetto street, with children playing with makeshift toys in whatever space remained between the stalls, carts and crowds, with the shouts of vendors and haggling housewives, and perhaps even the sharp whistle of the local constable. The recent film *Hester Street* recalls harshness of life back then with a touch of soothing nostalgia.

On its way westward, Hester Street runs into **Orchard Street**, which really was an orchard in the 18th century, and today boasts a jumble of cheap stores. Further west is **Eldridge Street**, where many of the 19th-century tenements are still standing, their gloomy façades redolent of the mean days before housing laws. Farther down Eldridge Street, at number 12-16, however, stands the opulent **Eldridge Street Synagogue** whose construction was financed by

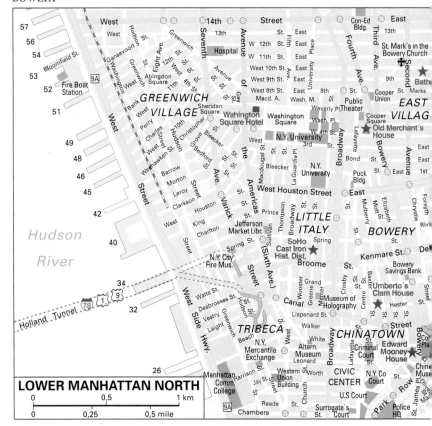

wealthy families. It is in a brilliant array of styles that typified the late 19th century, a little neo-Gothic, a little neo-Romanesque and a little Moorish. For a while the building was in sorry shape owing to general neglect, but was recently restored, and now houses a center documenting a century of Jewish culture in America.

Several blocks to the west comes the **Bowery**, a symbol of human dereliction. This wide lane got its name from the Dutch *bouwerij*, meaning farm. Later, it served as an evacuation route for soldiers during the Revolutionary War. During the 19th century, the street became an entertainment strip, featuring among others George Christy's Minstrel Shows and the

like. Jewish immigrants turned them into Yiddish theaters.

The Depression hit the Bowery hard. It became a hang-out for the homeless, the desperate, the disillusioned. The theaters turned into beer halls or distilleries. Fleabag hostels and dingy bordellos opened their doors to an insolvent clientele. It was the perfect setting for the poets and authors of the beat generation in the 1950s, who relished its special squalor. In the midst of this is one of the neighborhood's most spectacular buildings, the 1894 **Bowery Savings Bank** on the corner of the Bowery and Grand. It was the savings institution for poor neighborhood residents but features a Corinthian portico and scuptured lions.

The Bowery has started changing, especially as New York residents and businesses continue their endless search for cheap real estate in Manhattan. Gentrification has set in, and the derelicts have started moving out.

CHINATOWN AND LITTLE ITALY

Being called up for jury duty in New York City has a fringe benefit: The court buildings on Centre Street are close to Chinatown and Little Italy, two ethnic quarters known for, among other things, food. No visitor to the Big Apple, should miss an excursion to downtown Manhattan to see these sections where, in some

ways, time has stood still since the end of the last century.

The growth of Chinatown, began in the 1870s when Chinese immigrants living in San Francisco moved east mainly to escape violent discrimination. In New York they were for the most part left alone. In 1882, the Exclusion Act put a stop to immigration from China, but in the 1960s a generous quota system was introduced, which quickly pushed up the Chinese population. About 150,000 Chinese are currently living in Chinatown, most of whom are first generation. Thanks to the demographic explosion, Chinatown has long outgrown its traditional borders of Canal, Worth, Baxter Streets and the Bowery. (This area is now referred to as Old Chinatown.) It has spread into Brooklyn and Queens, and with some ethnic conflict, into neighboring Little Italy.

Life in Chinatown is not easy for the locals, who work hard, often in intolerable conditions and for low pay. Many see it only as a step on the way to better things, or as the only way to fulfill their fiscal duty toward a family in Taiwan or mainland China. Crime has increased, especially between rival gangs, whose skirmishes have been known to accidentally strike down innocent bystanders.

The years of self-imposed isolation from American society, isolation caused by, and self-imposed in reaction to, prejudice, have created a society within a society. Family associations, or *tongs*, which join together people with the same surname have regulated Chinatown since the end of the 19th century, helping immigrants, widows, and children, and defending Chinese against discrimination. They also ran protection rackets of sorts for businesses, had their hands in various illegal activities, and on occasion fought wars with each other for hegemony. The family associations still exist, of course, their power is still unchallenged and respected, their function as helpers and

community advisers seems to be absolutely necessary.

Chinatown is by no means a quaint, artificial place as is obvious from the first encounter on Canal and Mott Streets. It is as bustling, loud, exciting and devious as downtown Hong Kong or Taipei. Its restaurants number anywhere between 300 and 400, and they are known for being relatively inexpensive and high in quality even though the setting and service may at times seem on the dingy side.

It has all sorts of shops squeezed into brownstones, the air smells exotic, with snatches of typically New York wafts of fermenting garbage, steam, and exhaust fumes. Chinatown has quite a few obvious Chinese touches, such as pagoda-type roofs on telephone booths and street names written in Chinese. **Mott Street** is Chinatown's main street. At number 8 is the **Chinese Museum**, featuring a selec-

tion of exhibits from China such as a rickshaw and an 18-foot mechanical dragon. Along the street are vegetable and fish markets, thriving businesses since the immigration of the 1870s. The ice cream stores, however, are new.

Pell Street, named after a butcher from the pre-Revolutionary days, meets the east side of Mott Street, which was also named after a butcher. The fork of Pell and Dovers Streets is known as Bloody Angle because of the veritable butchery that took place there during the tong wars at the turn of the 20th century. Today Pell street has numerous restaurants.

Chatham Square is the site of the **Kimlau War Memorial**, a simple memorial with a characteristic pagoda top, dedicated to the Chinese Americans who were killed in action serving in the American army. Walking east of Chatham Square is not always recommended, at least not beyond the strip of restaurants. One block southeast, though, is a landmark of earlier generations that has now been adopted by the Chinese

Above: Night or day, the streets of Chinatown are always bustling. Right: Celebrating the feast of San Gennaro in Little Italy.

community. The **Mariners' Temple** on **Oliver Street** was originally the Oliver Street Baptist Church, but was bought by the mariners' organization in 1863 to serve as a mission for seamen and immigrants. Today the stone temple serves a largely Chinese congregation.

Across the Bowery from Chatham Square is **Division Street**, thus named in pre-Revolutionary times as the dividing line between the farms of James De Lancey, whose name was given to a main street on the Lower East Side, and Henry Rutgers. A shopping mall now stands where cattle once grazed. Going up the Bowery, near the huge **Confucius Plaza** on the corner of Pell Street is the city's oldest surviving row house. The 1785 **Edward Mooney House** belonged to a meat wholesaler who got the land when the afore-mentioned James De Lancey left the country after backing the losing side in the Revolution. It is regarded as a splendid example of Georgian architecture, filled with those little details which displayed Mr. Mooney's wealth.

Nearby, at 75 Bowery, is the **Sun Sing Chinese Theater**, practically hidden under the entrance to the **Manhattan Bridge**. Until 1950, it was Chinatown's opera house; now it is a movie theater showing mostly schmaltzy films made in Hong Kong.

Canal Street is a little of everything – more Chinese markets, banks, including the noticeable **Hongkong and Shanghai Bank**, and jewelry stores. But mainly, it is the pro forma dividing line between Chinatown and **Little Italy,** which officially begins at the corner of Mulberry Street. This ethnic enclave dates to the 1880s, but the population surged in the years between 1890 and 1924. After World War Two, the neighborhood declined somewhat as the children of the first generation moved out to the suburbs. In recent years, though, perhaps sparked by the vitality of the neighborhoods surrounding it, particularly SoHo, Little Italy has also undergone an economic transformation. The old standbys are still there, restaurants decked out in red velvet

59

and simple trattorias, but quite a number of newer places are competing for public favor. And Chinatown is also moving in in places. Suffice it to say, however, the dinner-time crowd is dense, especially on Sundays.

Gang violence in Italian communities has a special place in the annals of crime. And **Umberto's Clam House** at 129 Mulberry, offering good fare, has a special place in neighborhood crime folklore. It is the place where "Crazy Joey" Gallo was rubbed out, while celebrating his birthday in 1972. A place with a less macabre history is **Villa Pensa**, Little Italy's oldest restaurant, established in 1898. It has always drawn famous people from the entertainment world: Rudolf Valentino and Enrico Caruso were early fans of the place. Recently pop star Billy Joel wrote the song *Big Man on Mulberry Street,* while he was dining here. Across the street is the place for a

Above: Fire escape graphics on the façades of Soho lofts.

second dessert, **Ferrara's** (somewhat flashy, neon-lit), or the smaller, more authentic **Caffe Roma**.

Food is the mainstay of Little Italy it seems, and many come just to patronize the stores on Mulberry and Grand, that seem to have been directly transplanted from the Old Country. The **Italian Food Center** is a general store selling the staples, while **Alleva Dairy**, now over a century in business, sells cheese. **Piemonte's** sells pasta.

The area also has some interesting architectural sights, such as the former police headquarters on Broadway, a rich, baroque building that "turned condo" during the real estate boom of the 1980s. The **Puck Building** on Lafayette near Houston (pronounced how-st'n) is a neo-Romanesque extravaganza that was once the home of the humor magazine *Puck*.

SOHO AND TRIBECA

25 years ago, citizens were wary of venturing into the dark and deserted in-

dustrial neighborhoods of this part of Manhattan. Today, the area is a fashionable center for art-lovers and artists, models, actors, and shoppers – one indication of the changes New York has undergone in the last few decades.

SoHo, the area *So*uth of *Ho*uston Street, has a distinguished past. In the mid-1800s, it was virtually the city center of New York, with fashionable department stores and hotels. Polite society, however, was displaced and followed by commerce: Gradually, the area was taken over by the vast, cast-iron buildings of factories devoted to light manufacturing. By the 1960s, industry, too, had moved on, and these buildings were abandoned. There was talk of demolishing the empty hulks. Quick to see their possibilities, however, were artists, always on the lookout for cheap housing and studio space. As they moved in, tenanted, and renovated the lofts, SoHo gradually filled with galleries, smart shops and sophisticated restaurants. By the late 1970s the area had become so popular that only the most successful artists could afford it.

For the have-nots, one solution was **TriBeCa**, the *Tri*angle *Be*low *Ca*nal Street immediately to the south. In terms of architecture, history, and appearance, the area was similar to SoHo; the only difference was that it became trendy, and pricey, far more quickly. Rents have again forced out all but the high earners. Unlike SoHo, though, the neighborhood is not relentlessly chic; you can still stroll the streets without encountering hordes of shoppers and tourists.

TriBeCa's southern border is **Chambers Street**, just west of City Hall. Located here is a small patch of green called **Washington Market Park**. In 1880, this was the site of the vast Washington Market, which sold produce, eggs, cheese and candy. Today, other markets have replaced it, and the park is the domain of TriBeCa kids. Tiny, quiet **Duane Park** to the north is a plot of land

that was part of a Dutch colonial farm, and a property of the Duke of York.

With its 19-century Italianate buildings and the warehouses and trucks of a few dairy suppliers, the surrounding neighborhood seem much as it was a century ago. This impression is furthered by a group of buildings to the west: the **Harrison Street Houses,** restored 18th-century townhouses so quaint and perfect that most New Yorkers who see them, (usually from the vantage point of the restaurant **How's Bayou** across the street) immediately want to move in. They provide a striking contrast to the high-rise apartment complex looming over them. One reason they appear slightly out of place is that they're recent transplants, moved from their original site around the corner so that **Manhattan Community College** could be built.

East of the houses are two other notable buildings. The **New York Mercantile Exchange** at 6 Harrison Street was once the city's dairy trading center. Around the corner at 60 Hudson Street is the art deco **Western Union Building**, whose attractions include its unusual façade, featuring 19 subtly shaded colors of brick arranged in undulating patterns, and the acclaimed restaurant **Chanterelle** on the ground floor. For those of simpler tastes, north of Western Union is **Puffy's Tavern**, a dark, atmospheric bar that dates back to the days of Prohibition.

Northeast of Puffy's, in the area of West Broadway, White, Walker and Franklin Streets, is the "artsy" part of TriBeCa. The **Alternative Museum**, at 17 White Street, began as a showcase for minority and Third World artists; it now displays a wider range of art. **Artists Space**, at 223 West Broadway, focuses on less well-known artists, with a special interest in raw, developing talents. The **SoHo Photo Gallery** (in New York, names are not always indicative of location) at 15 White Street is the oldest co-op gallery for photographers in the

United States. You can see excellent experimental productions at **HOME for Contemporary Art and Theater** at 44 Walker Street. **Franklin Furnace**, at 112 Franklin Street, is a bastion of the avant-garde, with an archive of such disposable pop objects as postcards and record jackets, and fairly wild performance art.

Canal Street is all that divides SoHo from TriBeCa, but crossing it on foot is not as easy as one might think. Traffic streams toward the **Holland Tunnel**, which leads under the Hudson River to New Jersey. As sidewalks are lined with bargain stores and peddlers, pedestrians get in the way too.

On the other side of the street, you'll find the **Museum of Holography**. The three-dimensional images at the museum (11 Mercer Street) include portraits of celebrities, some of which blow kisses to passers-by. One block west**, Greene**

Above: Keeping an eye out for sales. Right: The Village truly earns its name especially on warm Spring days.

Street is known now for its galleries, shops, and luxury loft apartments. In the 1850s, however, when SoHo was the center of town, Greene and Mercer Streets were the city's red-light district. The houses to the south catered to sailors from ships docked on the Hudson. As one moved north, the establishments improved; social swells patronized these houses. Perhaps more than its notorious past, Greene Street is known for its architecture. It's the center of the **SoHo Cast-Iron Historic District**, five blocks of ornate, mint-condition buildings. Best on the block is the pale blue Second Empire structure with mansard roof at number **28-30 Greene**, nicknamed the "Queen of Greene Street."

Above all, SoHo is known for its art. The most important group of galleries is on West Broadway between Spring and Prince Streets; chief among them is the **Leo Castelli Gallery** (420 West Broadway), which showed Andy Warhol and Claes Oldenburg, among others, in the 1960s. Other notable galleries include Nancy Hoffman (429 West Broadway), the **New Museum of Contemporary Art** at 583 Broadway, which showcases new artists, and **568-578 Broadway**, housing a variety of artists and media.

Even for those without an overriding interest in art, a stroll down **West Broadway** is imperative. The street is packed with interesting shops like **Harriet Love**, selling the finest antique clothing, as well as stylish bistros such as **Jour et Nuit**. Walking here offers great people-watching and window-shopping opportunities. Because of the area's popularity, noteworthy spots have appeared off the main thoroughfare, as well. **Bebe Thompson** at 98 Thompson Street sells children's clothes that are more fashionable than most adults own. At **130 Prince Street** is a collection of art galleries and jewelry designers. **Zona**, at 97 Greene Street, seems more a gallery than a store in the way that it displays its spectacular wares

from the American Southwest. And for food lovers, a visit to the block-long, high-tech gourmet grocery **Dean & DeLuca** (560 Broadway) is a must. In its plethora of rarified, luxury products, the store seems a microcosm of SoHo.

GREENWICH VILLAGE

As its name implies, **The Village** is a city within a city, an independent community. Its maze of narrow streets overflows with colorful life: students and peddlers, businessmen and loiterers of all nationalities, in every imaginable outfit. A center for the hippy movement in the 1960s, the Village's low brownstone residences today house die-hards or would-be members of that generation side by side with young, affluent professionals. From stores to clubs, restaurants to pubs, the Village offers something for every taste. As befits a neighborhood of such diversity, the Village boasts a charming disorder even in its layout: there seems no rhyme or reason to the meanderings of its streets. Unlike the regimented grid of avenues further uptown, streets here crisscross and intersect at odd angles; one, Waverly Place, even crosses itself. Also unlike uptown with its broad pavements and blocky highrises, streets here have trees, uneven pavingstones, and open-air sidewalk cafés.

This folksy, small-town atmosphere is no accident. Neighborhood residents, generally politically active, fought to prevent the building of high-rises and helped bring about the passage of numerous landmark laws. As a result, many old buildings have survived; and the neighborhood streets have more light and air than do other parts of the island, where the skyscrapers all too often block the sunlight.

This, of course, is one reason why the Village has preserved so much of the quaintness that led notable writers and artists such as Henry James and Mark Twain, Jackson Pollock and Franz Kline, to live here in the past. And its varied cultural makeup promotes a kind of ease and

63

tolerance epitomized by the 1960, when beatniks and folk singers – Bob Dylan among them – converged here. Because of this tolerance – or a cause of it – the area is the visible center of New York's gay community.

8th Street is the main shopping street of the Village, a bustling stretch of shops catering to the young and trendy. Of note to fans of rock'n'roll is the **Electric Lady** recording studio between Macdougal Street and Sixth Avenue. Started by the late rock star Jimi Hendrix in the 1960s, it has since been used by many others in the rock pantheon. Around the corner on **6th Avenue** is **Balducci's**, an Italian extravaganza of a food store that is definitely worth a visit, despite the crowds (especially bad on Sundays). Across the street is the remarkable **Jefferson Market Library**, a former courthouse modeled after Neuschwanstein, the castle of Ba-

Above: Even Fidel Castro has a home in the Village. Right: Washington Square is the meeting place for a very diverse society.

varia's Mad King Ludwig II. Demonstrating this community's ability to organize, residents rallied to save this structure from its planned demolition.

The Village does have its more restrained side: On 9th, 10th and 11th Streets between Fifth and Sixth Avenues you can see the residences of prominent families of the 1830s. The headquarters of Forbes Magazine and the **Forbes Galleries** at Fifth Avenue are bastions of established wealth.

To most, the heart of the Village is **Washington Square Park**. Now a neighborhood hang-out, the park has an unsavory past: it began as a cemetery for victims of a yellow-fever epidemic in the early 1800s. It went on to become a gallows-field; the notorious Hanging Elm still stands at the northwest corner of the park. Today, the park is like a giant playground. Residents strum guitars, play frisbee or chess; often, acrobats or mimes perform; while a huge sidewalk art festival takes place in the fall and spring. A few years ago it was also a paradise for drug dealers: Community pressure and the resulting police action have reduced their presence somewhat.

The obvious landmark here is the **Washington Arch**, built of wood in 1889 to commemorate the 100th anniversary of George Washington's inauguration. The arch was reproduced in stone several years later. In 1913, the statues, *Washington at War* and *Washington at Peace*, were added; bodybuilder Charles Atlas is said to have posed for them.

Fortunate are the residents of the elegant townhouses around Washington Square, or the ex-stables on two side streets, **MacDougal Alley**, on the west side of the park, and **Washington Mews**, on the east side. The low buildings in these tiny alleys now contain luxury apartments many New Yorkers would kill to get their hands on. Most of them, however, belong to faculty members of **New York University**.

The buildings of this vast university surround Washington Square, while its students can be found throughout the neighborhood – one reason the Village maintains its youthful air. Favorite student hang-outs from time immemorial are the coffeehouses along **MacDougal** and **Bleecker Streets**. Although they're far from elegant, dark cafés such as **Caffe Borgia**, **Le Figaro** and **Caffe Dante** are historical loci for a cappuccino and a long conversation. True history buffs will opt for **Caffe Reggio**, on MacDougal since 1785, America's oldest café.

This area is also notable for its folk and jazz clubs. Gone are the days when the likes of Bob Dylan and Joan Baez graced the stage of the Kettle of Fish, but you can still catch folkies at the veteran **Bitter End** on Bleecker Street and **Speakeasy** on MacDougal, rock acts at the **Bottom Line** at Mercer Street and West 4th Street, and top jazz acts at the **Blue Note** on West 3rd and MacDougal.

South and west of the Bleecker Street coffeehouses is the old Italian part of The Village, a section that absorbed the immigrants spilling out of Little Italy. Between Sixth and Seventh Avenues, Bleecker Street is filled with Italian food stores that have been serving the neighborhood for generations. Midway down the block, **John's Pizzeria** always has a queue.

Across Seventh Avenue, the cluster of **Bedford, Barrow, Grove** and **Commerce Streets** forms one of the most charming stretches of the Village, if not the entire city. The early 19th-century townhouses on the narrow, tree-lined streets are in perfect condition, and some have definite eccentricities. Number **75 1/2 Bedford Street** is the narrowest house in the Village, a mere 9.5 feet wide. It was here that the poet Edna St. Vincent Millay lived after World War One, when the area was in full Bohemian flower. Millay was fond of a drink or two at the local pub, not easy during Prohibition, when bars were illegal. Her solution, and that of many others, was to head down the street to a speakeasy named **Chumley's** at 86 Bedford Street.

It masqueraded as a garage. Now, patrons can enter through the Bedford or the Barrow Street doors, the latter formerly used by regulars to make a fast exit when the police raided.

At the end of Bedford is **Christopher Street**, the center of gay life in New York, as evidenced by the plethora of specialized bookstores and bars. Not all cater to a primarily gay clientele, however: for example, the **Lion's Head** (59 Christopher), a hang-out that is popular with journalists, both gay and straight. Branching off Christopher, **Gay Street** was not named for the local scene, but for a prominent 19th-century family.

The stretch of Bleecker Street between Christopher and **Abingdon Square** to the west is lined with shop after shop specializing in French antiques, food and clothing. Unlike frenetic 8th Street, it is an upscale area, good for a leisurely stroll.

Above: The East Village Spring Festival brings out the best. Right: Guess whom I met on the way to the alehouse.

Nearby, the **White Horse Tavern** at the corner of West 11th and Hudson Streets was a favorite of poet Dylan Thomas, whose early death was the result of downing a reported 19 whiskys on the premises. North and west of the White Horse are Abingdon Square and the **Far West Village**, where more streets lined with brownstones, funky restaurants and quaint shops lead down to the Hudson River. Because it is less mainstream than the area around Washington Square, this section, to some people, is the real Village now.

East Village

Given the fairly renegade nature of this neighborhood, it's hard to believe that this, in the 1800s, was the chic part of town. The Astors, Vanderbilts and Delanos had mansions here. Today, the area is a mixture of ethnic neighborhoods and the avant-garde. Indian restaurants line 6th Street between First and Second Avenues; there is a Ukrainian section at

7th Street and Third Avenue; and the new-wave descendants of the counter-culturists of the 1960s and the punks of the 1970s inhabit Avenues A, B, C and D (dubbed "Alphabet City").

The western border of the **East Village** is Broadway; here, from 8th Street down to Houston, trendy, inexpensive clothing shops have proliferated, as have loud, usually Mexican restaurants. Music-lovers stop at the giant **Tower Records** building on Broadway at East 4th Street.

For more cutting-edge entertainment, the East Village has numerous venues. **Gas Station** on Avenue B has esoteric performance art. A block away, **Nuyorican Poet's Café** on East 3rd Street features, naturally, poets. **La Mama E.T.C.** on East 4th Street has been in the forefront of the off-Broadway avant-garde theater movement since its founding in 1962. The best known stage in this neighborhood, though, is the **Public Theater**, also known under the name **New York Shakespeare Festival**, located in the historic building that was once the Astor Library. International hits such as *A Chorus Line* and *Hair* originated here.

Down the street is an example of the wealth formerly associated with this neighborhood: the **Old Merchants' House**, on East 4th and Lafayette Streets. Both inside and out, this Greek Revival townhouse is exactly as it was in the 1830s, when the family of merchant Seabury Tredwell lived here. His daughter, forbidden to marry the man of her choice, devoted herself, instead, to the restoration of this house. Northeast of the Old Merchants' House is another historic site: **McSorley's Ale House**, on 7th Street and Second Avenue, dates back to 1854. Its men-only policy survived well into this century, making the pub a top target of the women's liberation movement.

Cooper Union, nearby, is a top school for architecture and design. Abraham Lincoln delivered a stirring speech here just before he was nominated as a Presi-

dential candidate and the American Red Cross was founded here. East of Cooper Union, **St. Mark's Place** was a bastion of hippie-dom during the 1960s that has since filled with youthful shops and restaurants. At the end of the block, at Second Avenue, is **Gem Spa**; during the 1960s, it sold rolling papers as well as its trademark egg creams, the quintessential New York Jewish drink of milk, chocolate syrup and seltzer. You can still buy the beverage from the present Indian owners. Just north of Gem Spa is another culinary landmark, the **Second Avenue Deli**, home of superlative pastrami. For a *schvitz*, the 100-year-old **10th Street Baths** are the only Russian-Turkish steam baths remaining in the city. Anchoring the neighborhood is **St. Mark's-in-the-Bowery Church**, the second-oldest church in the city, where Dutch governor Peter Stuyvesant and other generations of his family are buried. The church hosts events organized by artistic groups of the area, including theater, poetry and dance.

LOWER MANHATTAN
Accommodation

As people live and work in lower Manhattan, there are relatively few places to stay.

LUXURY: **Marriott Financial Center Hotel**, 85 West Street, New York 10006, Tel: 212/385-4900. **Vista International**, 3 World Trade Center, New York 10048, Tel: 212/938-9100. **Hotel Millenium,** 55 Church Street, New York 10007, Tel: 212/693-2001.

MODERATE: **Washington Square Hotel**, 103 Waverly Place, New York 10011, Tel: 212/777-9515.

Restaurants

LUXURY: **American Harvest**, new American cuisine, Vista International Hotel, 3 World Trade Center, Tel: 212/432-9334. **Bouley**, exceptional French, 165 Duane Street, Tel: 212/608-3852. **Chanterelle**, inventive, multinational cuisine, 6 Harrison Street, Tel: 212/966-6960. **Delmonico's**, clubby domain of financiers, 56 Beaver Street, Tel: 212/422-4747. **Gotham Bar and Grill**, elegant mix of classic and nouvelle, 12 East 12th Street, Tel: 212/620-4020. **Montrachet**, sublime French in TriBeCa setting, 239 West Broadway, Tel: 212/219-2777. **La Pactole**, exquisite French food, 2 World Financial Center, Tel: 212/945-9444. **The Restaurant at Windows on the World** and **Cellar in the Sky**, sophisticated restaurant with soaring views plus a wine cellar with a spectacular set menu, 1 World Trade Center, Tel: 212/938-1111.

EXPENSIVE: **Il Cantinori**, rustic Tuscan, 32 East 10th Street, Tel: 212/673-6044. **Duane Park Café**, sophisticated, 157 Duane Street, Tel: 212/732-5555. **Il Mulino**, sublime Italian, always crowded, 86 West 3rd Street, Tel: 212/673-3783. **Nice Restaurant**, great Cantonese food, 5 East Broadway, Tel: 212/406-9510.

Provence, bistro, 38 MacDougal Street, Tel: 212/475-7500. **Sloppy Louie's**, seafood, 92 South Street, Tel: 212/509-9694. **Tommy Tang's**, spicy Thai, 323 Greenwich Street, Tel: 212/334-9190. **La Tour D'Or**, popular lunch spot for Wall Streeters, magnificent views, 16 Wall Street, Tel: 212/233-2780. **Tribeca Grill**, upscale bistro/celebrity hangout partly owned by Robert De Niro, 375 Greenwich Street, Tel: 212/941-3900.

MODERATE: **Benito I**, 174 Mulberry, Tel: 212/226-9171, and **Benito II**, 163 Mulberry, Tel: 212/226-9012, both low-key trattorias. **Caribe**, funky Jamaican, 117 Perry Street, Tel: 212/255-9191. **HSF**, good dim sum, provides pictures for those who are not sure of the names, 46 Bowery, Tel: 212/374-1319. **Hwa Yuan**, good Szechuan,

40 East Broadway, Tel: 212/966-5534. **John Clancy's**, impeccable seafood, 181 West 10th Street, Tel: 212/242-0343. **Lucky Strike**, chic SoHo bistro, 59 Grand Street, Tel: 212/941-0479. **La Metairie**, rustic French, 189 West 10th Street, Tel: 212/989-0343. **One Fifth Avenue**, nautically decorated, comfy American food, 1 Fifth Avenue, Tel: 212/727-1515.

Peking Duck House, 22 Mott Street, Tel: 212/962-8208. **Phoenix Garden**, excellent Cantonese food, 46 Bowery, Tel: 212/233-6017. **Pierre's**, bustling bistro, 170 Waverly Place, Tel: 212/929-7194. **Silver Palace**, elegant, dim sum, 50 Bowery, Tel: 212/964-1204. **Sweets**, seafood, 2 Fulton Street, Tel: 212/344-9189.

Taormina, Neapolitan, 147 Mulberry, Tel: 212/219-1007. **El Teddy's**, wild Mexican joint, with replica of the Statue of Liberty's crown on the roof, 219 West Broadway, Tel: 212/941-7070. **I Tre Merli**, fashionable Italian, 463 West Broadway, Tel: 212/254-8699. **West Broadway**, French bistro with 1950s decor, 349 West Broadway, Tel: 212/226-5885.

INEXPENSIVE: **Benny's Burritos**, burritos, tacos and enchiladas in a young, noisy setting, 113 Greenwich Avenue, Tel: 212/727-0584. **Formerly Joe's**, neighborhood hangout with above average food, 230 West 4th Street, Tel: 212/242-9100. **Katz's Delicatessen**, vintage deli, the standard to which all others are compared, 205 East Houston, Tel: 212/254-2246. **Kin Khao**, colorful Thai, 171 Spring Street, Tel: 212/966-3939. **Luna**, cheap, funky, Southern Italian, 112 Mulberry, Tel: 212/226-8657. **Moondance Diner**, fancy diner food, 80 6th Avenue, Tel: 212/226-1191.

Pink Teacup, soul food, 42 Grove Street, Tel: 212/807-6755. **Salam**, Middle Eastern, 28 Greenwich Avenue, Tel: 212/741-0277. **Sequoia**, waterfront spot at the South Street Seaport, classic American and seafood, Pier 17, Tel: 212/732-9090. **Sugar Reef**, wild, West Indian, 93 2nd Avenue, Tel: 212/477-8427. **Tatiana**, French, 26 Wooster Street, Tel: 212/535-8779.

Tai Hong Lau, good Cantonese, 70 Mott Street, Tel: 212/219-1431. **Two Boots**, blend of Cajun and Italian, 37 Avenue A, Tel: 212/505-2276. **Universal Grill**, international food, 44 Bedford Street, Tel: 212/989-5621.

Cafés / Snacks

INEXPENSIVE: **Anglers and Writers**, cozy Village café, 420 Hudson Street, Tel: 212/675-0810. **Bridge Café**, at the waterfront, 279 Water Street, Tel: 212/227-3344. **The Cupping Room Café**, cozy SoHo brunch spot, 359 West Broadway, Tel: 212/925-2086. **Donald Sacks**, salads and sandwiches, 2 World Financial Center, Tel: 212/619-4600. **Kiev**, 24-hour Russian blintz parlor, 117 2nd Avenue, Tel: 212/674-4040. **McDonald's**, perhaps the most upscale fast food joint in the world, with a pianist, tuxedo-clad maitre d', 160 Broadway, Tel: 212/285-9026. **Madeline's**, quaint bakery/café, 177 Prince Street, Tel: 212/477-2788. **Café Picasso**, marble-filled café with garden, Italian sandwiches and pastries, 359 Bleecker Street, Tel: 212/929-6232. **Caffe Roma**, great Italian pastries, 385 Broome Street, Tel: 212/226-8413. **Royal Canadian Pancake House**, 54 varieties, 145 Hudson Street, Tel: 212/219-3038.

Festivals / Events

New York is famous for its street fairs; in spring, summer and fall, there is a good chance of running into one on any residential block downtown. Late **January** / early **February**: *Chinese New Year* fills the streets of Chinatown with revelers and festive dragons.

May and **September**: *Washington Square Outdoor Art Show*, artists offer their paintings for sale on the sidewalks.

First two weeks of **June**: The *Feast of St. Anthony of Padua*, Sullivan Street in south Greenwich Village, with Italian sausage stands and try-your-luck games.

Third week of **September**: *Feast of San Gennaro*, Mulberrry Street in Little Italy.

October: *Greenwich Village Halloween Parade* with costumes and floats, starting at Washington Square and heading north.

Local Transportation

The narrow streets of Lower Manhattan and the Village are impossible for driving or parking. Although the subways are filthy and noisy, they are the fastest way to get around.

The **East Side IRT** lines run to the East Village, SoHo, the Civic Center and Bowling Green; the **West Side IRT** to Greenwich Village, TriBeCa, the World Trade Center and Battery Park. The **8th Avenue IND** lines run to Greenwich Village, TriBeCa and the Financial District; the **6th Avenue IND** to Greenwich Village, SoHo, the East Village and the Lower East Side.

Buses head *downtown* to Greenwich Village and beyond on 9th Avenue, 7th Avenue and 5th Avenue; to the East Village, Lower East Side, Civic Center and South Street Seaport on 2nd Avenue. Buses run *uptown* on Hudson Street/8th Avenue, Church Street/6th Avenue, Park Row/3rd Avenue, and Water Street/1st Avenue.

Tours and Tour Companies

Citywalks, Bleecker Street from Bowery to Abingdon Square, west of Downtown, TriBeCa,

the World Trade Center and Battery Park City, Tel: 212/989-2456. **Eldridge Street Project**, a tour of the Lower East Side, Tel: 212/219-0888. **Lower East Side Walking Tour**, historic tour of the sites of Jewish immigration, 718/951-7072. **Lower East Side Tenement Museum Tours**, visits to the different ethnic neighborhoods of Chinatown, Little Italy and the Jewish section of the Lower East Side, Tel: 212/431-0233.

Lower Manhattan, a tour of the area around Trinity Church and Wall Street, Tel: 212/242-5762. **Radical Walking Tour, Greenwich Village, Part II**, an offbeat political tour of the Village, Tel: 212/941-0332.

Sidewalks of New York, tours of Historic Greenwich Village, Ghosts After Sunset (haunted Greenwich Village), SoHo Ghosts, Ye Olde Tavern Tour, (Village watering holes) and Hollywood East, Tel: 212/517-0201.

Sunrise Tours of the Fulton Fish Market, Tel: 212/669-9416. **Tours of the Federal Reserve Bank** (and their gold vaults) Tel: 212/720-6130. **Tours of the Old Merchant's House**, Tel: 212/777-1089.

Warnings / Words of Wisdom

Because Lower Manhattan is where the city started, and so much of it – except the towering monsters of the Financial District – is so small scale, visitors particularly love this part of town. On weekends or holidays the streets are overcrowded, and a visit during the week is recommended. This also applies to the Lower East Side and the shops of Orchard Street, unless doing battle for merchandise is an irresistible part of the experience. Greenwich Village is packed on weekends; sitting at an outdoor café on Sheridan Square, one can truly see anyone and anything walk by. Mimes and other street performers also turn up at weekends, because obviously they will draw the biggest crowds and make more money from contributions.

With so many New Yorkers concerned about crime these days, weekends in popular areas like The Village have lost a bit of their appeal, especially at night, when gangs of kids from less affluent neighborhoods "visit" the Village for criminal pursuits. However, they tend to stick to the smaller side streets, usually preferring the main thoroughfare of 6th Avenue between Bleecker and 8th Streets – so stay away from that stretch and from Washington Square Park at night. Both are usually fine during the day.

Tourist Information

New York Convention and Visitors Bureau, 2 Columbus Circle, New York 10019, Tel: 212/397-8222.

MIDTOWN MANHATTAN

UNION SQUARE
CHELSEA
GARMENT DISTRICT
THEATER DISTRICT
FIFTH AVENUE

14th Street, Manhattan, is one of several large streets that serve as unofficial divisions in the the city's grid. In this case, it is between Lower and Midtown Manhattan. And though this boundary is perfectly arbitrary, something over the decades has happened to change the character of the city on either side of it. Below 14th Street, people lead more laid-back lives, the neighborhoods are homogenous, bustling, colorful. As one presses northward from 14th Street, the atmosphere turns increasingly frenzied, garish, dangerous. Another territorial division is possible along the Fifth Avenue axis, which acts as a mirror. The east ranges socially from middle-class upward and the west middle class downward.

UNION SQUARE

Union Square, once only a bedraggled patch of green in the angle formed by Park Avenue and Broadway where they meet at 14th Street, has altered its image lately. In its earliest incarnation, in the early 1800s, it was a park enjoyed by prominent local families such as the Roosevelts. Later, it was a theater center

Preceding pages: Living in Midtown can be like living in a beehive. Left: The spires of St. Patrick Cathedral.

and a part of Ladies' Mile, a stretch of fashionable shops. By 1900, the shops had moved uptown and the neighborhood started to disintegrate socially and economically. The grand old homes became working-class tenements, and the square served as a meeting place for anti-establishment demonstrations and violent confrontations with police. Various labor and political organizations opened offices nearby to be close to the action, among them the Socialist Party, the Communist Party, the American Civil Liberties Union and the International Ladies Garment Workers Union. This communion of alternative thinkers and doers once led to the square being derisively referred to as "bughead square."

Throughout the 20th century, Union Square experienced a serious decline. By 1980, the park was used by drug dealers and users, businesses on the square were failing and buildings being abandonned. The process of gentrification set in, however, with new businesses and families moving into the high-ceilinged lofts and spiffy restaurants and shops opening to serve them.

Now this area and the surrounding **Madison Square** and the **Flatiron District** (briefly called SoFi, for south of Flatiron, a nickname that did not take) have become completely rejuvenated.

73

Two residents of **Union Square Park** that locals were pleased to see restored are the bronze statue of the **Marquis de Lafayette** offering his sword in the cause of American independence, created by Frederic Auguste Bartholdi, the sculptor of the Statue of Liberty; and the **Independence Flagstaff** symbolizing the forces of good and evil in a clinch during the American Revolution. At the **Greenmarket** held on Wednesdays and Saturdays genuine farmers sell the freshest fruits and vegetables, flowers, meats and cheeses at very good prices.

The **Con-Ed** (Consolidated Edison) building, belonging to New York's utility company, looms to the east of the park on 14th Street. Further along the street is a building of public interest that faithfully followed the neighborhood's fall and rise, the **Academy of Music**. It was the top theater in the late 19th century, standing

Above: The Chelsea Hotel is a legend since the Sixties. Right: Even automobiles in New York have apartment houses.

next door to the now-defunct Tony Pastor's Music Hall, the birthplace of American vaudeville. The Academy went from presenting top musical shows to hosting boisterous political rallies, to presenting rock'n roll performances in the 1970s, before becoming a popular rock/dance club, **The Palladium**.

CHELSEA

This section of brownstones and friendly cafés to the northwest of Union Square was once part of the estate of Captain Thomas Clarke, a retired British officer. He named it after the Chelsea Hospital in London, which specialized in caring for elderly and disabled soldiers. His grandson, Clement Clarke Moore, author of the famous poem *Twas the Night Before Christmas,* inherited the land and developed it as a distinguished residential area.

These plans went awry in the mid-1800s, when the Hudson River Railroad laid down tracks in the western part of

Chelsea. Breweries, slaughterhouses and glue factories moved into the area along with groups of immigrants looking for jobs and cheap housing. The Ninth Avenue El, an elevated railway, aggravated the local depression by casting a physical and acoustic shadow on the street. It was taken down after World War Two, but the western part of Chelsea has never really recovered. It remains one of the poorest neighborhoods in the city.

The eastern part of the area did better. Fashionable stores moved into the area in the 1870s and giant dry goods stores, featuring cast-iron structural elements, opened along 6th Avenue. Theaters from the late 19th century provided space for lucrative movie studios at the beginning of the 20th. By the 1920s, the fashion business had followed its clientele uptown and the movie industry had gone west to Hollywood where the light was better and the climate warmer. The neighborhood fell into disrepair. Urban renewal in the 1950s and 1960s cleared away some of the slums that had evolved in the meantime, and restoration work began on the Federal and Greek Revival townhouses.

Ethnically, the area is mixed: Japanese, Chinese and South American immigrants have moved in, adding to the Greek, Spanish and Irish enclaves of old. The biggest change in the 1980s was the rehabilitation of older, less grand buildings and restaurants on Eighth Avenue as well as the abandoned cast-iron structure buildings on Sixth Avenue for a yuppie clientele. Now, on the previously all-Hispanic stretch of Eighth Avenue from 14th to 23rd Streets, visitors will find dusty Cuban coffee shops next to sophisticated bistros. Over the last few years Chelsea has also become home to various performing arts companies, putting it in the same league as the West and East Villages in matters of cultural activity. The **Joyce Theatre** on Eighth Avenue, for example, was formerly a decrepit film

theater restored to its original Art Deco splendor to host visiting dance companies. Farther west, **The Kitchen**, in reality the kitchen of the erstwhile Broadway Central Hotel, presents young performers in various media, from video shows to standard, classic poetry readings.

Around the corner, the **General Theological Seminary** stands on a plot of land that it will always occupy on the block between Ninth and Tenth avenues and 20th and 21rst Streets. When Clement Clarke Moore owned the whole district, he donated the land for the seminary on the condition that it always be used for that purpose. A theological scholar, Moore taught Hebrew and Greek here. The area otherwise also boasts a number of beautiful Federal townhouses, including one, on the corner of 9th and 21st, which is currently used as a store. It has such rustic charm that it is hard to believe at times it is in the midst of Manhattan.

If walls could talk, the **Chelsea Hotel** at 222 West 23rd Street, would never stop. Located in the one-time theater dis-

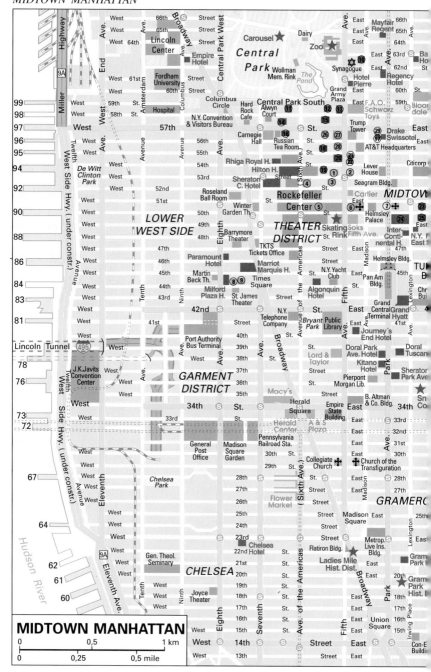

MIDTOWN MANHATTAN

| 0 | 0,5 | 1 km |
| 0 | 0,25 | 0,5 mile |

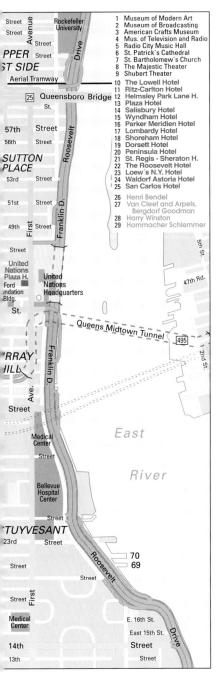

trict, it served as a stop-over for a long line of artists, including Sarah Bernhardt, Thomas Wolfe, Vladimir Nabokov, Arthur Miller, Brendan Behan and Dylan Thomas. In the 1960s and 1970s, it became truly notorious as rock stars such as Janis Joplin and the Sex Pistols carried on within its tolerant walls. The threshold of tolerance was reached when Sid Vicious, of the punk band the *Sex Pistols,* murdered his girlfriend Nancy Spungen there. Later, a film about their relationship, *Sid and Nancy,* was shot, appropriately, on location at the hotel.

The city's flower market, which begins at 26th Street and Sixth Avenue, is a diamond in the rough-and-tumble of the neighborhood. Like other markets, it is busiest in the early morning when fresh flowers arrive but the sensual show of smell and color, the exotic trees and flowers continues throughout the day.

Further north on Sixth Avenue, the tone becomes less charming and more blatantly commercial. Electronics and camera stores line the street, leading up to a massive bastion of consumerism. The glistening new **A&S Plaza**, a multi-level suburban-style mall anchored by the A&S department store, rises out of Herald Square. Next door to it is **Herald Center**, a strange, black glass vertical mall that was a commercial failure until the discount toy store **Toys 'R Us** moved in; it was also the subject of a scandal, when it was revealed that Ferdinand and Imelda Marcos had bought it using money of suspicious origin.

West of Herald Center is **Penn Station**, an ugly underground version of a previously grand train station, and **Madison Square Garden**, a cavern-like arena built on the site of the former station. It hosts concerts, sporting events and such happenings as the Democratic Convention of July 1992. The newly renovated **Paramount Theatre**, a concert venue, is on the other side, facing the magnificent colonnade of the **General Post Office**.

East-side Savvy

Chelsea residents have always had posh neighbors on their eastern flank. **Irving Place**, named after the writer Washington Irving, is a quiet street that connects 14th Street to **Gramercy Park** and is thereafter (that is its northward extension) called Lexington Avenue. The park was established in 1831 by the wealthy landowner Samuel Ruggles. Only those who bought the plots of land around the park were allowed to use it, a practice that continues today: local residents pay an annual fee for the key. This exclusivity and privacy in the midst of the city turmoil has attracted many distinguished citizens, Samuel J. Tilden, a former governor of New York State, and a presidential candidate for the Democratic Party in 1876, lived at No. 15, now the **National Arts Club**. Next door, the

Above: Gramercy Park is an oasis in the midst of New York. Right: The Empire State Building, once the tallest building in the city.

Players Club, for actors, was the home of the actor Edwin Booth (brother of John Wilkes Booth, Lincoln's assassin) until his death in 1893.

One of the most beautiful blocks of houses in what is known as the **Gramercy Park Historic District** is on 19th Street between Irving Place and Third Avenue; the exquisitely restored 19th-century townhouses and stables were the rooms and "offices" of an artists' colony in the 1930s.

A block north, at 20 East 20th Street, is the **Theodore Roosevelt Birthplace**. Teddy Roosevelt, the rough-riding man, the statesman who "spoke softly and carried a big stick," probably the most overtly imperialistic of all American presidents (he was the 26th), lived in these rather comfortable circumstances until his teens. The house was later destroyed, but Roosevelt's sisters had it rebuilt in mirror image to their uncle's house next door. It is open to the public and features five floors displaying period furniture and family memorabilia.

Slightly west of the Roosevelt house on Broadway is the **Ladies Mile**, another historic district. The ornate building at 881-887 was formerly the home of the Arnold Constable Dry Goods Store and is much admired for its two-story mansard roof. The building at **901 Broadway**, a construction in typically pompous mid-19th-century style, was originally home to Lord & Taylor, a department store now located on Fifth Avenue and 38th Street. Several blocks north at the intersection of Broadway, Fifth Avenue and 23rd Street is the unique **Flatiron Building**, which has given the entire neighborhood its name. The building itself was named for its shape, which is similar to that of the household device used to press clothes. On its completion in 1902, it was the tallest building in the world.

Across the street is **Madison Square**, now a fairly quiet park where locals walk their dogs. It has had a varied history. It was a hunting ground, then a pauper's graveyard. On their slow uptown migration, fashionable society settled the area for a while around the mid-1800s. Madison Square Garden was located here for a while before its move uptown. This old "Garden" building became notorious when millionaire Harry K. Thaw killed architect Stanford White there, designer of elaborate homes for many wealthy New Yorkers. Thaw thought that White was paying too much attention to Mrs. Thaw, the glamerous ex-showgirl Evelyn Nesbit.

On **Madison Avenue**, which begins on the eastern edge of Madison Square, is an impressive building that film directors like to use as a background when shooting films featuring the city on location. It has an interesting square tower with a clock on each face, inspired by the campanile of St. Mark's in Venice. This massive building with its lavish Italian-marble lobby and huge, vaulted entrances houses the headquarters of the Metropolitan Life Insurance Company.

Over on Fifth Avenue, a little to the north are two churches of contrasting character. The first is the somewhat severe, marble **Collegiate Church**, a Dutch Reform Church built in 1628 by Peter Minuit, the first Dutch governor of what was then called New Netherland. Its most famous minister is Dr. Norman Vincent Peale, author of the widely read *The Power of Positive Thinking*. Around the corner on 29th Street is the no less beautiful **Church of the Transfiguration**, also known as the Little Church Around the Corner. Its fame rests on the liberal attitude of the church fathers who, in 1870, went ahead with the funeral of an actor when other area churches refused. A number of actors later joined the parish in gratitude and solidarity, among them Edwin Booth and Gertrude Lawrence.

Empire State Building

A few blocks north of these churches is the building that once upon a time stood out alone on the skyline of New York.

The **Empire State Building**, built in 1931, was the world's tallest building at the time. Before its construction, the site contained two mansions belonging to the Astor family. In the early 1890s, William Waldorf Astor moved to Europe, and had a hotel built on the site of his house. His aunt, Mrs. William Astor more or less did the same with the neighboring mansion. Thus was born the Waldorf-Astoria.

Following a fire, the buildings were demolished and the hotel moved to a new site on Park Avenue where it is still operating as one of New York's finer accommodations.

As for the Empire State Building, as an office building opened during the Depression, it had a difficult time finding tenants at first. But its symbolic value for New York was undeniable, especially after King Kong climbed it in the 1933 film *King Kong*. During World War Two,

Above: Even fashion, from sweatshop to show, has its district in New York. Right: One way to keep an eye out on one's car.

a bomber brushed its 79th floor. And there is another notorious and grisly fact: the Empire State Building has always been a popular site for suicides; the first occurred in 1933.

Diagonally across the avenue is the former **B. Altman & Company**, a fine department store that catered to the carriage trade when it opened in 1906. It was a typical New York consumer institution, but its conservative style and the vigilant competition ultimately forced it out of business in 1989. The grandiose, palace-like building will probably be revamped to serve yet another business purpose.

A few blocks north, at 38th Street, is a store that, with its emphasis on quality merchandise, put it in direct competition with the former Altman. **Lord & Taylor**, which moved here from its original site on the downtown Ladies' Mile, has become most well known for its windows at Christmas. In December, 1905, it began the tradition of replacing the merchandise in its windows with Christmassy scenes;

the weather, it seems, was unseasonably warm that year and shoppers did not feel like looking at heavy sweaters and coats. The pretty displays were such a hit that they are now featured every year.

To the east of Lord & Taylor at this point on Fifth Avenue is **Murray Hill**, an area named after a certain Robert Murray who had a house here during the Revolutionary era. As legend has it, Mrs. Murray detained the British leader General Howe and his chief officers by offering them tea, allowing American troops to escape up the West Side.

After the Civil War, the area became attractive to the upper crust, who built their mansions along Fifth, Madison and Park Avenues. Quite a number of old carriage houses and townhouses survive in the cross streets, recalling those bygone days. **Sniffen Court**, a particularly well preserved stretch on East 36th Street between Lexington and Third Avenues, consists of a mews of ten exquisite carriage houses. Another fine example of these 19th-century residences is the 45-room brownstone located at **231 Madison Avenue**. Built originally for a banker named Anson Phelps Stokes, J.P. Morgan bought the house for his son in 1904. It is now being restored to serve as an addition to the **Morgan Library** nearby. The library, a massive, elaborate palazzo was built in 1906 to house Morgan's extensive collection of books, manuscripts and drawings, which include examples from the Middle Ages and the Renaissance, including original Gutenberg editions. Morgan's office in the library has been kept in the same condition he left it upon his death in 1913.

GARMENT DISTRICT

Life west of Fifth Avenue in the 30s and points north has a more populist feeling about it. The districts that are lined up next to each other here never fail to awe, inspire, amuse and frighten the less hardened outsider. Heading west on 34th Street, the first major intersection one arrives at is **Herald Square**, which was

named for a newspaper, the *New York Herald,* which, until 1921, occupied a palazzo-style building north of 35th Street. Neither the building nor the paper is around any more. The block between 34th and 35th Streets and Seventh Avenue and Broadway is occupied by **Macy's**, the grand-daddy of New York department stores. Founded in 1858 by a Quaker from Nantucket Island, the store always had a straight-laced image. Since the mid-1970s, however, the store has worked to improve this, and has become quite fashionable. One can find anything and everything on its 2.2 million square feet of retail space. And during Advent it is one of the best places for children to meet up with a dyed-in-the-wool New York Santa Claus.

During the 19th and early 20th centuries, the area west of Macy's was known

Above: Yellow cab salad, not unusual in Midtown Manhattan. Right: Times Square is both gaudy and decadent depending on the time of day.

for its rowdy dance halls, beer parlors, "cat houses," and other dens of vice. It was nicknamed Tenderloin District by the police, who considered it the choicest place to pick up a little graft. Some of the seediness remains, of course: The area around Tenth Avenue in the 30s and 40s is the infamous tough neighborhood known as **Hell's Kitchen**, which provided the backdrop to *West Side Story*.

7th Avenue between 23rd and 42 Streets has recently been renamed **Fashion Avenue** for its concentration of factories and showrooms serving the rag trade, as it is called. The real heyday of the area was in the 1920s, when the garment industry was set up here to keep it separate from the retail tier which had established itself in the great palaces of Fifth Avenue.

The garment district provided thousands with work, but often in miserable conditions and for miserable pay. It is hard to imagine how pople could work for ten hours a day in poorly ventilated, cramped sweatshops in New York's notoriously hot, muggy summers. It is hardly astonishing, then, that the International Ladies Garment Workers' Union (ILGWU) had considerable success in the area.

In recent years, manufacturing has shifted downtown in large part to the sweatshops of Chinatown, or to Asia outright; the showrooms, however, remain here. As a result, traffic is impossible during working hours as double-parked trucks and workers wheeling garment racks clog the streets.

A few blocks west is an area with a multi-ethnic mix of food shops, with Italian predominating. It's an enjoyable place to stroll around and pick up an interesting snack. A few blocks furth to the west between Eleventh and Twelfth Avenues on 34th Street is the **Jacob K. Javits Convention Center**, a glass city-within-a-city. The neighborhood is unfortunately a no-man's land and the design of the center is cold and slick. Only those

who have to attend shows there are encouraged to go.

42nd Street Discoveries

42nd Street is special, everyone knows, but mainly for the aura of of its western section where illicit activities have thrived longer than anyone can remember. It's a sleazy place, from its denizens to the XXX-rated entertainment touted by the movie-house marquees. Lately, developers have been taking advantage of tax breaks to put up new buildings and basically clean up the neighborhood. Though everyone except pimps, pushers and other profiteers of poverty will welcome the change, there are those who fear that the area will go to the other extreme and become sterile.

People arriving by bus in Manhattan will inevitably run into 42nd Street: the **Port Authority Bus Terminal** sprawls over the blocks between 40th-42nd Streets and 8th and 9th Avenues. Considering its size (it's the largest bus sta-

tion in the world), the Port Authority is quite efficient. But the trashiness of the surrounding neighborhood often slips inside, and in cold weather it also becomes one refuge for many of the city's homeless. Travelers are cautioned to keep a sharp eye on their belongings and tuck their wallets into safe places.

The heart of 42nd Street is without a doubt **Times Square**. It is here that the famous ball drops on New Year's Eve, and the garish neon signs light up the nights. The square owes its name to a resident newspaper. *The New York Times* moved to what was still called Longacre Square at the turn of this century. The mayor immediately changed the name to honor the paper. Because of the paper's conscientious international coverage, the neighborhood then became known as the "Crossroads of the World."

THEATER DISTRICT

The "Great White Way" also begins on Times Square. The nickname refers to the

river of lights formed by the theater houses lining Broadway. These are legitimate businesses that produce the world-famous Broadway shows. Because of the up and down nature of the Broadway theater, however, the **Theater District** goes through fits and starts. Almost on an annual basis, critics deplore the state of the "Fabulous Invalid," the Broadway Show, and in some seasons their nickname seems quite appropriate. With increasingly high labor costs and ticket prices, shows have to be absolute hits just to hang on. Quite a number fail, the sight of a darkened theater is not unusual.

The beautiful Broadway theaters are not only threatened by poor box office sales. Development has swept some off the map. In order to build the towering **Marriott Marquis Hotel**, several vintage theaters were razed and a giant, barn-like replacement was erected on its

Above: Acting begins at a tender age. Right: The modern design of the Jacob Javits Convention Center.

ground floor. The theater community protested loudly for months.

The Broadway theaters document American theater history. In the **Shubert Theater**, on West 44th Street, Katharine Hepburn appeared in *The Philadelphia Story*; Barbra Streisand made her Broadway debut in a show called *I Can Get It For You Wholesale;* and *A Chorus Line*, the longest running Broadway musical, took up residence for 6137 performances.

Down the street, the **St. James Theater** housed classics such as *Oklahoma!*, *The Pajama Game* and *The King and I.* The **Majestic** showcased *The Music Man*, *Carousel*, and now has, for years to come, *The Phantom of the Opera.* **Martin Beck Theater** nearby presented some great classics of the stage as well, with some classic performers: the Lunts in *Reunion in Vienna*, Katharine Cornell in *The Barretts of Wimpole Street,* and the debuts of Arthur Miller's *The Crucible* and Tennessee Williams's *Sweet Bird of Youth.* A couple of blocks north at the endangered **Barrymore**

Theater, Fred Astaire danced in *The Gay Divorcee* and Marlon Brando electrified audiences and became a star in *A Streetcar Named Desire*. The vast **Winter Garden** presented Fanny Brice and Josephine Baker in *The Ziegfeld Follies*, followed, decades later, by *West Side Story* and *Cats*. In the midst of all these theaters, in a very obvious construction on 47th Street between Seventh Avenue and Broadway, is the **TKTS** booth selling tickets at half price. During holidays the line often goes round the block by 3 p.m. when tickets go on sale.

On the northern end of the theater concentration, the streets are packed with restaurants and office buildings. One of the newest is the **Equitable Center**, a striking modern building that contains a huge mural by Roy Lichtenstein and several of the area's most upscale restaurants. Farther north is deli country, shared by the glitzy **Stage Deli**, a place that names sandwiches after stars and New Yorkers' favorite **Carnegie Deli**.

The Carnegie is always jammed, customers have to share tables with other parties, and the service is often rushed and rude, but the Carnegie offers New York's finest pastrami, and it is a quintessential city experience.

Critics, producers, playwrights, actors and other practitioners of the theatrical trade have long claimed that only the great, splashy, tinsely shows actually have a chance on Broadway. The more high-brow stuff has consequently relocated to what is known as "off-Broadway," especially to the houses of **Theater Row**. This block of formerly abandoned buildings on 42nd Street between Ninth and Tenth Avenues now hosts a lineup of good, less expensive theaters (for example, the **Lack Theater Alliance**, and the **Chelsea Theater Center**), complete with trendy restaurants for the hungry audiences. Not surprisingly, the next development was off-off-Broadway theater, which has spread throughout the city.

This neighborhood has other points of interest besides theater. The great ballroom **Roseland**, on West 52nd Street, opened in 1919 and hosted most of the major performers of the great jazz era of the 1920s and 1930s. It still features ballroom dancing several days a week.

All the way west, on the Hudson, are the great passenger liner piers; liners usually arrive and dock on Saturdays. A couple of blocks south is the **Intrepid Air Space Museum**, a veteran aircraft carrier now stocked with fighter planes and helicopters and open to visitors. The newest acquisitions are a submarine and a destroyer that operated in Vietnam. Those who want to crawl through the carrier's control bridges and command centers, be warned: There is usually a wait.

East on 42nd

As one heads east on 42nd Street from Times Square, the atmosphere changes completely. **Bryant Park**, located at Sixth Avenue, watched over by the slim

Grace and N. Y. Telephone Company Buildings, breaks up the harsh city landscape with some pleasant vegetation. In 1853, it was the site, during America's first World's Fair, of the Crystal Palace, a beautiful domed glass pavilion which burned to the ground five years later. During the Civil War, the space was used as a staging ground for troops heading off to battle the Confederates. It lingered as a vacant lot until 1834 when it was finally landscaped into an enjoyable park named after an American poet and journalist, William Bryant. For a while in the 1980s it became one of the gathering point of the turbulent New York drug scene. It lost all attraction as a quiet spot for a lunch break for New Yorkers sweltering in the local offices and shops. Thanks to a massive redevelopment project, the drug dealers have been chased away and the park is open again to the regular public.

Above: Busy Grand Central Station. Right: Anywhere else beside New York the Helmsley Building would be in dubious taste.

The eastern half of the park's block is occupied by one of New York's great treasures, the magnificent **New York Public Library**. Stone lions, *Patience* and *Fortitude,* greet visitors who have scaled the imposing front steps. The interior is as grandiose as the exterior, with mighty columns supporting vaulted ceilings. The library owns nine million volumes and 21 million documents.

Grand Central Terminal, east of the library, is another grandiose edifice. It was completed in 1903. At the time, the railroad yards between 42nd and 45th Streets were covered. But the neighborhood east of them, now the fashionable **Turtle Bay,** was anything but fashionable. Slums, slaughterhouses and breweries had settled in around the Third Avenue and Second Avenue Els (elevated railways). During the 1920s and 1930s the area gradually changed in character, though the cattle pens remained until 1947 when the United Nations moved in.

The southern façade of Grand Central facing the south side is notable for its

group of statues representing Mercury, Hercules and Minerva, and for its clock, 13 feet in diameter. New lighting has made this side of the station even more attractive at night.

The vast (160 feet wide, 470 feet long, and 150 feet high) **Main Concourse** inside is also worth a closer look. The ceiling has been decorated with the signs of the Zodiac, and the floors are of Tennessee marble with Italian *bottocino* marble trim, but in order to examine this carefully, you will have to make sure you do not come at rush hour. This beautiful building was in danger of being torn down by developers a few years ago. It was saved by a concerned group of citizens led by Jacqueline Onassis.

East of Grand Central are a number of interesting skyscrapers that keep visitors staring upward into the heavens.

Some time should be taken to walk a loop along **Park Avenue** where two buildings around 50th Street command attention. **St. Bartholomew's Church** is an intricately detailed, domed, Byzantine structure that is the only low-rise on overbuilt Park Avenue. As such, it has been the focus of a long-running battle between the church fathers, who want to sell the "air rights" to a developer, and conservationsists who would like to see it remain exactly as it is. The parties have reached a deadlock.

Down the block is the venerable hotel the **Waldorf-Astoria**, which with its elegant twin towers, looks like something out of a Fred Astaire-Ginger Rogers movie, especially after its recent restoration. The days in which well-heeled guests would arrive in their private underground railroad cars are long gone; now the toniest guests (including diplomats, movie stars and, occasionally, the President of the United States) arrive by limousine and stay in the private Towers annex.

Two other important constructions are the **Pan Am Building**, a 59-story rectangle that was supposedly shaped like an airplane wing (it has a helicopter landing pad on its roof); and the **Helmsley Build-**

87

ing, the former New York Central and New York General Building, which is painted in gold leaf and beautifully illuminated at night.

Another little detour starting on 42nd street is up Lexington Avenue to 53rd Street for a peek at the **Citicorp Center**. The distinctive sloping glass paneled roof facing south was originally designed as a solar collector but now it only serves as a vent. The building houses the **Market at Citicorp Center**, three levels of shops and restaurants. More important, in this always-bustling town, is that there are tables and chairs available to foot – sore pedestrians.

Back on 42nd Street, one of the most spectacular buildings in the New York skyline, the **Chrysler Building**, is an Art Deco wonder with abstract friezes of automobiles, flared gargoyles depicting

Above: The United Nations is becoming more crowded as the century progresses. Right: Exclusive jewelry is on offer in the Trump Towers.

1929 hood ornaments and a spire resembling an automobile grille. The lobby is also worth a look, for its African marble designs and ceiling featuring a depiction of the building.

Less stunning, but equally famous is the **Daily News Building** (even further east). It served as the workplace of Clark Kent, the reporter who changes himself into Superman every now and then to go chase the baddies. In the *Superman* comic book and movies, the newspaper is known as the *Daily Planet.*

Across the street and east of the News Building is one of New York's more beautiful indoor atriums, the 12-story extravaganza that fills the glass interior of the **Ford Foundation Building**. Alongside the trees is even a small pond. And finally, closing off 42 Street on the east is the world famous **United Nations** complex. John D. Rockefeller Jr. donated the money to purchase the land, previously occupied by slaughterhouses.

This development, the **General Assembly Building** and **Secretariat** were built in the late 1940s by an international committee of twelve architects. Now, it is most interesting to visit when the General Assembly is in session from September to mid-December.

North of the U. N. complex, the now exclusive **Beekman** and **Sutton Place** developments took a long time to achieve their present status. When Sutton Place was established in 1875, it was in wild territory facing an island with a prison and an insane asylum as its only buildings. In 1921 J.P. Morgan's daughter moved there, signalling the beginning of a trend.

Now these streets, especially 48th and 49th Streets, contain rows of beautiful townhouses with quaint gardens that are quite a sight in New York's concrete jungle. Local residents have included such distinguished stars as Katherine Hepburn, Leopold Stokowski and Judge Learned Hand.

FIFTH AVENUE

If midtown Manhattan has a flagship of sorts, an aorta funneling all the city's life forces, then it is Fifth Avenue from 42nd Street to Central Park. It was a top address even at its inception in the post-Civil War era, when railroad tycoon Jay Gould moved there, and the Vanderbilt family members tried to outdo each other in by building one lofty mansion after the other. Today, just a few of those buildings survive. Instead, what is visible in bulk are the towering skyscrapers of modern Manhattan business that replaced them.

Just off the Avenue, on West 44th Street, is a hotel notable not only for its accommodations but for its history as well. Mention the **Algonquin** and images of clubbiness and literary tradition come to mind; writers have always been drawn to this cozy, wood-paneled place. Meetings of the famous wits of the Round Table, Alexander Woollcott, Robert Benchley and Dorothy Parker among them, put the hotel on the map. Down the

street from the Algonquin, camouflaged among ordinary storefronts, is a remarkable building, the home of the **New York Yacht Club**. Sailing ship sterns, ocean waves and dolphins have been shaped into its façade. Until American sailors lost the *America's Cup* to Australia in 1983, the trophy had made its home here for over a century. It is now in San Diego. A few blocks up on 47th Street between Fifth and Sixth Avenues is a street devoted to the art of selling jewelry. This is the **diamond district**, with window after window filled with trays of gems. Bargaining skills count for a lot here, but given the array of merchandise, many people would not buy anywhere else. An estimated $400 million in gems is turned over daily here.

Saks Fifth Avenue near 49th Street is the next main stop on the way up north. It originally stood on Herald Square, but was transferred to the present location in 1924. It has stuck to elegance and a certain restrained style in the face of the general inclination toward trendiness.

The merchandise at Saks still recalls the dignity of the one time carriage trade. Next to Saks is a monument of an entirely different nature, **St. Patrick's Cathedral**, a dramatic Gothic cathedral that is the largest Catholic church in the United States and the eleventh largest in the world. When it was completed in 1879, it was too far out of town for most of its parishioners; now, of course, it is in the dead center. It is especially well-positioned as a grandstand for parades down 5th Avenue; the current cardinal, John O'Connor, a conservative thinker who, some think, tends to forget the fact that State and Church are separated in the USA, receives those parading by if he agrees with their position, or pointedly snubs them if he does not.

Across Fifth Avenue from St. John's is one of the major landmarks of New York, the 19-building, 22-acre complex of

Above: A youthful Prometheus watches over the Rockefeller Center Plaza. Right: The Museum of Modern Art is always exciting.

Rockefeller Center. John D. Rockefeller, Jr. took long-term leases on this land, originally to house the relocated Metropolitan Opera House. During the Great Depression, however, the directors of the Opera changed their minds and Rockefeller decided to develop the plot himself. The centerpiece is the 70-story **General Electric Building**; surrounding buildings house the corporate offices of Time Warner Publishing, Exxon and Simon & Schuster. The main focus, however, is the skating rink: during the summer months, it is an outdoor café but starting in October it becomes an ice rink. Skates can be rented. Another sight at the rink in December and early January is the gigantic Christmas tree. It usually stands over 60 foot high and is decorated with 20,000 colored lights.

Behind Rockefeller Center, on Sixth Avenue and 50th Street, is another landmark of New York entertainment: **Radio City Music Hall**, an art deco palace that from its beginning in 1932 has housed variety shows, featuring its famous house

act, the high-kicking Rockettes. For 40 years, Radio City was also *the* place to premiere a film. In the late 1970s, it, like Grand Central Terminal, was threatened with demolition and was saved by a group of concerned citizens, again including Jacqueline Onassis. Now, the Rockettes are still going strong; the hall is also used for pop concerts.

North of Radio City on 6th Avenue is a lineup of office buildings known as the **Concrete Canyon** for its ability to block out all light from the sky. This area's interesting sights are located on the side streets between 5th and 6th Avenues. Three are the **Museum of Television and Radio** on West 52nd Street, a vast archive of programs with facilities for visitors to view selections; the **American Crafts Museum** on West 53rd Street, a collection of contemporary folk crafts; and the **Museum of Modern Art**. MoMA, as it is familiarly known, has one of the world's finest collections of modern art, including works by Picasso, Matisse, de Kooning and Wyeth. Sculp-

ture is also represented extensively, as are film, design and photography. Also notable, if less obvious, is the entire stretch of 52nd Street between 5th and 6th Avenues; its nickname is **Swing Street**, to commemorate its place in the history of jazz. Starting in the late 1930s, its nightclubs, many of which were former speakeasies, began to draw the great musical innovators such as Charlie Parker and Dizzy Gillespie. Midway down the street, however, is a former speakeasy that has lost much of its original populism. The **21 Club**, identifiable by the jockey figures outside, became a private club-like celebrity haunt, the home away from home for power brokers in the worlds of show business and politics.

East of the 21 Club on 52nd Street at 5th Avenue is one of the few surviving 19th-century mansions that once lined the avenue. The site was once the property of William Vanderbilt. He owned a kind of Loire-Valley-like chateau across the street, but displeased by the growing

91

commercialization of the area, he sold it to the businessman Morton F. Plant, the Commodore of the New York Yacht Club. Plant built a five-story, Italian-style palace of marble and granite on the site but over the years, he too began to find the area too commercial, so he moved. According to New York gossip Plant gave his palazzo to Pierre Cartier for a string of pearls, said to be worth $1 million. Other stories have it, though, that William Vanderbilt re-entered the picture, bought Plant's real estate and rented it to Cartier for $50,000 a year. Whichever, in 1917, **Cartier** opened its doors in that exquisitely elegant location, and has been doing business there ever since. Perhaps to acknowledge its special beauty, the owners wrap it in red ribbon like a gift.

The eastern side of Fifth Avenue also merits some attention, particularly Madison Avenue where, at 50th Street, one

Above: A derivative view of the Yellow Brick Road. Right: Blending into the scenery on Lexington Avenue.

finds another stately vestige of a bygone era. The **Villard Houses** are a century-old group of six houses whose architecture was based, once again, on Italian models. They were commissioned by the publisher Henry Villard. The Archdiocese of New York later owned them and sold them to real estate developer Harry Helmsley; he in turn restored them and incorporated two of them into the **Helmsley Palace**. Purists are somewhat offended by this kind of architectural hooliganism, but are at the same time relieved that they were not torn down.

North on Madison is a building that also received a great deal of attention but more for its shape than its history. The **AT&T Headquarters** on 55th-56th Streets is referred to as the Chippendale building because the top curves of the roof were designed to resemble a piece of furniture in that style. It was greeted with scorn upon completion in 1982; over the years, though, people have gotten used to it. And younger visitors are drawn to it for its **InfoQuest Center**, a hands-on

museum of technology that is fun for even the computer illiterate.

Architectural sights in the mid-50s are as important as the shoppers' oases that have opened their doors here. All the big names of the fashion industry, and most of New York's super department stores, are located around here: **Mark Cross, Gucci**, **Bijan** (ultra-luxurious clothing for men), **Bulgari**, **Fendi**, **Harry Winston** and **Henri Bendel**. A special stop is **Steuben**, the designer of crystal sculptures that are often purchased by the city for gifts to visiting heads of state, a solid reference if there ever was one. **Fortunoff** is a very fine jeweler with a wide selection of jewelry in many styles and at many prices.

Since doing such heavy shopping is often tiring, there are several places to stop in this stretch. **Elizabeth Arden** has a salon on Fifth Avenue with a famous red door; it's the perfect place for a facial or massage. **Paley Plaza**, a pocket-sized park on 53rd Street just east of Fifth Avenue, is a surprising respite featuring a cooling waterfall nestled in between shops. The regal **Peninsula** and **St. Regis Sheraton Hotels** are soothing spots for afternoon tea.

Acute Consumerism

57th Street is another crossway that has to be investigated on its own. Off to the east, around Lexington Avenue, is a store that visitors enjoy even if they have no intention of buying. **Hammacher Schlemmer** is full of gadgets, sometimes ingenious, sometimes daffy inventions that one definitely will not find anywhere else. But who knows, some of these weird items might become standard. After all, H-S was the first store to carry the steam iron and the pressure cooker, oddball inventions in their day.

Within eyeshot, two blocks north of Hammacher-Schlemmer, is the consumer center *par excellence,* the place even the Queen of England visits when she is in town. **Bloomingdale's** is not a department store, it is a marketing phenome-

non; a multi-level compendium of trendy items, presented in such a dazzling way that only the truly strong of will can resist a good spend. Given the store's success, it is no surprise that marketing managers make pilgrimages here to study the local technique.

A trail of exclusive shops (**Chanel**, **Laura Ashley**, **Buccellati** and **Hermes**) lines the way westward from H-S to the intersection of 57th and Fifth, the most fashionable shopping intersection in all of New York. On these four corners, the department store **Bergdorf Goodman** and its temple of jewelry **Van Cleef & Arpels** face off against the new **Galeries Lafayette** and **Tiffany's**.

The latter two are housed in the ostentatious new **Trump Tower**, which also contains several floors of upscale shops. Trump Tower is such a symbol of grandiose excess that visitors flock in just to

Above: The Plaza, more than a luxury hotel, it's a legend. Right: The Trump Tower, a Garden of Eden for well-heeled consumers.

look at the lobby which is panelled in peach-colored marble and boasts a pleasant, cooling waterfall.

A few blocks west on 57th Street is the world-famous **Carnegie Hall**, built by the philanthropic industrialist Andrew Carnegie. Tchaikovsky conducted the New York Philharmonic here at the opening concert in 1891. He was followed by a long string of great conductors (some famous composers as well), including Gustav Mahler, Arturo Toscanini, Leopold Stokowski and Leonard Bernstein. Pop stars also used the stage and the giant hall (Simon and Garfunkel, for example). Some say it has the best acoustics in the world and now, after a massive 1986 restoration, its physical beauty matches the sound. The history of the hall is carefully chronicled in the neighboring **Carnegie Hall Museum** in the **Carnegie Hall Tower**.

Right next to the hall is the **Russian Tea Room**, a red, green and gold extravaganza, always lit with Christmas lights, which is the place to eat blini with caviar and watch producers try to talk major movie stars into deals. By coming here, these stars are not being shy; the biggest names get the most visible banquettes: in the bar and the front of the room. The very back and upstairs are considered, literally, Siberia. Down the street from Carnegie Hall is another haven for artists, the **Art Students League**, a neo-Renaissance palace. Every important exhibition at the turn of the century was held here; many still are. Nearby is a temple with a completely different tone: the **Hard Rock Café**. The Cadillac fins over the entrance were the subject of a neighborhood battle a few years back; the Hard Rock won and got to restore the fins. The lines out the door and the ear-splitting music and brouhaha inside testify to the enduring popularity of this place. In competition with the Hard Rock, a new loud, star memento-studded restaurant has opened down the block. **Planet Hollywood** is the movie star's Hard Rock, a repository of film memorabilia, including those donated by its co-owners, Arnold Schwarzenegger, Sylvester Stallone and Bruce Willis.

North of this stretch of competitive restaurants is a building that is so intricate and magnificent that even rushed New Yorkers stop and stare. **Alwyn Court**, at 7th Avenue and 58th Street, has terra cotta dragons and other decorations covering every inch. In a city in which so many buildings are glass boxes, this rococo concoction is a dazzler. **Petrossian**, the neighboring store, is New York's leading caviar emporium.

The End of Midtown

For its part, Fifth Avenue proceeds to Central Park at 59th Street, another busy intersection. **FAO Schwarz** is a parental nemesis, one of the world's finest toy shops. Before Christmas, the lines go around the block; only the truly stalwart or greedy dare to venture in. Across the street is a fairly formal park, **Grand Army Plaza**, anchored by the circular **Pulitzer Memorial Fountain**, a little monument funded by a bequest in the late publisher's will. Also prominently displayed in the Plaza is a statue of Civil War hero General William Tecumseh Sherman that was displayed at the World Exhibition in Paris in 1900. It has been here since 1903 but no one took special note of it until recently, when it was so garishly regilded by Donald and Ivana Trump that it seemed to be made of neon. Those concerned were reassured that it would tone down with age. The since-divorced Trumps took interest in the statue after they bought the **Plaza Hotel** on the southwestern corner of the intersection. This turn-of-the-century masterpiece of neo-Renaissance design had once been the most exclusive hotel in the city. Its list of past guests includes Eleanor Roosevelt, Mark Twain, F. Scott Fitzgerald and Frank Lloyd Wright, who made it his New York headquarters. The Plaza has a pleasant, luxury restaurant.

MIDTOWN MANHATTAN
Accommodation

LUXURY: **Drake Swissotel**, 440 Park Avenue, New York 10022, Tel: 212/421-0900. **Grand Hyatt**, Park Avenue at Grand Central, New York 10017, Tel: 212/883-1234. **Helmsley Park Lane**, 36 Central Park South, New York 10019, Tel: 212/371-4000. **Marriott Marquis**, 1535 Broadway, New York 10036, Tel: 212/398-1900. **Parker Meridien**, 118 West 57th Street, New York 10019, Tel: 212/245-5000. **Peninsula New York**, 700 5th Avenue, New York 10019, Tel: 212/247-2200. **Plaza**, 5th Avenue at 59th Street, New York 10019, Tel: 212/759-3000. **Rhiga Royal**, 151 West 54th Street, New York 10019, Tel: 212/307-5000.

Ritz-Carlton, 112 Central Park South, New York 10019, Tel: 212/757-1900. **St. Regis Sheraton**, 2 East 55th Street, New York 10022, Tel: 212/767-0525. **United Nations Plaza**, 1 U.N. Plaza, New York 10017, Tel: 212/355-3400. **Waldorf-Astoria**, 301 Park Avenue, New York 10022, Tel: 212/355-3000.

EXPENSIVE: **Doral Park Avenue**, 70 Park Avenue, Tel: 212/687-7050. **Doral Tuscany**, 120 East 39th Street, New York 10016, Tel: 212/686-1600. **Dorset**, 30 West 54th Street, New York 10019, Tel: 212/247-7300. **Hilton**, 1336 6th Avenue, New York 10019, Tel: 212/586-7000. **Inter-Continental**, 111 East 48th Street, New York 10017, Tel: 212/755-5900. **Kitano**, 66 Park Avenue, New York 10016, Tel: 212/685-0022. **Loew's New York Hotel**, 569 Lexington Avenue, New York 10022, Tel: 212/752-7000. **New York Marriott East Side**, 525 Lexington Avenue, New York 10022, Tel: 212/755-4000. **Sheraton Centre**, 811 7th Avenue, New York 10019, Tel: 212/581-1000. **Sheraton Park Avenue**, 45 Park Avenue, New York 10016, Tel: 212/685-7676.

MODERATE: **Gramercy Park**, 2 Lexington Avenue, New York 10010, Tel: 212/475-4320. **Chelsea**, 222 West 23rd Street, New York 10011, Tel: 212/243-3700. **Paramount**, 235 West 46th Street, New York 10036, Tel: 212/764-5500. **Salisbury**, 123 West 57th Street, New York 10019, Tel: 212/246-1300. **The Algonquin**, 59 West 44th Street, New York 10036, Tel: 212/840-6800. **Shoreham**, 33 West 55th Street, New York 10019, Tel: 212/247-6700. **Lombardy**, 111 East 56th Street, New York 10022, Tel: 212/753-8600. **Wyndham**, 42 West 58th Street, New York 10019, Tel: 212/753-3500.

BUDGET: **Journey's End**, 3 East 40th Street, New York 10016, Tel: 212/447-1500. **Milford Plaza**, 270 West 45th Street, New York 10036,

Tel: 212/869-3600. **The Roosevelt**, 45th Street and Madison Ave., New York 10017, Tel: 212/661-9600. **San Carlos**, 150 East 50th Street, New York 10022, Tel: 212/755-1800.

Restaurants

LUXURY: **Le Bernadin**, exceptional seafood, 155 West 51st Street, Tel: 212/489-1515. **21 Club**, the point here has never been the food, just being able to afford it, 21 West 52nd Street, Tel: 212/582-7200. **La Côte Basque**, distinguished French cuisine, 5 East 55th Street, Tel: 212/688-6525. **The Four Seasons**, site of the power lunch, 99 East 52nd Street, Tel: 212/754-9494. **La Grenouille**, a ladies-who-lunch hangout, 3 East 52nd Street, Tel: 212/752-1495.

Lutèce, best French, 249 East 50th Street, Tel: 212/752-2225. **Palio**, good Italian, 151 West 51st Street, Tel: 212/245-4850. **The Palm**, the largest lobsters and steaks in New York, 837 2nd Avenue, Tel: 212/687-2953. **Rainbow Room**, atop Rockefeller Center, the height of sophistication, 30 Rockefeller Plaza, Tel: 212/632-5100. **The Quilted Giraffe**, unusual nouvelle French, 550 Madison Avenue, Tel: 212/593-1221. **San Domenico**, Bolognese cuisine, 240 Central Park South, Tel: 212/265-5959.

EXPENSIVE: **Bice,** Milanese trattoria, 7 East 54th Street, Tel: 212/688-1999. **Chefs, Cuisiniers Club**, superlative new American cuisine cooked by chefs for their fellow chefs and others, 36 East 22nd Street, Tel: 212/228-4399. **China Grill**, inventive blend of French, Californian and Chinese, 51 West 52nd Street, Tel: 212/333-7788. **Coffee Shop**, hip Brazilian, 29 Union Square West, Tel: 212/243-7969. **Da Umberto**, Tuscan trattoria, 107 West 17th Street, Tel: 212/989-0303. **Eze**, Provençal, 254 West 23rd Street, Tel: 212/691-1140. **Gallagher's Steak House**, 228 West 52nd Street, Tel: 212/245-6370. **Lola**, hot Caribbean, gospel brunch, 30 West 22nd Street, Tel: 212/675-6700.

Hatsuhana, best sushi in town, 17 East 48th Street, Tel: 212/355-3345. **Jezebel**, fabulous soul food, 630 9th Avenue, Tel: 212/582-1045. **Lespinasse**, multinational, in the St. Regis Sheraton, 2 East 55th Street, Tel: 212/339-6719. **Le Madri**, Italian mothers do the cooking, 168 West 18th Street, Tel: 212/727-8022. **Old Homestead**, steakhouse, vast portions, 56 9th Avenue, Tel: 212/242-9040.

Positano, southern Italian food, 250 Park Avenue South, Tel: 212/777-6211. **Remi**, glorious Venetian food, 145 West 53rd Street, Tel: 212/581-4242. **La Reserve**, exceptional French, 4 West 49th Street, Tel: 212/247-2993. **Russian Tea Room**, luxurious place to see celebrities, 150

West 57th Street, Tel: 212/265-0947. **Sumptuary Restaurant**, creative California-New York blend cuisine, 400 3rd Avenue, Tel: 2212/989-0303. **Trattoria Dell'Arte**, with huge antipasto bar, 200 West 57th Street, Tel: 212/245-9800. **Union Square Café**, 1 East 16th Street, Tel: 243-4020. **The Water Club**, good seafood in a fancy barge, East 30th Street at East River, Tel: 212/683-3333.

MODERATE: **Cabana Carioca**, good Brazilian, 123 West 45th Street, Tel: 212/581-8088.

Carnegie Deli, New York delicatessen, 854 7th Avenue, Tel: 212/757-2245. **Claire**, seafood, 156 7th Avenue, Tel: 212/255-1955. **Periyali**, traditional Greek, 35 West 20th Street, Tel: 212/463-7890. **Prix-Fixe**, barn-like restaurant, set menu, 18 West 18th Street, Tel: 212/675-6777. **Rosa Mexicano**, traditional Mexican, 1063 1st Ave, Tel: 212/753-7407. **Trixie's**, good Southern food, 307 West 47th Street, Tel: 212/582-5480.

BUDGET: **Big City Diner**, fun, funky diner, 572 11th Avenue, Tel: 212/244-6033. **Friend of a Farmer,** tasty American fare, 77 Irving Place, Tel: 212/477-2188. **Broadway Diner**, Theater District diner, 1726 Broadway, Tel: 212/765-0909. **Café Iguana**, fun Tex-Mex, 235 Park Avenue South, Tel: 212/529-4770. **Cadillac Bar**, noisy Tex-Mex, 15 West 21st Street, Tel: 212/645-7220. **Hamburger Harry's**, solid burger joint, 145 West 45th Street, Tel: 212/840-2756. **Hour Glass Tavern**, low priced prix-fixe but you are given just one hour to eat, 373 West 46th Street, Tel: 212/265-2020. **Joe Allen's**, simple, theatre hangout, 326 West 46th Street, Tel: 212/581-6464. **Karen's Taste of the Tropics**, tiny Caribbean spot, 374 West 46th Street, Tel: 212/586-7769. **Landmark Tavern**, historic waterfront tavern, 626 11th Avenue, Tel: 212/757-8595. **Live Bait**, crowded bar/Southern restaurant frequented by models, 14 East 23rd Street, Tel: 212/353-400. **Pete's Tavern**, 129 East 18th Street, Tel: 212/473-7676.

Bistros

EXPENSIVE: **Café Un Deux Trois**, Theater District bistro, 123 West 44th Street, Tel: 212/354-4148. **Orso**, excellent Northern Italian bistro, 322 West 46th Street, Tel: 212/489-7212. **Chelsea Central**, cozy American bistro, 227 10th Avenue, Tel: 212/620-0230. **La Colombe D'Or**, popular Provençal bistro, 134 East 26th Street, Tel: 212/689-0666.

Espace, 9 East 16th Street, Tel: 212/463-7101. **Mesa Grill**, fashionable bistro, 102 5th Avenue, Tel: 212/807-7400. **Lescale**, French bistro, 43 East 20th, Tel: 212/477-1180. **Sam's**, casual American bistro owned by actress Mariel Hemingway, 152 West 52nd Street, Tel: 212/582-8700. *MODERATE:* **Bellevue,** modest bistro, 496 9th Avenue, Tel: 212/967-7850. **Chez Josephine**, excellent French bistro, 414 West 42nd Street, Tel: 212/594-1925. **Chez Napoleon**, old-fashioned Theater District bistro, 365 West 50th Street, Tel: 212/265-6980. **Les Halles**, French bistro, 411 Park Avenue South, Tel: 212/679-4111. *BUDGET:* **Le Madeleine**, casual bistro, 403 West 43rd Street, Tel: 212/246-2993.

Transportation

Cabs are readily available on all streets in the midtown sections. On the West Side, the Theater District, Garment District and Chelsea, the **West Side IRT**, **6th Avenue** and **8th Avenue IND** lines are the proper routes. The Nr.10, Nr. 11, Nr. 5 and 6 bus lines also travel the West Side in both directions.

For the East Side, Union Square, Gramercy Park, Murray Hill and Midtown east, the **East Side IRT** line and Nr. 104, Nr. 14, Nr. 101 and Nr. 102 buses are the ones to take.

Tours and Tour Companies

Tours of Carnegie Hall, 1, 154 West 57th Street, Tel: 212/247-7800. **Circle Line**, boat cruise around Manhattan, Pier 83, West 42nd Street at Hudson River, Tel: 212/563-3200.

NBC Studio Tours, 30 Rockefeller Plaza, Tel: 212/664-4000.

New York Public Library Tours, 5th Avenue, 40th-42nd Streets, Tel: 212/661-7220.

Sidewalks of New York, **Chelsea Saints and Sinners**, **Murder Tours of Midtown**, Tel: 212/517-0201.

United Nations Tour, East 45th Street and 1st Avenue, Tel: 212/963-7113.

Festivals / Special Events

March 17: *St. Patrick's Day Parade* moves down 5th Avenue.

Easter Sunday: *Easter Parade* moves down 5th Avenue.

May: *Memorial Day Parade* moves down 5th Avenue, late May. *Ninth Avenue Food Festival*, from 35th to 57th Street.

July 4: *Independence Day Fireworks,* colorful display over East River.

October: *Columbus Day Parade* moves down 5th Avenue.

November: *Thanksgiving Day Parade* moves down Broadway to Macy's.

Early December: *Christmas Tree Lighting*, takes place at the Rockefeller Center.

Tourist Information

New York Convention and Visitors Bureau, 2 Columbus Circle, New York, N.Y. 10019, Tel: 212/397-8222.

UPPER MANHATTAN

CENTRAL PARK
UPPER WEST SIDE
COLUMBIA
UPPER EAST SIDE
HARLEM

Today downtown is history; midtown is work; but for many, uptown Manhattan is the essence of New York, or just plain home. Here is the hallmark grid-like layout typical of New York; here, in a small area, is the social and ethnic diversity so characteristic of this melting-pot city. From Central Park to Harlem, from the artsy Upper West Side to the cool elegance of the Upper East Side, from German Yorkville to the Hispanic enclaves in the East 100s, from the ivory towers of academe at Columbia University to the medieval ones of the museum-cum-monastery The Cloisters, Upper Manhattan is perhaps more diverse, and has more cultural treasures, than any other part of the island.

The border of Uptown is 59th Street, running along the foot of Central Park. Between Fifth Avenue and Central Park West, the street is known as **Central Park South**, a pleasant place to stroll. On one side, fancy hotels alternate with apartment buildings, while restaurants such as **Rumpelmayer's** and **Maxim's** offer upscale dining for the denizens of both. On the other, a low stone wall separates sidewalk from the trees of Central

Preceding pages: Central Park, 843 acres of landscaped greenery. Left: Small talk with a wiener ad in Uptown Manhattan.

Park proper; at intervals, rows of horse-drawn carriages await passengers well-heeled enough to pay their fares (which run at about $34 for half an hour).

At the southwest corner of the park, Central Park South intersects with Broadway, Eighth Avenue, and Central Park West in a traffic hub known as **Columbus Circle**. A statue of Christopher Columbus beckons north. Information about New York City in a variety of languages can be found at the headquarters of the **New York Convention and Visitors Bureau**, located on the second floor of an architecturally outlandish edifice nicknamed the "Lollipop Building." This bureau (it is closed on weekends) offers everything from current brochures on sights and attractions to bus and subway maps, restaurant and shopping guides, and discount tickets to Broadway shows.

CENTRAL PARK

Perhaps the best place to start a tour of Upper Manhattan is in **Central Park** itself. Not only does it offer shady walks through fields and meadows, past odd bits of statuary or rock outcroppings; the park also gives the visitor a chance to see New Yorkers at their best. On a sunny weekend, the locals turn out in force: Young men and women on roller-blades,

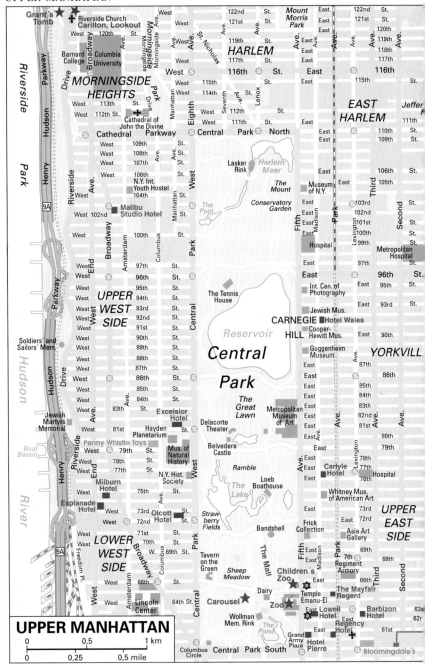

UPPER MANHATTAN

```
0          0,5              1 km
|----|----|----|----|
0      0,25        0,5 mile
```

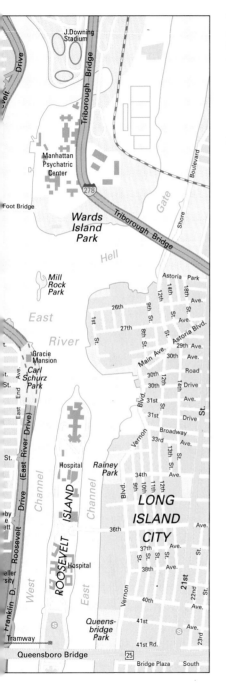

outfitted with protective padding in a rainbow of Day-Glo colors, zoom in and out of the crowds; family groups, armed with strollers, tricycles and balloons, seek picnic spots; Tai Chi classes practice in inscrutable silence under a tree, while nearby, Eastern European folk dancers execute elaborate steps to the music of a portable tape recorder. Although the roads are closed to cars on weekends, traffic is still heavy: Armies of joggers contend with the many cyclists. But the colors are bright, spirits are high, and, at the sight of kites flying in the spring breezes of the Sheep Meadow, many people come truly to understand the over-used phrase "I love New York!"

This 843-acre oasis seems so natural that even most New Yorkers think of it as a piece of nature which has been pre-served from urban development. Not so. Every tree, every lake was part of a care-fully thought-out plan, and placed with the gentle precision of an artist's brush stroke. Central Park is the result of the rigorous efforts of 3000 workers, 400 horses, a 14-million-dollar annual budget and more than a century of planning and hard labor. Back in 1857, the land that was to become New York's beloved park was a vast and ugly eyesore filled with garbage, stone quarries and pigsties. It was populated by strays: cats, dogs and squatters who camped on the land and eked out livings by pig-farming and moonshining. Finally, residents of the city had had more than they could stomach. They determined that a contest should be held for the design of a park to replace this swampland. From 33 en-trants, two designers were chosen. They were Frederick Law Olmsted, a frail-looking Connecticut Yankee who was ap-pointed Park Superintendent, and Calvert Vaux, a short, slight Englishman. Their collaboration, a plan called *Greensward*, was the origin of today's Central Park.

The park reaches from Central Park South at 59th Street to Central Park North

at 110th, bounded by Fifth Avenue to the east and, on the other side, the appropriately-named Central Park West. Entrances divide the surrounding wall at frequent intervals all around the park. While maps exist to guide your steps should you feel compelled to see all of the park's noteworthy attractions, one of the best ways to visit Central Park is to ramble with no particular aim in mind. You're sure to see a host of things you never expected; and the ring of skyscrapers towering over the treetops will help guide you back to the urban world if you lose your bearings.

The southern entrance to the park is right across from Grand Army Plaza at 59th Street. Just inside the park is a serene body of water known, simply and logically enough, as **The Pond**. Moving north, one may hear the jarring strains of rock'n'roll music emanating from the

Above: Musicians give some of their best out in the open. Right: The Sheep Meadow in Central Park has not seen many sheep.

Wollman Memorial Rink, which is open to skaters on wheels in the summer, and on blades in the winter.

Nearby, there's the **Gotham Miniature Golf Course**, featuring scale models of various New York City landmarks, (a recent addition to the park, donated by the downwardly-mobile New York City mogul Donald Trump). Behind the golf course, but seemingly from another age, the 19th-century **Dairy** with its brightly-painted eaves and high-pitched slate roof houses the park's **Visitor Information Center**, where free maps, brochures and events schedules are available.

To the left, there's a twang of hurdy-gurdy music from the pipes of an authentic-looking antique **Carousel**. This merry-go-round features 58 ornately hand-carved and brightly painted wooden steeds, some of which rise and fall as they move round and round and round. On a busy weekend, lines are long, and the horses are ridden by veritable squadrons of children – most laughing and squealing, a few uncertain about what to think of the experience, and requiring the hand of an accompanying parent.

Central Park boasts not one but two zoos: the **Central Park Zoo** and the adjacent **Children's Zoo**. Admission is currently only $1 per adult and $.25 for children. Recently refurbished, the zoo today is a state-of-the-art facility. Over one entrance, marvellous mechanical zoo animals dance for a few moments every time the hour strikes on the **Delacorte Clock**. At the entrance to the Children's Zoo, youngsters are delighted by the sign "No Adults Unless Accompanied by a Child" at the entrance. If they wheedle enough with their offspring, parents may be allowed in to peek through the windows of the fanciful animal houses at the little creatures inside.

The vast expanse of **Sheep Meadow** hasn't actually seen grazing sheep since 1934. Replacing them on the grass are people, picnicking, sunbathing, playing

frisbee, or flying kites. Adjacent to the meadow**, The Mall** is a peaceful walk lined with elm trees and statues of Shakespeare, Robert Burns, Sir Walter Scott and others. Also nearby is the restaurant **Tavern on the Green**, esteemed more by socialites than gourmets, whose twinkling Christmas lights outlining the tree branches brighten night-time New York all year round.

The curving form of the **Central Park Bandshell** provides a backdrop for various summer concerts, speeches and all sorts of performance art. The shell attracts a wide variety of performers. Some days see amateur musicians – occasionally a little *too* amateur – giving impromptu "concerts" all around the area. But the bandshell also hosts its share of great performers.

72nd Street is one of Uptown Manhattan's main east-west arteries, which means that it, like 66th, 79th, 86th and 97th, cuts across the park. Passing beneath this street along a tiled arcade as you walk north from the bandshell, you'll come to **Bethesda Fountain**, an ornate three-tiered fountain named after the Biblical pool in Jerusalem said to possess healing powers. This vantage point offers a view of the rowers on the lake; if this inspires you, both boats and bikes can be rented from the **Loeb Boathouse**.

A splendid cast-iron bridge crosses the narrowest part of the lake and leads to **The Ramble**, a heavily wooded area of twisting paths that has several hundred species of birds. It is easy to get lost in The Ramble. If the skyscrapers at the park's periphery don't help you, try looking at the lampposts. Each post bears a metal tag with a number, the first two digits of which indicate the number of the nearest cross-street, while the last two show which half of the park you're in (even numbers for the eastern half, odd for the west). At least you'll know where you are standing in The Ramble.

Strawberry Fields, west of Bethesda Fountain, is perhaps the most-visited section of the park. The tear-shaped expanse of lawn is a memorial park to former

Beatle John Lennon, who was shot by a mentally disturbed "fan" in front of his apartment house nearby. Yoko Ono, Lennon's wife, donated the area, which is named after the Beatles' hit.

East of the fountain, across the park from Strawberry Fields, is **Conservatory Pond**. This pond is distinguished by being the site for the Saturday-morning regattas of model sailboats. In his children's classic *Stuart Little*, author E.B. White immortalized this race when his mouse-hero was engaged by a boat-owner to pilot his model craft to victory. When one looks at the boats, the idea of a creature captaining one of them doesn't seem so far-fetched: some of the models are six feet high, and perfect replicas of the real thing. There are more sights for children here: the statue of **Alice in Wonderland** sitting on a giant mushroom, or the story-tellers who narrate at

Above: Bethesda Fountain is a cool place to meet on a Summer day. Right: Rollerskating is one way to keep fit and get around.

the feet of the **Hans Christian Andersen Statue** on summer weekends.

Theater in Central Park isn't provided only by street musicians and oddballs, of which the park certainly has more than its share. At the **Swedish Cottage**, marionette shows are presented every week for a mere $2. On a larger scale, the nearby **Delacorte Theater** is home, in summer, to top-notch productions of the New York Shakespeare Festival TK, presented free of charge. The prospect of free quality entertainment in a city where standard theater tickets cost around $80 draws huge crowds, so come early. But these crowds are nothing in comparison to those drawn by Opera in the Park. The Metropolitan and City Opera companies stage a few open-air performances each summer on the **Great Lawn**, an oval expanse of meadow. For such performances, the meadow is literally carpeted with the blankets of picnickers and waiting for the evening's entertainment to begin. Other concerts are equally, if not more, popular; in 1990, singer Paul

Simon drew an inordinately large segment of the city's population.

Overlooking lawn and theater is **Vista Rock** and the Gothic Revival **Belvedere Castle**, whose tower is an even better look-out point. The castle is used as an information center where exhibits and classes for children are held; there's also a weather station here. Descending from here, you'll come to the **Shakespeare Garden**, planted with shoots of hawthorn and other plants from the garden of Shakespeare's house in Stratford-upon-Avon, England.

East of the Great Lawn is another notable Central Park monument, the old and somewhat worn obelisk: **Cleopatra's Needle**. The wear is understandable; as the obelisk is 3500 years old – although in fact it has nothing to do with Cleopatra. This granite monument was a gift to the city from Egypt. It was first moved by the Romans, who brought it to Alexandria in 12 B.C.; its second move, in A.D.1880, brought it to New York. Its deterioration is due as much to its age as to the city's humidity and pollution.

Walking north past the back of the Metropolitan Museum (whose every expansion involves heated dispute with park officials opposed to the museum's encroachment on their turf) you'll come to the huge **Reservoir**, extending some ten city blocks. The path around the Reservoir is a favorite with joggers, although all are advised to avoid the area after nightfall. North of the reservoir, the park is less heavily visited, as the neighborhoods outside the park's confines grow progressively more questionable as one gets up into the 100s. Still, there are many recreational possiblities, notably the **Tennis House**, as well as lawns, **The Pool** and **Lasker Rink**. At 105th Street near Fifth Avenue is **Conservatory Garden**, the park's only formal gardens, bequeathed by the Vanderbilt family. Very popular free tours and free concerts are given here in the summer.

Central Park at night is, unfortunately, a place to avoid, unless you're in the midst of one of the crowds going to an open-air concert or theater production. Particularly since the case of the "New York Jogger," when a young woman jogging around the reservoir after dark was attacked and raped by a band of teenagers, New Yorkers are wary of the park's all-too-quiet paths. Central Park, for all its beauty, is still in New York, and it's wise not to forget this fact however green its lawns and trees,

UPPER WEST SIDE

Central Park is not all that Upper Manhattan has to offer – far from it. The neighborhood between Central Park West and the Hudson River, from 59th Street up to about 104th or so, is one of New York's most vibrant in terms of culture, shopping, restaurants. As the neighborhood flourished during the 1980s, changing in character from "experimental" to "in," it retains a new vibrancy, even if

prices for food, clothing and rent have rapidly overtaken those of other, more established neighborhoods.

The Upper West Side is a picture-book example of gentrification. Twenty years ago, Columbus Avenue was still a questionable address: today, it's one of New York's most chic shopping streets, lined with brand-name boutiques and glassed-in cafés advertising brunch specials. The same process of upgrading is now occurring on Amsterdam Avenue, one block west, which has until now retained a larger complement of family shoe-repair shops, corner grocery stores, and the like, as well as its Hispanic population. In 1957, Leonard Bernstein and Stephen Sondheim captured the flavor of life in the neighborhood in their immortal *West Side Story*. Today, there's still a strong sense of racial contrast. Cross streets in the area of the 80s are filled, on

Above: Al fresco dining while watching the sights of Upper West Side. Right: Basketball is one of the most popular team sports.

summer days, with Hispanic families sitting on their stoops, or groups of young people listening to "ghetto-blasters" – a very different picture from that one block to the east or west, where nattily-dressed people move briskly toward the store or restaurant of their choice.

The rapid change in the neighborhood is evident in other ways, too. Upper Broadway, in particular, is lined with homeless people, either carefully spreading out old magazines, dog-eared books, and very used clothing on the sidewalk in the hopes that someone will buy something, or, more directly, begging for money. Sometimes the contrast is very painful, particularly when hungry parents and children station themselves in front of high-priced delicatessens like Zabar's. One of New York's less attractive sides is the fact that, to most residents, these people come to seem just a part of the urban landscape.

To orient yourself in the Upper West Side, you need only know that the regular North-South, East-West grid of avenues

and numbered streets is intersected by Broadway, which runs diagonally north to 72nd Street before straightening out and proceeding uptown in a more regular North-South line. Each of the area's avenues has its own particular character. **Central Park West**, running along the park, is known for its large, spacious apartments in distinguished buildings. Many of these are the work of architect Emory Roth, whose style and influence pervades the area. The next avenue, **Columbus**, is now known as the area's center for trend. Virtually all of the small businesses remaining are being forced out by rents which have, in light of the desirability of retail space here, risen sky-high. **Amsterdam Avenue**, one block over, is, as mentioned above, likely to fall victim to the same fate, although it still retains its Hispanic flavor. The Upper West Side's public school is on Amsterdam, surrounded by a chain-link fence.

Lined with everything from movie theaters to sushi bars, the opera house to Woolworth's, the Upper West Side sec-tion of **Broadway** can only be described as "eclectic." Some areas look downright down-market, with discount drugstores and boutiques selling cheap clothing; and some patches are too new to feel anything but artificial, such as stretches in the 80s where new high-rise condominiums were put in during the 1980s. Suffice it to say that the ambience of Broadway changes from block to block.

North of 72nd Street, **West End Avenue** is not zoned for business; hence, this is a residential street in the New York sense, lined with blocky apartment build-ings. Lovely as some of these are, the prime interest which this avenue holds for visitors is that it's the best place in the area to find a taxicab. Running along the Hudson, the next avenue over is **River-side Drive**, a quiet, pleasant street lined with brownstones and apartments, giving access to the long, narrow green strip of Riverside Park, designed by Central Park's creators Olmsted and Vaux. From here, you can look out over the river to the landscape of New Jersey.

Walking up Broadway from Columbus Circle, one of the first things to catch the eye is **Lincoln Center of the Performing Arts**, a spacious plaza of white stone to the left at 66th Street. Home to the Metropolitan and New York City Operas, the New York Philharmonic, the City Ballet, and several other major groups, Lincoln Center was designed as a solution to the increasing inadequacy of the city's antiquated performance spaces. The "New Met," as the opera is called, opened in 1966, and all three of the main buildings were operating by 1970; still, many old-timers speak nostalgically of the "Old Met," on 39th Street and Broadway, which has since been torn down.

Today, the "New Met," with its distinctive six-story-high arched glass windows, with gigantic Chagall tapestries peeping through, is Lincoln Center's most striking building. Flanking it to the right and left are **Avery Fisher Hall** (hailed by

Above: Could this be the long arm of the music scene at Lincoln Center?

some as an acoustic nightmare, although the New York Philharmonic Orchestra plays bravely on) and the **New York State Theater**, home to the New York City Opera and Ballet. Behind the Met at the right, the **Vivian Beaumont** and **Mitzi E. Newhouse Theaters**, which present spoken dramas and musicals, share a building with the **Library and Museum of Performing Arts**, housing an extraordinary collection of sheet music, records and tapes. (See the chapter on *Performing Arts* for more information.) Central to all of these stages is the fountain at the middle of the plaza; sitting here, or at a table of the café which sprouts up on the plaza in the summer, you can do a lot of people-watching.

Across 66th Street is another well-known space: **Alice Tully Hall**, a recital and concert facility adjacent to the world-renowned **Juilliard School**. Talented students from all over the world compete for places in Juilliard's top-notch music, dance, and theater programs; in music, the school is virtually without equal.

It's hard to believe that, a mere 100 years ago, a ramshackle farm stood in the rural terrain of what, today, is the busy intersection of 72nd and Broadway. Soon thereafter, large apartment buildings began to crop up all around, setting the mold for the character of the area. One of the most renowned is the **Ansonia**, an ornate masterpiece of Art Nouveau architecture completed in 1901. The building has traditionally been home to artists and performers, even before the advent of the Lincoln Center down the street; some floors have music studios available to students and teachers on an hourly rental basis. Famous tenants of days gone by include author Theodore Dreiser and baseball great Babe Ruth – certainly a performer in some sense of the word.

Grand Apartment Houses

Those with a real interest in architecture and grand apartment houses are advised to return to Central Park West, which contains examples a-plenty. Considering the uniform sedate tone of the street as a whole, the variety of architectural styles is particularly striking. The **Century Apartments** and the **Prasada Apartments** (25 and 50 Central Park West, respectively) demonstrate the French Empire style; farther north, Art Deco **55 Central Park West** made a film appearance as Spook Central in the popular film *Ghostbusters*. At 67th Street, the **Hotel des Artistes** sports a remarkable neo-Gothic façade. Originally built with extra-high ceilings to accommodate the needs of artists, the building now accommodates wealthy people with a taste for the outré. Past residents include dancer Isadora Duncan, film star Rudolf Valentino and author Noel Coward.

The yellow brick building at 72nd Street is one of New York's most renowned. When it was built in 1881, critics complained that it was so far uptown that it might as well be in Dakota terri-

tory. Ever since, the building has been known as the **Dakota**. Rank upon rank of stars have lived here, including Judy Holliday, Lauren Bacall, José Ferrer and Gilda Radnor. An idea of the tremendous size of the Dakota's apartments can be gleaned from the film *Rosemary's Baby*, part of which was set here; the stately edifice was also the point of departure for a (fictional) journey back in time in Jack Finney's classic New York novel *Time and Again*. It was here, furthermore, that John Lennon was shot in 1980 as he returned home with his wife from a late-night recording session. Ironically, Lennon once said that he liked living in the area because it was so busy that he was allowed to come and go unremarked

Certainly, Central Park West houses more than its share of celebrities. At the **Langham** (135 Central Park West), Woody Allen filmed parts of *Hannah and Her Sisters* in Mia Farrow's apartment. Topped with Roman temples, the towering **San Remo Apartments** at 145-146 Central Park West have, over the years, been home to Rita Hayworth, Raquel Welch, Dustin Hoffman, Paul Simon, Tony Randall and Diane Keaton. When Madonna tried to buy an apartment there, she was rejected by the other tenants; even by the other celebrity residents of the building, her lifestyle was considered just too flamboyant. Finally, Sherlock Holmes fans will know that Basil Rathbone, the cinema's quintessential Sherlock, lived at **The Kenilworth** (151 Central Park West). To architecture buffs, the building will be of interest purely as a study in exotic excess.

As long as you're on Central Park West, a visit to the **New York Historical Society** may be just the thing to put Manhattan in its proper historical perspective. This ornate 19th-century stone building contains rooms furnished in 17th- and 18th-century style, a silver gallery, a collection of Audubon watercolors and one of Tiffany lamps, as well as a library of

priceless books, documents and manuscripts.

Virtually next door is the mammoth **American Museum of Natural History**, described in detail in the chapter on *Galleries and Museums*. One branch of it, the **Hayden Planetarium**, is located on 81st Street: Here, visitors recline in comfortable chairs to watch the projections on the domed ceiling of the **Sky Theater**. In addition to the shows on the mysteries of the universe, there's the **Guggenheim Theater** with its 360-degree screen and many exhibits on the sun and moon, stars and planets, the possibilities of extraterrestrial life, and the like. Of course, all this makes the planetarium extremely popular with children; it's likely to be crawling with classes on school outings if you arrive there on a weekday.

Further north, between 261-267 West 94th Street and 260-266 West 95th Street,

Above: The massive mausoleum to Ulysses S. Grant on Riverside Drive. Right: The stone carvings of St John the Divine.

there's a double row of townhouses which bear the name **Pomander Walk**. Assembling British cottages, these were built to resemble the stage sets for the play of the same name. Humphrey Bogart and the Gish sisters were residents here, perhaps attracted by the ambience.

Strolling back down Broadway or Columbus Avenue, one notes how new co-ops and slick restaurants contrast with old ma-and-pa stores, dry-cleaners, and the like. Some of the new arrivals are innovative and amusing enough to please everyone. Columbus Avenue features stores like **Only Hearts**, devoted entirely to items shaped like hearts, emblazoned with hearts, talking about hearts; or **Maxilla & Mandible**, featuring a wide range of bones from common and exotic animals. Possibly related, **Murder Inc.** on Broadway sells only murder mysteries or books having to do with the subject (except, one presumes, for how-to volumes). An excellent range of books on every subject can be found a few blocks downtown at **Shakespeare & Co**.

Hunger pangs are easy to still in this area. The quintessential New York delicatessen, **Zabar's**, located at the corner of Broadway and 82nd, features an extraordinary selection of every kind of food, from knishes to prepared salads to more varieties of smoked salmon than you can count. Each week, Zabar's sells 10,000 pounds of coffee and ten tons of cheese. Upstairs, there's a full range of kitchen supplies, from luxuries to the basics. Another noteworthy, if much smaller, deli is **Barney Greengrass, the Sturgeon King**, on Amsterdam between 86th and 87th (next door to the **Popover Café**). To accompany whitefish salad or lox from either of these establishments, the bread of choice is an **H&H Bagel** from the Broadway store just across from Zabar's; 70,000 of the doughnut-shaped, boiled and baked rolls are produced by hand here every day.

West, Riverside Park has fewer attractions to boast, but it's a favorite with neighborhood numerous joggers, cyclists, and children. **Grant's Tomb**, final resting place of the Union General in the Civil War, who was President from 1868-76, can be found in the park at 122nd Street; while in summer, music from open-air concerts at the **Soldiers and Sailors' Memorial** wafts downtown on the river breezes. At 82nd Street the **Jewish Martyrs Memorial** recalls the holocaust. At the **79th Street Boat Basin**, some hardy New Yorkers dwell on their houseboats year-round. On a clear day, standing by the river, it's possible to see up as far north as to the **George Washington Bridge**, or downriver, from some spots (and with the aid of binoculars) to the Statue of Liberty. Events such as the Bicentennial or Miss Liberty's birthday were celebrated with Independence Day parades up and down the river of tall ships from around the world; for these events, the park was so jammed with people that it was difficult to find a place to watch.

COLUMBIA

North of 96th Street, Broadway seems to get more run down. The buildings are shabbier, the shops are seedier, and the people have a less affluent air. But there's more here than at first meets the eye. On 112th Street between Amsterdam and Columbus is the massive **Cathedral Church of St John the Divine**, the "largest Gothic church in the world." Under construction since 1892, the cathedral is still far from done; working on it, stone-cutters are trained in techniques that were used centuries ago. Their work can be admired in the Stonecutting Yard. The church has five naves and hosts organ concerts, whereby one can only admire the skill of performers who have to come to grips with a long echo.

A couple of blocks further uptown, Broadway has the air of a college town, lined with bookstores and affordable student-type restaurants. And for good reason: This is the campus of one of New York's oldest educational institutions,

Columbia University, and its sister college, **Barnard** (Columbia began admitting women in 1988; Barnard, however, still does not admit men). A heavy iron grille separates the urban cityscape of Broadway from the green quadrangle of the campus with its libraries, classroom buildings and dorms. Established in 1754 as "King's College," the University has seen many changes come to this part of New York.

The college's students, faculty and staff have created a demand for housing, which has made this area, in places, pleasant to live in. The residential streets along the river comprise a neighborhood known as **Morningside Heights**. On 120th Street, **Riverside Church** features not only the world's largest carillon (74 bells) and the world's largest (20-ton) bell, but also a congregation known for its openness and its activism in questions of social and human rights. The observa-

Above: The Upper East Side is a mainly residential area of New York City.

tion deck atop its 426-foot-high tower affords a spectacular view of the city (although it's wise to go at times when the carillon is silent; from here, the bells are deafeningly loud).

UPPER EAST SIDE

On the other side of Central Park, Manhattan's East Side is another world. This is an ultra-expensive, exclusive universe of clean streets, ivy-covered townhouses, designer boutiques, museums, antique stores and art galleries. Upper East Side prides itself on offering the best of everything to the city's elite; and those who live there can afford to pay for it.

The Upper East Side is wider than the Upper West Side: that is, there are more North-South avenues on this side of the park. Running along Central Park is **Fifth Avenue**, which loses its business zoning when it meets the park, taken up instead with residential dwellings and, for a stretch, Museum Mile. On Fifth Avenue, the word *residential* means spacious, luxurious and exorbitantly-priced; this is some of the most expensive real estate in the world.

If Fifth Avenue is residential, **Madison Avenue** more than makes up for it. In this street, New York's consumerism achieves its full flowering. It's here that international fashion designers have their boutiques, here that the most exclusive hairdressers set up shop. Jewelry and Italian leather, antique rare books and fine wines: Everything sold here is characterized by exclusivity, fine craftsmanship, and astronomically high prices. There are an abundance of Italian pastry shops and luncheon parlors for shoppers (or window-shoppers) longing to rest their weary feet; but nothing on Madison Avenue is cheap, not even food.

As if streets here were meant to alternate in character, **Park Avenue** returns to the sedate decorum of residential Fifth Avenue – and even takes it a step further. The stylish and reserved pace here makes every day seem like Easter Sunday. Many of the passers-by are fashionable residents walking their dogs, or the wealthy patients of exclusive Park Avenue doctors and cosmetic surgeons. Even the ever-present New York City panhandlers keep a low profile on Park Avenue – perhaps because of the impeccably uniformed doormen standing before the huge old apartment buildings. This rarefied environment appears to be the sole province of the wealthy, the powerful and the well-dressed.

Known to New Yorkers as "Lex," **Lexington Avenue** returns the visitor to the "real" New York: hectic, bustling, dirty, lined with shops. This is another shopping street, but without the exclusivity of Madison. Only two blocks over, **Second Avenue** is, quite simply, one of the longest restaurant rows in the world. Between its shops and apartment buildings are chic restaurants and hamburger hideaways, as well as purveyors of Chinese, Indian, Thai, African and every other national cuisine imaginable. The avenue is also home to a host of second-hand stores, some featuring bargain discards from the swells over on Park.

First Avenue was once the capital of New York's young "swingle" (swinging single) scene. These days, it is a bit more subdued. The clubs are still there, but the clientele has aged, and in this age of AIDS most singles swing a lot more carefully today than they used to. First Avenue also has its share of attractive apartment buildings.

Closest to the East River are **York Avenue** and, between 79th and 90th Streets, **East End Avenue**, both largely residential. **Sotheby Parke Bernet**, or Sotheby's, at 72nd Street, is a world-renowned fine-arts auction house that came into being when London's prestigious Sotheby's merged with New York's Parke Bernet. As well as offering remarkable collections of art, the auctions held here every other week make fascinating theater, with high drama and much excitement. At other times the collections are open to public viewing.

Upper East Side Sights

The Upper East Side could be said to begin at **Grand Army Plaza,** directly in front of the **Plaza Hotel.**

Walking through the doors of the Plaza, one is transported into a bygone age. Sitting among the green fronds and fountain of the **Palm Court** restaurant at the center of the lobby, listening to live music, is much the same as it must have been decades ago: the epitome of elegant, prosperous New York. Quite a different tone reigns, however, in **Eloise's Room**. Hilary Knight's book *Eloise*, about a mischievous little girl who lives in the hotel, has been such a favorite with generations of children that the Plaza has recreated her room for them to see – although many will be disappointed that the replica is so much tidier than the original.

East of Grand Army Plaza, on Lexington, is New York's favorite department store: noisy, trendy **Bloomingdale's**. The store offers everything from designer apparel to furniture to, incredibly enough, spy and surveillance items. Fall usually sees the store organized around some theme, such as "France" or "India;" the store's detractors say that such themes give buyers an excuse to buy, foreign handicrafts cheap *in situ* and sell them in New York, during the season, at an immense profit. To the east of "Bloomie's," near the entrance of the Queensboro Bridge, is the Aerial Tramway which, until the F-train was granted an extra stop, was the only way people living on **Roosevelt Island** in the East River could make it to Manhattan.

Although Manhattan is not generally thought of as one of the world's most re-

Above: The Metropolitan Museum of Art, the oldest in the city and the largest in the western world. Right: The modern interior of the Fifth Avenue Synagogue.

ligious cities, there are some beautiful places of worship on the Upper East Side. One of these is the **Christ United Methodist Church** on Park Avenue and 60th Street, designed during the Depression to look centuries old. Inside is a Byzantine-style sanctuary that glitters with golden hand-laid mosaics. To the north, at 5 East 62nd Street, is the **Fifth Avenue Synagogue**. Set in the limestone walls are pointed oval stained-glass windows with striking abstract designs.

A few blocks further up Fifth Avenue, at 65th Street, is the **Temple Emanu-El**. This world's largest Reform Jewish synagogue can seat 2500 worshippers. Supported by marble columns, the mammoth ceiling and great arch are covered with delicate, intricate, colorful mosaics reminiscent of Middle Eastern mosques.

The **Seventh Regiment Armory** is one block north on 66th and Park. This huge brick structure is still used as a military headquarters; there's even space inside for tennis courts and a shelter for the homeless. The massive central staircase and wood-paneled lobby hearken back to an earlier era. Today, the building hosts many posh events. One of New York's ironies is the contrast between the many wealthy people in attendance and the homeless down and out New Yorkers getting a night's sleep in the shelter down the hall.

Farther to the North, Madison Avenue combines a broad range of shopping outlets with a blend of upscale international residents. Plaques by the doorways of some of these elegant buildings reveal that they're home to such organizations as the German **Goethe House**, which hosts art exhibitions, films and lectures. The **China Institute in America**, **Ukrainian Institute**, the **Hispanic Society of America**, the **American-Irish Historical Society** and the **Japan Society**, each dedicated to increasing American appreciation of its respective culture, are located near one another.

A more direct appreciation of the German culture can be gleaned by visiting the stretch of the Upper East Side known as **Yorkville**, from the mid 70s up to 96th Street between Park Avenue and the Hudson River. Numerous Eastern European and German immigrants settled in this area: German, Czech and Hungarian influences can still be seen in the area's restaurants and shops.

Reaching from Gracie Square at 84th Street up to 90th Street, over the Franklin D. Roosevelt Drive (FDR drive to locals), is a stretch of green called **Carl Schurz Park** named after a German immigrant who made it all the way to the Senate. The park surrounds **Gracie Mansion**, built in 1799 by businessman Archibald Gracie, and residence of New York's mayors since Fiorello LaGuardia's day in the 1930s. When Ed Koch was Mayor, he opened the Federal-style mansion to the public; tours of it are still given on Wednesdays.

Above Yorkville, the neighborhood between 86th and 96th Streets from Fifth to

Park Avenues is known as **Carnegie Hill**. Today, the name doesn't have many associations for the average New Yorker but in days gone by, this was a suburb where tycoons of the past like Andrew Carnegie, the Astors and the Vanderbilts constructed mansions suited to their positions as the pillars of Manhattan's commerce and society. This area later became known as "Millionaire's Row." Most of the old families are now gone, but new millionaires have, in many cases, taken their place.

The neighborhood is also home to many art galleries, not to mention the stretch of Fifth Avenue between 82nd and 104th Streets, which was, not so very long ago, rechristened "Museum Mile." Among the most impressive museums here is the Metropolitan Museum between 80th and 84th Streets, a fine arts emporium, and four blocks north the Guggenheim Museum whose architecture alone is well worth a look. (For details, see the chapter *Museums and Galleries.*)

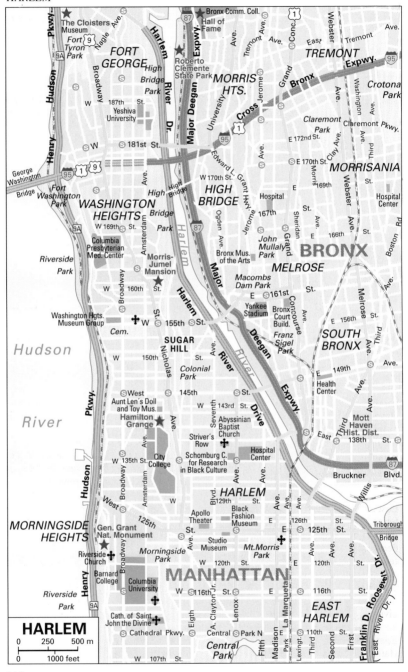

HARLEM

Few other places in the world trigger more terror, curiosity and fascination than the area north of 110th Street in Manhattan. The name **Harlem** bears the double association of the flowering of black American culture earlier this century and crime which has run rampant in recent decades, creating in areas an urban landscape that appears literally war-torn, after years of grinding poverty.

At the turn of the century, Harlem was a well-to-do suburb, accounted one of New York's three most exclusive neighborhoods, and containing some of the city's most beautiful homes. After World War One, the area attracted American blacks anxious to escape the prejudice and poverty of such places as the rural South. The presence of outstanding black artists, musicians and thinkers ushered in an era known as the Harlem Renaissance. Unfortunately, the Great Depression in the 1930s hit this neighborhood particularly hard. After World War Two, when much of America was booming, Harlem was suffering from housing shortages and chronic unemployment. While many people left the area altogether, those who stayed continue to suffer from the latter problem. Enforced idleness has increased the incidence of drug use and crime. Attempts are being made at rehabilitation; still, a visitor's first reaction is likely to be one of shock.

As one moves farther "up" the Upper East Side, the ambiance changes, characterized by the strains of Latin music coming from boom-boxes rather than sedate decorum. North of 96th Street, one notes fewer and fewer well-groomed people, and is more likely to hear *gracias* at the end of a sentence than *thanks*. Townhouses and luxury apartment buildings give way to tenements as the neighborhood metamorphoses into overcrowded **East Harlem**. Also known as Spanish Harlem because of its predominately Puerto Rican and Latin American population, the neighborhood reaches from around East 96th to West 120th Streets, from Lexington to Lenox Avenues. It is probably best not to walk here; anyone determined to see it should take a cab.

To its residents, this neighborhood is known as *El Barrio* (Spanish for "the neighborhood"), and an important cultural highlight is **El Museo del Barrio** (5th Avenue at 105th Street), devoted to exhibiting Puerto Rican and Latin American art and culture. Another center of local color is the market called **La Marqueta**, on Park Avenue (which, here, has a very different complexion from further downtown) from 111th to 116th Streets. At La Marqueta, everything from tropical fruits and vegetables to herbs and spices is for sale. Indicating the blend of cultures in New York, however, is the fact that African goods are also available, as well as all the required "fixins" for soul food. A short visit here leaves no doubt in one's mind as to why New York is sometimes called "Little Puerto Rico."

A curious pocket of East Harlem is the stretch from 114th to 120th Streets between Second Avenue and the East River. This area is tenanted primarily by a tenacious group of Italians who keep the streets in front of their tidy brownstones clean enough to eat pasta from.

125th Street, also known as **Martin Luther King Jr. Boulevard**, is the heart of Harlem. On Saturday morning, it beats with a vengeance, as hundreds of shoppers pick through the goods sold on the streets in front of the famed **Apollo Theater**. Countless legendary stars have appeared at the theater, including Billie Holiday, Ella Fitzgerald, Duke Ellington, Count Basie and Aretha Franklin. Wednesday night is amateur night at the Apollo: At this raucous event, promising talents are greeted with appreciative screams and foot-stomping, while displeasure is expressed in catcalls and thrown tomatoes. The theater is well-pa-

trolled, so visitors needn't worry. Also on 125th Street (at Fifth Avenue) is the **Studio Museum in Harlem**, a small but excellent museum devoted to African, Afro-American and Caribbean artists. Home to many art treasures, it possesses a permanent collection of painting, sculpture and photography, as well as a gift shop selling African and black American-inspired items. Nearby, on **126th Street**, the **Black Fashion Museum**'s brownstone houses the work of black fashion designers, as well as costumes from black plays and films.

The **Schomburg Center for Research in Black Culture** is located on Lenox Avenue between 135th and 136th Streets. This branch of the New York Public Library has the world's largest collection of books and papers documenting black history and literature. Lenox Avenue, by the

way, is the name Sixth Avenue bears on this part of the island; Seventh Avenue in Harlem is known as **Adam Clayton Powell Jr. Boulevard**. This street was named for a local son who led the **Abyssinian Baptist Church** (132 West 138th Street) to become the city's most influential black church in the late 1930s; Powell was elected to the United States Congress in 1945. The church, one of the oldest and, by all accounts, most imposing in Harlem, was built in 1808.

Two Harlem neighborhoods, in particular, stand out. One is a string of handsome townhouses on 138th and 139th streets, between Seventh and Eighth Avenues. Before Harlem was known as a black neighborhood, many black families went to great pains to move into these homes; the street has been known as **Striver's Row** ever since. Perhaps the most famous region of Harlem is **Sugar Hill**, the area from 143rd to 155th Streets between St. Nicholas and Edgecombe Avenues. Former residents include Cab Calloway, Duke Ellington and Bill

Above: Today, Harlem represents the troubled heart of African-American culture. Right:The Abyssinian Church in Harlem.

"Bojangles" Robinson; today, it is considered to be the best address in Harlem.

For another Harlem experience, **Sylvia's** restaurant, on Lenox Avenue between 125th and 126th Streets, is said to have the best home-cooked soul food outside the American South. There may be no better way to top off a visit to Harlem than with a heaped platter of ribs, collard greens, grits and black-eyed peas.

Washington Heights

Many city residents seldom have the occasion or desire to go north of the George Washington Bridge. They're missing out on an colorful blend of African, Greek, Armenian, Jewish, Irish and Puerto Rican cultures. The neighborhoods known as **Washington Heights** and **Inwood** offer all of these – as well as institutions such as the **Hispanic Society of America**, the **American Academy of Arts and Letters** (both on Broadway between 155th and 156th Streets), and the **Columbia Presbyterian Medical Center** (Broadway between West 165th and 168th). **Yeshiva University**, on 186th Street and Amsterdam Avenue, is the oldest center for Jewish studies in America, housed in a colorful, neo-Romantic building. Naturally, it is surrounded by kosher bakeries and butcher shops.

From 192nd north to Dyckman Street is another masterpiece of landscape architecture by Central Park's Olmsted: Fort Tryon Park. The park is a bequest of millionaire John D. Rockefeller, as is the museum set in a part of the fort itself, called **The Cloisters**. This is a glorious reconstruction of French and Spanish monastic cloisters, housing much of the Metropolitan Museum's medieval collection, including paintings and tapestries, carved rosary beads of wood and ivory, gold and enameled pieces, manuscripts, sculptures and stained-glass windows. Surrounded by flower and herb beds meant to hearken back to the Middle Ages, the museum has a disorienting effect: a tranquil piece of medieval Europe in the confusion of Manhattan Island.

UPPER MANHATTAN
Accommodation

Upper Manhattan can boast some of the best hotels in the world.

LUXURY: **Barbizon**: A delightful hotel with pastel walls, pink marble floors, small but adequate rooms. 140 East 63rd Street, New York 10021, Tel: 212/838-5700. **The Carlyle:** old-world style at its finest, rooms decorated with antiques, 35 East 76th Street, New York 10021, Tel: 212/744-1600. **The Lowell Hotel:** A real find, cozy, fashionable, distinctive, some of the rooms have wood-burning fireplaces, 28 East 63rd Street, New York 10021, Tel: 212/838-1400.

The Mayfair Regent: The lobby is a designer's dream, antique-filled and almost like a museum. Ultraplush rooms and suites, along with excellent service, provide *la dolce vita* for jet-setters, 610 Park Avenue, New York 10021, Tel: 212/288-0800. **The Pierre**: Dignified elegance abounds. The rich and powerful who do not have to show it to know it stay here, some of the suites overlook Central Park, 2 East 61st Street, New York 10021, Tel: 212/838-8000. **The Regency**: Warm and efficient service in the midst of marble and gilt. 540 Park Avenue, New York 10021, Tel: 212/759-4100.

MODERATE TO BUDGET: **Empire**: A clean, bright budget hotel right across from the Lincoln Center, Broadway at 44 West 63rd Street, New York 10023, Tel: 212/265-7400. **Esplanade**: Huge rooms in the hundred-dollar-range, some with a view of the Hudson River, 305 West End Avenue, Tel: 212/874-5000. **Excelsior**: Charming hotel, attractive rooms. Very inexpensive by New York standards, 45 West 81st Street, Tel: 212/362-9200. **The Milburn**: An old-world hotel, rooms have kitchenettes, 242 West 76th Street, New York 10024, Tel: 212/362-1006.

Olcott: This hotel in the heart of the Lincoln Center district serves as a home-away-from-home for artists and businessmen from abroad, 27 West 72nd Street, New York 10024, Tel: 212/877-4200. **Wales**: The affordable place to stay on the Upper East Side, gracious rooms that a third and fourth guest can stay in for $5 each, a remarkable bargain in New York, 1295 Madison Avenue, Tel: 212/876-6000.

BUDGET: There is precious little to recommend in this category in Upper Manhattan for travelers on a shoestring. The best are the following: **New York International Youth Hostel**: A renovated, 19th century Gothic-style building with dormitory accommodation at rock-bottom prices. No service, bring your own towels and sheets, 891 Amsterdam Avenue, Tel: 212/932-2300.

Malibu Studios Hotel: clean and comfortable rooms in the $40 range, 2688 Broadway (at West 103rd Street) near Columbia University, Tel: 212/222-2954.

BED AND BREAKFAST: Another option growing in popularity is the bed and breakfast where guests stay in a spare room in someone's apartment. Booking through an agency is presently the only way to set this up without personal contacts. Agencies offering a range of possibilities: **Urban Ventures**, Tel: 212/594-5650, **City Lights Bed and Breakfast Ltd.**, Tel: 212/737-7049 and **Bed, Breakfast (and Books)**, Tel: 212/865-8740. Reservations for Bed and Breakfast should be made as far in advance as possible.

Restaurants

There is no shortage of restaurants, cafés and snackbars in Upper Manhattan, and no way, without devoting an entire book to the topic, of covering all the good ones. Do not be afraid to experiment and discover special favorites among the hundreds of restaurants not listed here.

Aureole, 34 61st Street between Madison and Park, Tel: 212/319-1660. **Café des Artistes**, 1 West 67th Street between Central Park West and Columbus Avenue, Tel: 212/877-3500. **Le Cirque**, 58 East 65th Street, in the Mayfair Regent Hotel, Tel: 212/794-9292. **Dallas BBQ**, 1265 Third Avenue at 73rd Street, Tel: 212/772-9393. **El Caridad**, 2199 Broadway at 78th Street, Tel: 212/874-2780. **Primavera**, 1578 First Avenue at 81st Street, Tel: 212/861-8608. **Sylvia's**, 328 Lenox Avenue between 126th and 127th Streets, Tel: 212/534-9414. **Tavern on the Green**, Central Park West and 67th Street, Tel: 212/873-3200.

For socializing and drinking: **Elaine's**, 1703 Second Avenue between 88th and 89th Streets, Tel: 212/534-8103. **Jim McMullens**, 1341 Third Avenue, at 76th Street, Tel: 212/861-4700. **Wilson's**, 201 West 79th Street, corner Amsterdam Avenue, Tel: 212/769-0100.

For an uptown hamburger hankering: **Jackson Hole Wyoming Burgers**, 232 East 64th Street between 2nd and 3rd Avenues, 517 Columbus Avenue at 85th Street, 1270 Madison Avenue at 91st Street and 521 Third Avenue at 35th Street.

Transportation

Do not even think about renting a car. Traffic is horrendous, parking impossible or a daunting expense. And getting around Upper Manhattan is relatively simple. It is tough to get lost because it is laid out in a grid: The streets run east-west horizontally, and the avenues are basically running north-south vertically. Most numbered streets are one way with traffic on even numbered streets going east, traffic on odd numbered streets going west. Avenues basically alternate, with First Avenue going north, Second Avenue going south, and so forth. Fifth Avenue runs right down the middle dividing the city into east and west.

Taxi's continually cruise the streets looking for passengers, and a wave of the arm will usually flag one down, except, so it always seems, when it is raining or during rush hours. There are also radio cabs which will arrive ten to fifteen minutes after a call. Recommended firms are **All City Taxi**, Tel: 212/796-1111, **Battery City Car and Limo Radio Group**, Tel: 212/947-9696 and **UTOG**, Tel: 212/741-2000.

The fastest, though not the most luxurious, way to get around Upper Manhattan is by subway. During rush hour, passengers feel like tightly packed sardines in a filthy can. Master skills in pushing and shoving are required in order to get in and out of the cars. However, other times of day are less crowded and next to walking, it is the most popular mode of transportation. A free map is available at any subway token booth. Routes follow color-coded lines. The fare is currently $1.15, and always threatening to rise. Purchase tokens at the entrances of most subways and ride as far as desired in any direction. Transfers are allowed any place where the routes intersect and are marked with a circle.

Slower, but more scenic, is the bus. The flip side of the subway map shows the bus routes. At every bus stop, the route for that particular bus is posted. A good way to really see and experience New York is on foot, with a pair of good walking shoes or sneakers.

Tours

There are myriad of individual tours to choose from. Walking tours are a good idea for first-time visitors with plenty of time, and the best way to get a taste of Uptown Manhattan. Tours of Harlem are highly recommended.

Harlem Renaissance Tours, 18 East 105th Street, New York 10029, Tel: 212/722-9534, works closely with the Harlem Visitors and Convention Association, the Apollo Theater and the Uptown Chamber of Commerce. Gospel tours, theater and jazz tours, taste of Harlem international food tours, and more, including special interest tours, multilingual guides.

Harlem Your Way! Tours Unlimited, 129 West 130th Street, New York 10027, Tel: 212/690-1687. Tours for individuals or groups, including daily walking tours, Sunday gospel tours, jazz tours, black art and culture tours.

Penny Sightseeing Company, Tel: 212/410-0800, walking tours and Sunday gospel trips to Harlem. For personalized walking tours of Harlem with a resident, phone Ron Spence, Tel: 212/368-1876, the sole guide for his firm **Harlem Renaissance**.

As for other areas of Upper Manhattan, a variety of tours are offered by **Columbia University**, Tel: 212/280-2838, the **Museum of the City of New York**, Tel: 212/534-1672, and the **New York Historical Society**, Tel: 212/873-3400. A number of naturalist and special interest tours, focusing on history, weather, plants, rocks and animals, are offered at no charge in Central Park by the **Park Rangers**, Tel: 212/397-3080.

Wild Man Steve Brill, Tel: 212/360-8165, leads tours of several Upper Manhattan Parks, including Central Park, focusing on edible weeds and plants in the urban environment.

The **92nd Street YMCA/YWHA**, Tel: 212/427-6000, offers art and cultural tours, as well as neighborhood walks, among an extensive year-round tour program.

Festivals / Special Events

Third Sunday in **June**: The largest of several *Puerto Rican Day Parades* takes place, up Fifth Avenue to 86th Street. **July 4**: the best seats in town for *Macy's Fireworks* are in Riverside Park.

July and August: *Summer Festival* in Central Park with a series of plays and concerts. At the same time, the *Mostly Mozart Festival* occurs at Lincoln Center, including free and bargain concerts at Avery Fisher Hall.

July: A *Japanese Oban Festival* features dancing in Riverside Park Mall, at 103rd Street. An *Indian Festival* takes over the Central Park Mall, with singing, dancing, food and clothing stalls. The *Fiestas de Loiza Aldea* is a recreated Puerto Rican festival, with dancing, music and food on Ward's Island, across the footbridge from 102nd Street and East River Drive.

August: *Fiesta Folklorica*, international festival of dancing and singing in Central Park. The city's largest German-American festival is the *Steuben Day Parade*. Honoring one of George Washington's generals, the parade moves from 61st Street to 86th Street on Fifth Avenue.

Late November: On Thanksgiving, the city's largest parade of all, the *Macy's Thanksgiving Day Parade*, begins uptown at 79th Street and Central Park West, heading downtown to Herald Square via Broadway. Famous for giant balloon figures, marching bands, floats, celebrities and the kick-off to the Christmas season.

Tourist Information

New York Convention and Visitors Bureau, 2 Columbus Circle, New York 10019, Tel: 212/397-8222.

MUSEUMS AND GALLERIES

From art to fire-engines: If you want to go see any kind of exhibition or museum, New York is the right city to be in. As everything else about the city, New York's museums are on a grand scale. To avoid exhaustion, visitors have to be selective and accept that it's impossible to see more than a small percentage of what the city has to offer. But stamina will be rewarded with some fascinating displays, as well as some of the greatest art treasures in the world.

Museum Mile

For those who like their viewing route to be well-traveled and well-signposted, there's always Museum Mile. Many of New York's best and most renowned museums are located along a single stretch of upper Fifth Avenue, known as Museum Mile.

The grand-daddy of all New York museums is the Metropolitan Museum of Art, on Fifth at 82nd Street. Rivaling many in Europe, this illustrious collection includes some of the greatest old masters in the world, and is expanding at a rapid rate, necessitating additions to the building such as the Lila Acheson Wing and the infamous new 20th-century wing. The "Met" also contains a stunning collection of African art. Frequently, blockbuster shows such as the Tutankhamun exhibit or the Manet retrospective are hung here. For these, it's often necessary to wait for hours in line for tickets, then deal with the crowds of people filing by the works.

Frank Lloyd Wright's design for the Guggenheim Museum (1071 Fifth, at 89th Street) is a work of art in itself.

Preceding pages: The Cloisters on Manhattan's northern tip. Left: The Metropolitan Museum of Art is one of New York's most important centers for art.

Starting at the top, the viewer walks down a ramp spiraling around the round building until reaching the bottom. The museum has just reopened after the addition of another wing to the edifice. This has given rise to a host of accusations that Wright's original concept has been abused, not to say destroyed. Visitors will have to judge for themselves.

Other Museum Mile venues include the Smithsonian, or Cooper-Hewitt, Museum, located in the Andrew Carnegie Mansion at 2 East 91st Street, where the National Museum of Design's collection of decorative arts, considered by many to be the finest in the world, is on display. And a stunning, comprehensive array of Judaica, including painting and sculpture, decorative arts and coins, is on show at the Jewish Museum (1109 Fifth, at 92nd Street). Photo buffs head further uptown to the International Center of Photography (1130 Fifth, at 94th Street), which displays the works of such major 20th-century photographers as Cartier-Bresson. All three of these museums also feature rotating exhibitions.

Two Upper East Side museums are omitted from the Museum Mile roster by an accident of geography rather than quality: the Frick Collection and the Whitney Museum of American Art. The mansion of steel millionaire Henry Clay Frick at Fifth Avenue and 70th Street is home to the collector's stunning legacy of European old masters paintings as well as the appropriate furniture and decorations. (Those whose taste runs to mansions should also take in the Pierpont Morgan Library, a marvelous collection of medieval and Renaissance manuscripts and sculpture housed in the former home of its namesake, at 36th Street and Madison Avenue.)

A few blocks away, at 945 Madison Avenue (75th Street), the architecture of the Whitney is anything but beautiful. Walking inside, however, is as good as a basic 20th-century art history course for

familiarizing oneself with the major movements of art in America from the turn of this century to the present. Every two years, the Whitney Biannual exhibition furnishes material for controversy, debate, and hand-wringing about the state of contemporary art. But in New York, the last word in modern art is had by the Museum of Modern Art (11 West 53rd Street near Fifth Avenue). Renovations in the 1980s brought the building's appearance up to the standards of its collection, which includes pearls by Cézanne and Picasso, Pollock and De Kooning. The superb painting collection, displayed over two floors, is supplemented by a photography collection, an outdoor sculpture garden, and a room for rotating exhibitions by modern masters from Andy Warhol to Richard Serra.

Above: School children are often taken to the Metropolitan to get an eyefull of the great masters. Right: Frank Lloyd Wright's unusual architecture is almost as noteworthy as the Guggenheim's collections.

Off the Avenue

The East Side, however, doesn't hold a monopoly on museums. Furthermore, not every New York museum is devoted to art. Prime example is the Museum of Natural History, at 81st and Central Park West, a rival in size to the stately "Met" across the park. It could be argued that the artistic sensibilities of New York children are decisively influenced by the experience of entering the darkened rooms, where the sole source of light is life-sized dioramas illustrating the animal life of various areas, from elephants to grizzly bears to the unforgettable blue whale suspended from the ceiling of the sea room. A special aspect of this show is the dinosaurs. The museum also has halls devoted to the art and culture of primitive tribes; rocks and minerals; and, of course, the Planetarium.

At 1 East 53rd, off Fifth Avenue, the Museum of Broadcasting includes some 20,000 tapes of radio and television programs, from the dawn of these media to

the present. Exhibits are devoted to several of the century's leading lights in the field. On the other side of Fifth, the American Craft Museum (40 West 53rd) is what the name implies, and also offers visitors the chance to participate by creating their own works. A major institution is the Museum of the American Indian, now uptown at Broadway and West 155th Streets, but scheduled to move downtown in the near future. This is the country's leading museum in the field, increasingly important as people struggle to keep history and the old traditions and knowledge alive.

This is only a sampling of the many museums big and small which the city has to offer. More specialized collections are housed in the New York City Fire Museum, the American Numismatic Society, Aunt Len's Doll and Toy Museum, and the Asia Society Gallery, to name a few. For exhaustive listings, check with the New York Convention and Visitors Bureau, or such magazines as the *New Yorker* or *New York*.

Gallery-hopping

Renowned as the cultural capital of the United States, New York draws artists from all over the country. No matter that the art scene in other cities is flourishing more and more, New York is still the number-one location for artists both starving and successful. The starving ones aspire to enter and the successful ones take for granted the rank upon rank of galleries which exist to display their works. Gallery owners, meanwhile, try to cater to the short attention span of the American public by constantly scouting for new trends and talents, keeping their regular stable of exhibitors while changing their offerings as much as possible. All of which makes keeping up with the New York "scene" a full-time job.

There are three major "gallery rows" in New York: SoHo, 57th Street and uptown on Madison Avenue. Not surprisingly, the tenor of these venues tends to reflect that of the surrounding neighborhood: near Madison, one may find classic prints

129

tastefully hung in an elegant building on a quiet side street, while in SoHo, concept art (including, perhaps, video displays, graffiti, or broken Coke bottles) lies scattered across the floor of a vast loft in what used to be a factory. On 57th Street and in SoHo alike, galleries can be tucked away, up stairs or down, and there are more of them than at first meet the eye, even in gallery-packed SoHo (where a casual observer might not suspect that there are more than 200 art galleries within five square blocks).

Given this diversity and the fluctuating nature of the scene, it's difficult to keep track of everything that's happening at any one time. Before making a New York gallery tour, pick up a copy of the *Art Now Gallery Guide* (generally available in the galleries themselves), which gives a comprehensive listing of current New York shows. Although one can never know quite what to expect in a New York

Above: A gallery in SoHo is the place to look at art and buy it on occasion.

gallery, the guide helps one to prepare an itinerary before taking the plunge.

There's no need, however, to be intimidated by the New York art scene. Galleries exist so that people can look at the work; generally, they are quieter than museums and more accessible, because smaller. It's possible to look at a show or two without feeling inundated by art, as one often does in a large museum. And there are other advantages to looking at works by living artists: show openings, where artists and potential buyers hobnob while sipping wine from plastic cups; or some days when short-staffed galleries ask the artists to come in and keep an eye on things while their show is hanging.

Madison Avenue

In art as well as fashion, Madison Avenue specializes in known quantities. Its galleries are housed in stately old townhouses, and display works which are by, if not conventionally "old," certainly accepted "masters." M. Knoedler & Co., for example, feature works by Abstract Expressionists (sometimes known as the "New York School"); Hirschl and Adler Galleries have European Impressionist works as well as a dazzling array of American paintings and sculpture. More Impressionists at Wildenstein & Co. Gallery; works from the earlier part of this century can be seen at Acquavella Gallery, Barry Friedman Gallery (specializing in Art Nouveau and Symbolism), and La Boetie Gallery. In an even more classic vein, the Colnaghi Gallery displays 16th to 19th-century English paintings, drawings, sculpture and furniture. Some of the finest prints in the world are hanging at David Tunick Gallery, just off Central Park.

Midtown Galleries

The 57th Street galleries are sandwiched between – and sometimes located in – office buildings, several floors above the hustle and bustle of the midtown crowd. Some buildings house several galleries (notably "The Gallery Building" on West 57th), enabling the art viewer to see a bewildering variety of styles and works in quick succession. Although there's still an emphasis on big names, the art here tends to represent what's happening today, rather than (as on Madison) fifty to a hundred years ago.

One of the elder statesmen of the New York art scene, Sidney Janis has brought together some of the best of contemporary European and American art in his gallery, where exhibitions are of museum quality. Pace, also widely renowned, has a prestigious roster of major modern American and European artists, generally well displayed. It would be hard, however, to classify the work at the Holly Solomon Gallery, known in the art world for showing the provocative and the avant-garde. Be prepared for anything.

Other fine galleries in the area include Blum/Helman, owned by the man who gave Andy Warhol his first US show and put on early exhibitions of Jasper Johns, Robert Rauschenberg and Roy Lichtenstein. Frumkin/Adams was a bastion of contemporary figurative art when it was only Frumkin; now, times have changed, and it also shows abstract works.

The Marian Goodman Gallery is the place to find many highly regarded European avant-garde artists not yet known in the United States.

All-American, on the other hand, is the Kennedy Gallery, devoted to American art from the American Revolution up to today. Located in a skyscraper office building, the elegant Marlborough Gallery remains a major exhibitor of important American and European artists, such as the witty Red Grooms, whose satiric New-York-based works have taken over the gallery and its outdoor sculpture terrace on more than one occasion. And the Robert Miller Gallery is a joy, not only because of its fine exhibitions, but also because of the gallery's elegance and pleasant staff.

Downtown Galleries

In a city given to extremes and quick changes, SoHo is one of the most changeable of neighborhoods. Nowhere is this better exemplified than in its galleries. New ones open and close, artistic styles sweep the area to fall into ignominy a year or two later. Here, the *Gallery Guide* is a necessary tool; chances are its information, which appears monthly, is still current.

Some SoHo standbys do exist, among them those mentioned in the section on *SoHo*. Other worthwhile venues are Brooke Alexander, Cooper, and Michael Walls. While uptown galleries tend to go with big names, some SoHo dealers are still willing to take a chance on a young unknown. The spirit of exploration and adventure, therefore, is required from dealers and viewers alike.

SHOPPING

There's no question about it: New York is a consumer's paradise. One criticism often leveled at the city, in fact, is that it places too much emphasis on merchandizing, marketing and, simply, money. But this emphasis means that, for a visitor, one of the best ways to get a feeling for the "Real New York" is by shopping. Whether strolling and looking in the windows of an elegant boutique or searching for tangible souvenirs of a trip to the city, one quickly gets to know a neighborhood's geography and personality when one embarks on a shopping expedition in New York.

Even specific, hard-to-find items aren't difficult to procure in this "city with everything." Discount designer clothes, discontinued china patterns and out-of-print books are all readily available; other

Above: Red hot items at Bloomingdale's, the epitome of consumerism in New York. Right: Strolling in style in the city.

stores specialize in everything – from wearable art to Provençal fabric to antique music boxes and wind-up toys. If searching for something particular, or particularly esoteric, referring to the Yellow Pages will probably be helpful. In the course of strolling through most New York neighborhoods, however, one is likely to encounter enough merchandise to satisfy one's wildest dreams.

Serious shoppers looking for the typical New York shopping experience head either for the area around 57th Street and Fifth Avenue, or for Madison between 50th and 86th Streets.

The 57th Street area combines the bustle of New York with international designer chic. Whether you are looking for thousand-dollar fashion separates or street vendors selling African imports to passing tourists, this, the veritable heart of New York, is the place to be. Trump Tower (725 Fifth Avenue, at 57th Street) has become famous as the quintessential address for the crème de la crème, filled with fabulously expensive luxury boutiques for clothing and jewelry. Other notable names on Fifth include chic department stores Henri Bendel, Bonwit Teller, Bergdorf Goodman, and Saks Fifth Avenue (further downtown, at 49th Street). 57th Street, meanwhile, boasts such brand-name boutiques as Ann Taylor, Laura Ashley, Chanel and New Yorkerpar-excellence Norma Kamali.

Here, too, are the outlets of the well-known luxury "gadget" emporium Hammacher Schlemmer (147 East 57th) and the exclusive main branch of the art bookstore Rizzoli (31 West 57th).

Quite a different clientele patronizes F.A.O. Schwarz, a "department store" at 767 Fifth devoted entirely to children's toys, which is as elaborate, excessive and confusing as any adult emporium in the city. And three avenues to the East, at 59th and Lexington Avenue, is Bloomingdale's. To some, this is the premiere shopping address in Manhattan, and far more affordable than its Fifth Avenue cousins. Around Bloomingdale's, the shopping scene is a different world: bargain shoe shops, branches of clothing-store chains, and fast-food outlets.

"Affordable" is not a word applicable to Madison Avenue. Walking here gives one a very different picture of the city. Street wear is impeccable, stores are elegant, prices high. Madison Avenue doesn't have quite the aura of big-city business found on 57th Street, (although traffic uptown can be very heavy at rush hour). After all, it's catering to clients of boutiques like Yves St. Laurent (855 Madison), Giorgio Armani (815 Madison), or Ralph Lauren, housed in an imposing edifice on the corner of 72nd St, at 867 Madison. But Madison also houses smaller shops, such as Go Fly A Kite, which suits its merchandise to its name. Browsers looking for china, crystal, silver, or similar "housewares" will want to stop in at Lalique, Pavillon Christofle (both at 680 Madison), or Gem Antiques (1088 Madison).

Prices may not be much lower on the West Side's Columbus Avenue, but the clientele is significantly different. Free of the burden of tradition and established wealth, the shops around here are more varied and eclectic. Between branches of well-known chains such as The Gap and International Express are places like The Down Quilt Shop (518 Columbus) or Handblock (Columbus and 83rd), which sells hand-crafted items from clothing to ceramics. Penny Whistle Toys, at 448 Columbus (other branches at 132 Spring Street and 1283 Madison Avenue), is one of the leading toy stores in the city. There's also Mythology, for devotees of science fiction and Dungeons and Dragons; some of Columbus's other whimsical stores are mentioned in the section on the Upper West Side.

Shops in Greenwich Village range from discount purveyors of Indian cotton to the Erotic Bakery, whose confections are all distinctly suggestive. Bleeker Street is a main shopping artery here, with clothing stores, gourmet food and

the unique Bird Jungle, whose feathered denizens also include brilliantly-colored South American parrots. 8th Street is another center for Village consumers; store windows are filled with leather, second-hand clothes, row upon row of shoes. Capezio, on MacDougal near 8th, sells a variety of fashions as well as a complete range of the dance equipment for which the store is famous.

In New York, art and shopping seem to go hand in hand: The city's main gallery centers are also its shoppers' paradises. Madison Avenue, 57th Street and SoHo have in common interesting art galleries, a variety of stores and high prices. SoHo, however, specializes in the unique and outré rather than the established and accepted, and browsing in its eclectic stores is a wonderful way to see a colorful slice of New York. West Broadway, Prince, Spring, Greene, Mercer and Broome

Above: Great deals can be found on every street corner. Right: In Midtown Manhattan most of what glitters is really gold.

Streets are all shopping meccas. If you're tired of looking at art, drop by Zona, where displays of products from the American Southwest create a very un-New York atmosphere, or Comme des Garçons, an outlet for the well-known avant-garde Japanese clothing label. Azzedine Alaïa's original boutique is also located in SoHo.

Businessmen have to shop, too – in New York, everyone shops – and the area around Wall Street offers more than its share of consumer possibilities. In the cobbled streets and docks of the South Street Seaport, "old-timey" wooden signs advertise such stores as Museum Books and Charts Store, purveyors of rare maps, prints, model ships, and all things nautical. On the waterfront, the giant red building of Pier 17 houses one of the city's few All-American shopping malls, selling everything from clothes to books to food in three floors of stores. On the other side of the island (not a long walk, here at Manhattan's narrow tip) is the World Financial Center, at the foot of the

World Trade Center. Here, branches of upscale luxury shops such as Barney's New York or Godiva Chocolates cater to the business crowd. Bargain-hunters will do better at nearby Century 21 (12 Cortlandt Street), a discount paradise for men, women and children.

The Lower East Side, the area bordered by The Bowery, Houston Street, and the East River, is historically New York's garment district. Logically enough, therefore, it offers plenty of garments for sale. First-timers may be a bit put off by the presentation – racks of clothing on the sidewalk, pawed through by crowds of shoppers, with nary a changing room in sight – but no one can argue with the prices. This is one of the few places left in the city which offers real bargains. Grand Street specializes in linens; for clothing, luggage, and accessories, try Orchard Street between Houston and Canal.

As rents rise, retailers, like residents, are forced to seek out new neighborhoods in which to set up shop. One area which has profited is the so-called Flatiron District. Earlier in the century, the area between 9th and 23rd Streets around Broadway, Fifth and Sixth Avenues, was known as the "Ladies Mile" because of the couturiers and milliners along its sidewalks; now, again, the area is beginning to offer prime shopping. Older tenants like Paragon Sporting Goods Center share the neighborhood with fashion names Emporio Armani or a Joan and David shoe store. The Strand bookstore, at 828 Broadway, is a "must" for booklovers – "must" is certainly a good word to describe the atmosphere of this warehouse-like establishment where shelf upon shelf of used books, in no discernible order, offer hours of pleasure for hard-core browsers. Another "don't miss" is The Last Wound-Up, on 19th St. With its motto "If it winds up, it winds up here," the store offers everything from watches to novelties, Chinese wind-up

toys to gorgeous antique music boxes worth thousands of dollars.

Herald Square is for shoppers who love crowds, noise, lots of pushing and shoving, and suburban-type shopping malls. Macy's and A&S are the major department stores here; the former a New York classic; the latter a more recent arrival at the heart of the glass-walled mall, which has been struggling since it opened in the 1980s. To the north, discount appliances, including cameras, computers and software, line the area around Broadway between about 34th and 50th Streets.

All of which leaves souvenir-hunters with plenty to choose from. What, in the end, is a "typical" New York purchase? The answer could be anything from vacuum-packed lox from Zabar's to a Big Apple piggy-bank, a fabulously expensive classic suit from New York designer Donna Karan to a New York Yankees baseball cap. But one thing is certain: very few people leave the city empty-handed, at though many may have empty wallets.

SPORTS

New York's sporting public likes its teams victorious. While this may not be enough to distinguish New York from other cities, the sheer number of the teams certainly is. Baseball, football, basketball, hockey, tennis, horseracing, taking place at Yankee Stadium, Shea Stadium, Madison Square Garden, Flushing Meadows, Aqueduct or Belmont, keep sports fans busily occupied, at least for that part of the year when their sport of choice is in season. The teams and individual competitors had better be good, too, as the New York public is famously vocal in its approval or criticism. After all, the term "Bronx cheer" (known elsewhere as a "raspberry") was coined at the city's own Yankee Stadium. Fortunately, the exuberance of loyal fans has been rewarded over the years: City teams have often won world championships.

Above: Not everyone outside the USA understands football, but it's a great show.

But the city is also fertile ground for participant sports. Staying fit has become something of an obsession with New York's urban dwellers, and numerous health clubs, parks (approximately 10 percent of the city is reserved for parks) and public beaches provide fine settings for working up a sweat and having a good time to boot. Keep in mind, however, that popularity in New York breeds congestion. Weekend joggers and bike riders virtually take over the parks.

Spectator Sports

Although they have been somewhat less successful in recent years, the New York Yankees have won more world championships than any other team. The Yankees are also the last of the "original" New York baseball teams, since the Giants' and the Brooklyn Dodgers' emigration to California. For these reasons, a visit to Yankee Stadium, at 161st Street in the Bronx, is something of historic pilgrimage for faithful fans. More recent arrivals on the scene, the New York Mets have stolen some of the Yankees' thunder of late. After the "Miracle Mets" of 1969 and 1972, the team went through a long slump, but pulled out in the mid-1980s to win the World Series in 1986, an occasion celebrated with a ticker-tape parade down Wall Street, in true New York style. Mets home games occur at Shea Stadium, in Flushing, Queens.

But it's not always necessary to travel out to these stadiums in order to see top-notch professional sports. At the heart of Manhattan, Madison Square Garden (36th Street and 7th Avenue) is home to basketball's New York Knicks and hockey's New York Rangers, depending on the season. The Garden also hosts a wealth of sports and entertainment events, such as the Ice Capades; professional tennis tournaments; track and field events; or, every spring, the Ringling Brothers Barnum and Bailey Circus, a New-York sized classic dubbed "the Greatest Show on Earth." Call (212) 465-MSG1 for ticket information.

The Knicks are another New York team which has seen moments of greatness alternate with long slumps. Recently, the acquisition of a new coach has restored the flagging spirits of players and fans alike, and superstar Patrick Ewing generally gives the opposition a run for its money. Information about the team can be had from the Knicks hotline (212/751-6310). The Knicks may be the only basketball team officially from the Big Apple, but in the world of hockey there are two New York teams: the Rangers and the Islanders. The latter play at Nassau Coliseum in Uniondale on Long Island (516/794-4100).

The New York Giants won the 1991 Super Bowl, and don't you forget it. Once fixtures at Yankee Stadium after the baseball season was over, the Giants have now acquired their own stadium across the river – that's right, Giants Stadium is in New Jersey (The Meadowlands, East Rutherford, (201) 935-8222). The New York Jets, who used to share Shea Stadium with the Mets, have also emigrated to the Meadowlands (201/421-6600), both teams presumably having discovered what urban residents have been bewailing for years, how hard it is to find a home in the city. Games are played weekly, generally on Sundays, during the brief September-December season. Most tickets are sold on a seasonal basis.

The Mets, the Jets, and the Nets – attempting to compete with them, the organization OTB (Off-Track Betting) tried to dub its clients the "Bets" in an ad campaign of the 70s. The name may not have stuck, but horseracing – and betting – are alive and well in New York. Trotters race daily at Yonkers Raceway in Yonkers (off Highway 87 north of the Bronx), while, when the football teams allow them space from January to August, trotters and pacers also race at the Meadowlands, as well as at Roosevelt Raceway, Westbury, Long Island.

For fans of Thoroughbred horse racing, a well-known name is Belmont Park, (718/641-4700), where the Belmont Stakes, the last of the three races that comprise the Triple Crown, are held in early June. The track is open from May to July and August to October. Aqueduct Racetrack, on Rockaway Boulevard, (718/641-4700), conducts a racing season from October to May. There is no racing on Tuesdays at either track. And, even if they aren't called "the Bets" any more, people still patronize the more than 100 **OTB** branches in the five boroughs. This organization (212/704-5118), the first such in the United States, takes bets on Thoroughbred and harness races throughout the country.

The biggest tennis competition in the city is held in August and September. As the US Open is one of four international grand slam tennis events, tickets to late rounds are hard to come by. For information contact the US Tennis Association,

Flushing Meadows Park, Flushing, NY 11368, 718/271-5100. The Tournament of Champions is held in August at the West Side Tennis Club in Forest Hills, 718/268-2300.

Participant Sports

Among the hordes of visitors to New York City every year, there must be some who are in tip-top physical condition and would like a slightly different view of the city's boroughs. Such hardy souls should consider entering the New York City Marathon. The 26-mile course winds through all five city boroughs, although participants may not have much time for sight-seeing. Among the approximately 20,000 runners who take part each fall are world-class athletes bent on victory and hobby joggers who want to see if they can finish. At least two million

Above and right: Rollerskating and jogging are some of the participant sports offered by the parks in New York City.

people line sidewalks and rooftops to watch this colorful event; after all, unlike most sporting events in New York, people can watch this one for free. Entry forms are available from the Road Runners Club, P.O. Box 881, FDR Station, New York 10150, (212) 860-4455. A similar event for cyclists, but without the emphasis on winning, is Citibank's Five-Borough Bike Tour, held in May. Cyclists can enjoy speeding in a mile-long pack along avenues closed to traffic. Equally enjoyable tours, however, can be made in the city's parks. Cars are banned, for example, from some Central Park roads from 10 a.m. to 3 p.m. and 7 p.m. to 10 p.m. weekdays, and all weekend. Other car-free tours can be made in Riverside Park, Battery Park Esplanade downtown (both of which have the addded attraction of river views of New York Harbor), and Brooklyn's Prospect Park. For bicycle rentals, try AAA Bikes at the Loeb Boathouse in Central Park (212/ 861-4137); Bicycles Plus at 204 East 85th Street (212/794-2201); or Pedal Pusher at 1306 2nd Avenue (212/288-5592).

If the idea of riding through the park on something other than wheels appeals, turn to Claremount Riding Academy (173-177 West 89th Street, (212) 724-5100), the only riding stable in Manhattan. The Academy rents horses with English saddles for a turn around Central Park's reservoir along the bridle path. Culmitt Stables (51 Caton Place, Brooklyn, (718) 438-8849), provides a similar service in Prospect Park.

For a simple afternoon workout, the health club services offered by many hotels will probably be at least adequate. Walk-ins may use the facilities at Manhattan's Know Sweat (217 East 12th Street, (212) 254-4531), or the Vanderbilt YMCA (224 East 47th Street, (212) 755-2410), as well as other YMCA facilities throughout the city.

Skaters, take note: The only year-round ice rink in New York City is the in-

door Sky Rink on the sixteenth floor of 450 West 33rd Street (212/695-6555). Probably the city's most famous rink is the one at Rockefeller Center (50th Street at 5th Avenue), where, at Christmastime, hundreds of skaters circle under the enormous Christmas tree, often in the company of Santa Claus, under the eyes of thousands of spectators. Central Park's Wollman Memorial Rink is jammed on weekends. All rinks offer skate and locker rentals.

Tennis, anyone? Try contacting Central Park's Tennis House, near 94th Street (212/397-3194), for information on the required court reservations. Reservations are taken up to two days in advance at the U.S.T.A. Tennis Center, at Flushing Meadows Park (718/592-8000). Furthermore, various tennis clubs throughout the city offer private courts; try Columbus Racquet Club, 795 Columbus Avenue (212/663-6900); HRC Tennis, East River Drive at Wall Street (212/422-9300); or Manhattan Plaza Racquet Club, 450 West 43rd Street (212/594-0554).

Dedicated joggers need no guide to induce them to leave their beds for a morning run, but may be interested to know that the track circling Central Park's Reservoir measures 1.5 miles, while Riverside Park between 72nd and 116th Streets is 2.25 miles. Neither of these is recommended in the evening. Self-motivated swimmers looking for a place to get their feet wet will find public pools at Asher Levy Place (East 23rd Street Pool, 212/397-3184); 342 East 54th Street (212/397-3148); and 35 West 34th Street (212/397-3193). More swimming can be done in the breakers off Long Island; the biggest and best beaches in the area are Jones Beach (516/785-1600) and Robert Moses State Park (516/669-0449). Nearer the city, beaches are more crowded and often less than clean; still, Queens' Rockaway Beach and Brooklyn's Coney Island draw mammoth crowds on summer weekends. For seekers of quieter times by the waterside, a better bet might be the Atlantic beaches on Staten Island, at Wolfe's Pond Park or Great Kills Park.

139

EATING AND DRINKING

Those who proclaim with professorial assurance and in stentorian tones that America lacks gastronomic culture are either ignorant of the country's history, or have never been to New York. Nowhere is the meltingpot more visible, more accessible than in the city's gastronomic life. Just about every national style between the Far East and the Far West, North Cape and Cape Hatteras can be found somewhere in the New York streets. Any palate, any penchant, any depth of pocket or purse can be satisfied dining in New York City. There are well over 15,000 eating outlets (ranging from carts to luxurious restaurants) to choose from, and many serve fine food.

American food is the food of other cultures, sometimes mixed and sometimes pure, and New York is its greatest showroom. On the most expensive turf in the country, in the heart of midtown Manhattan, even fast food, often seen as quintessentially American, leaves its styrofoam cocoon behind and blossoms into a hundred aromatic flowers. The humble hotdog peddler, who once forlornly guarded a little cart full of wan wieners and soggy sauerkraut as an alternative to the breadline, has pushed to the forefront of international cuisine. At last count there were 7754 licensed vendors, many of them recent immigrants with pride in their national dishes: On the streets of Manhattan you can find Italian sausages, Chinese dumplings, Jewish knishes or kosher hotdogs, Mexican tacos, German bratwurst, Japanese yakitori, Caribbean roti, Argentine empanadas and New York cheesecake for dessert. This street cuisine is the ideal way to eat on hot summer days, when the lunchbreak is too short, the restaurants full and the city streets too alive to leave.

Fast food in New York also means pizza, sold from hundreds of shoe-box-

Above: Fast food on New York's streets has become exotic. Right: The club sandwich, a far cry from nouvelle cuisine.

like parlors spread throughout the city. It is sold by the slice, a unit much larger than its name implies, dripping with oil and cheese, and accompanied by ice-cold bubbleless soft drinks that have no real flavor even at room temperature. Fast food is also felafel sandwiches in pita bread drowned in tahini, a Lebanese contribution; or the Greek version, with strips of lamb and tzaziki. It is what New Yorkers call a hero, a medium-sized white-bread loaf, stuffed by most local delis with cold (or warm) cuts, cheese and salads of choice. And then there are the bagels, hard doughnut-shaped rolls of raised dough (rye, pumpernickel, wheat, white, with raisins), served spread with melted butter, cream cheese, lox, pastrami, or whatever one fancies.

"Typical" in New York, however, is in the mind of the beholder. For those used to stretch limousines, Concorde and a bottomless credit rating, it might be any of the first-rate French restaurants in Midtown, whose names are almost inevitably preceded by the definite article, whose gender is inevitably correct, as the owners and operators are usually French: La Grenouille, Le Cygne, Le Bernardin, La Côte Basque, La Caravelle, Le Perigord. (An exception to the definite-article rule is the Lafayette; but it *sounds* as if it had an article.) In this category of French and if-you-have-to-ask-the-price-you-can't-afford-it, there is also the Auréole and Le Cirque, both located a little further uptown, and downtown Bouley and Chanterelle, the latter being exceptionally well decorated.

Equally typical of New York is a restaurant where the food is second-rate, but men are not allowed to enter without a jacket and tie. On the other hand, like the Metropolitan Museum, a taste of New York's ethnic foods is a must. Furthermore, the price is generally right.

On West 55th Street The Carnegie Delicatessen is arguably the ultimate Eastern European Jewish delicatessen, with deli-

cious pastrami, juicy coleslaw, huge sour pickles. One sandwich is enough for two meals here. A somewhat simpler place, but perhaps a shot more genuine is Katz's Delicatessen, while Bavarian *Weisswurst* with pretzels, washed down with *Weissbier*, taste just as it does in the *Heimat* around East 86th Street. Sylvia is the Queen of Soul Food, the African-American cuisine. She serves up ribs, chicken, beans and greens, rice and biscuits in the middle of Harlem, on Lenox Avenue between 126th and 127th Streets. Brazilian specialties, another derivative of the African experience, are available at Cabana Carioca II (West 45th), where the recommended beverage is a rum concoction named the *caipirinha*. A peculiar strain of food is served at the El Caridad. Half the neighborhood is usually waiting for a place at a formica table for a heaped plate of Cuban-Chinese food.

Eating in Chinatown often means overcoming the unfamiliar, hectic surroundings, but the atmosphere may be more genuinely Chinese than in those places

where most customers are white and middle class. Chinatown, however, is an eater's paradise, though at times the appearances are deceiving. Some of the best restaurants (Little Szechuan, Siu Lam Kung, Wong Kee, for example) are stuffed into basements, their waxcloth-covered tables are shared by all customers, their waiters stern, over-worked, but very efficient. Many restaurants are open all night. Portions are huge, but customers are welcome to a doggie bag, an American tradition that none but the snooty will forswear. The decor of the Silver Palace, once called a *dim-sum* heaven, is more traditional. It is a mammoth hall decorated with dragons. Guests choose finger-food off carts as the waiters pass by.

Eating in Little Italy, north of Canal Street, is a joyful experience. Umberto's is where Joe Gallo was gunned down,

which has endowed it with macabre notoriety. Puglia is an inexpensive little place, always crowded on weekends, and where tipsy guests who do not know each other lock arm in arm at long tables and sing Italian songs they do not know either. Ferrara's across the street is the place to go for dessert. An alternative is a trip to the Village to hang out in one of the many cafés there.

Italian food, of course, is not restricted to Little Italy. The Primavera in the 60s is a fine, albeit expensive, place. Belmont, the Bronx's Little Italy, also has a number of restaurants to choose from.

6th Street in Manhattan has grown into Little India. The scent of curry fills the air, here, and it seems sometimes that the restaurateurs all have the same muzak tape. Some of the restaurants are intimately tiny, others have delightful, quiet gardens out back. The one thing they have in common is quality and good value for the dollar. The BYOB system (Bring Your Own Bottle) has a moderating effect on the prices.

Above: The deli of old takes on a chic look.
Right: The Russian Tea Room, one of the most resilient institutions of the better crust.

But New York cuisine is not restricted to ethnic and international foods. The city's restaurants also excel in real American food. One standby is "surf and turf;" and the "surf" offerings, i.e. seafood, of this harbor city can be excellent. A notable address in this regard is the Oyster Bar at Grand Central Station, where chowders and filets are served along with oysters on the half shell amidst Art-Deco elegance. Another option for good seafood is out in City Island in the East Bronx.

New York steak has become famous, and some would say it's as good at one of the lesser spots like Spark's, The Assembly Steak House, or The Palm (East 45th Street/Second Avenue). The Gotham Bar & Grill, however, combines culinary and visual delights. It's a chic place arranged in a former warehouse, has a number of levels, interesting lighting, and, most of all, it is consistently good (and expensive).

And no one should point a finger at the traditional hamburger. It comes in all shapes and sizes in New York (try the Jackson Hole Wyoming Burgers, the Burger Joint, the Corner Bistro or Hamburger Harry's).

An experience, of course, is the famous Hard Rock Café, whose logo, emblazoned on thousands of T-shirts, has spread around the world. It tends to be very crowded though, and the managers take their hard rock quite seriously: The volume of the music in the place is enough to blast the relish off your burger.

The Broadway Diner is a place to get basic American diner food: BLTs, hamburgers, the stew of the day, milk shakes, the lot washed down by a bottomless cup of coffee. In fact, just about any diner offers the same deal, and corner diners are also great spots for people-watching.

New Age left its mark on American cuisine, giving rise to a number of restaurants whose names are sometimes as imaginative as their menus. The Four Seasons, which has been around for some time, has dishes that borrow quite a few elements from the Orient. The same ap-

plies to the The Quilted Giraffe, which offers Japanese-American dishes in a slick, post-modern grey and black setting. The Sign of the Dove has a French influence. It is situated in a beautiful indoor garden. Another outgrowth of the New Age is the multitude of health-food, vegetarian restaurants for those people who intend to live forever.

In New York, as in many other large towns, the local imagination sometimes seizes upon some restaurant and disproportionately inflates its reputation. The reason is often that a star has picked it as a place to eat, and it suddenly becomes popular. It is wise to remember that gossip columnists are not necessarily good food critics.

A number of places, however, have distinguished themselves mainly because they attract stardom. Witness the Club

Above: The Hard Rock Café is famous for great burgers and a lot of loud music. Right: At McSorley's, where they still throw saw dust on the floor.

"21", where a so-so hamburger costs $24. The *Russian Tea Room* is truly Russian, and can be counted on to have the best *blinis* in town, and some star or other very famous face hanging out in the middle of the forever-Christmas decor.

Drinks

The drinker's equivalent of the typical diner can be recognized by a three-colored neon beer sign flashing in the window. The bar tenders have seen it all, they mix efficiently, chatter away at the same time, and when they get friendly, they even start mixing their own creations. Some places have become quite popular, not to say hip. Pete's Tavern and McSorley's in the Village have a beery reputation, if you can reach the bar. The Union Square Cafe and the Soho Kitchen and Bar have become the hang out of the self-conscious yuppie crowd, while the grumpies (grown up mature professionals) prefer Jim McCullens, which serves good pastas, pizzas, burgers and salads

and a first-class selection of more than 100 wines by the glass. After an evening at the theater people grab a nightcap at Joe Allen, or better yet, Whiskey, where the waiters either were seen or will be seen on the stage at some point and you can spot the faces.

A Table!

It is impossible to make a general assessment of the service in New York restaurants. It ranges from terrible to perfect, with every shade in between. Many of the posh places have excellently trained staff, some of the smaller ethnic places are owned and operated as family businesses. The alleged rudeness of Chinese waiters in the little spots in Chinatown is in fact stress. The gruffness of deli- and diner-counter staff is frequently an offshoot of typically dour New York humor and should not be taken personally. A large number of restaurants also hire students or struggling actors, beginner models and starving writers.

When the waiter/actor comes to a table to recite the specials, the result is often a dramatic monologue preceded by a casual "Hi, I'm ..., I'm your waiter tonight." Feel free to interrupt and ask prices if that information has not been worked into the act. The staff are often friendly and outgoing.

Some customer/waitperson traditions have to be respected or accepted. The first is, that the customer gets bread and water, after sitting down. The water might be omitted if a severe drought is on the land. Secondly, tipping is 15 percent and important. The reason is that the waitpeople are officially paid under the minimum wage, and the tips are an important source of income. Part of that money goes to the busboy, the person who brings the amenities and clears the table. Also, tips are important if you want to return to the restaurant and enjoy your meal. And finally, if the food is not good, don't forget: The waiter is not responsible for the cook's divagations so make your complaint to the manager.

145

NIGHTLIFE

"The city that never sleeps" – a fitting epithet for New York. Walking down Broadway at two in the morning, one sees more activity and life on the street than one encounters in many other cities at midday. Meanwhile, the clubs are just starting to warm up at this hour.

Of course – this being New York – some night spots have exacting standards. Bouncers stand at the doors of the "in" clubs and reject the inappropriately-dressed out of hand. Finding the right balance between high fashion and looking as if one doesn't care about how one looks can be difficult, but can guarantee entry into a club. Another problem for the uninitiated is knowing which club happens to be "in" at the moment. In fickle New York, last week's big scene could be this week's Siberia – Studio 54, for example, the latest word in the 1970s, was a joke in the 1980s, and closed altogether by the 90s; and tourists now flock to the Palladium, formerly reserved exclusively for New York chic-eria.

For dancing, there are always plenty of venues, "in" or not; once you get out on the floor, "in" might not matter so very much anyway. City (124 West 43rd Street, 212/869-2088) has been through a number of incarnations – Shout, Xenon, and the Henry Miller Theater – before arriving at its present name; today, it's a frantic, moderately-priced dance club near Times Square. Down the street, Laura Belle (120 West 43rd Street, 212/819-1000), a relative newcomer, is a clubby place where the young and the famous come to dance. For those who need a lot of room to move, the vast Red Zone (440 West 54th Street, 212/582-2222) measures 14,000 square feet, and features huge movie screens.

Preceding pages: New York displays a million points of light at night. Left: What good is sitting alone in your room?

Au Bar (241 East 58th Street, 212/308-9455) is an ultra-fashionable place catering to young, oh-so-stylish Europeans (fondly known as *Eurotrash*) and models. Tatou (151 East 50th Street, 212/753-1144) has an illustrious past: formerly an opera house, it became a supper club where Edith Piaf and Judy Garland performed. Now, it is elaborately decorated, invoking the spirit of New Orleans, with a disco and private club upstairs.

When Limelight (47 West 20th Street, 212/807-7850) first opened its doors, it sent shock waves through the neighborhood. This disco is located in a former church, complete with spires and stained-glass windows. The shock was caused more by its flouting of taboos, such as staging of mock crucifixions and other such spectacles. Today, it has become an accepted establishment.

Nell's (246 West 14th Street, 212/675-1567) was another trend-setting club when first it opened, all the more popular because it was nearly impossible to get in. Now, the club's harsh turn-them-away-at-the-door policy, has relaxed, and individuals not personally known to the doorman can sometimes gain entrance.

The Pyramid Club (101 Avenue A, 212/420-1590) displays a colorful side of New York's night life. This East Village club caters to a clientele ranging from transvestites to yuppies. In the old days, the club used to let in assorted "street people" to add a touch of local color. Not for the easily shocked, it offers a genuine East Village experience.

Easier to take and more welcoming to all, Peggy Sue's (University Place at 13th Street, 212/260-4095) is a "down home" place to drink a beer and dance.

Once the very latest word in New York clubs, The Palladium (126 East 14th Street, 212/473-7171) has decorations by artists including Keith Haring and Jean-Michel Basquiat. It's not as fashionable as it used to be, but this means that you can get in to see the huge, multi-story

dance floor and the variegated works of art. Every room is different, and don't overlook the bathrooms.

More Elegant Nightspots For Dancing

Those who prefer a more restrained tone to the rambunctious club scene don tuxedos or sequined gowns and head for the Rainbow Room (30 Rockefeller Plaza, 212/632-5000). Refurbished and re-polished to its former sleek, Art-Deco glamor, this club, located on the 65th floor of Rockefeller Center, is admittedly pricey, but remains one of the most romantic places in New York, complete with a vista of twinkling city lights.

The Copacabana (10 East 60th Street, 212/755-6010) can't match the Rainbow Room for elegance, but it has a long and colorful history. The club has been a hangout for baseball stars, gangsters and movie stars (Lucille Ball met Desi Arnaz in the club); performers have included many top names, including the Chairman of the Board, Frank Sinatra. Here, you can dress up, smoke a cigarette in a jeweled holder, and watch for a mafia hit.

Formerly fallen into disrepair, Roseland (239 West 52nd Street, 212/247-0200) was revamped in the mid-1980s in an attempt to restore some of its previous luster. Within these walls, visitors can still hear the big-band sound and watch the fancy steps of practiced ballroom dancers. The dance floor is half a block long, and to give high steppers inspiration, a wall-length display contains shoes of famous dancers past and present, from Ruby Keeler to movie tough George Raft to tap master Gregory Hines.

Live Rock'n'Roll Clubs

Above: Happy hour is the opener to a night on the town. Right: Getting dressed up for the night is part of the fun.

On any weekend, a major rock act could be playing Radio City Music Hall, The Paramount Theater, or Madison

Square Garden. But apart from those big-name events, vistors can be assured of a night of good live music at one of many smaller theaters and clubs.

A favorite Village nightspot, the Cat Club (76 East 13th Street, 212/505-0090) is popular with visiting rock'n'roll stars, who just may hop onstage in the course of an evening. CBGB (315 Broadway at Bleecker Street, 212/677-0455), another long-time Village venue (not to say "dive"), was once the center of the punk rock movement; the cutting-edge music still clearly takes precedence over decor. More up-market than CBGB, The Bottom Line (15 West 4th Street, 212/228-6300) pulls a young crowd from surrounding New York University. But bigger names tend to play here, as well. One of the club's most illustrious alumni, a young unknown named Bruce Springsteen, went on from The Bottom Line to the covers of *Time* and *Newsweek* and sold-out 50,000-seat arenas.

The Lone Star Café, with its trademark iguana atop the building, was long a Village landmark; locals mourned when it went out of business a few years ago and a suburban real estate developer bought the iguana. Now, they console themselves with the Lone Star Roadhouse uptown (240 West 52nd Street, 212/245-2950). Not quite as authentic in feel, this club still features Texas-style rhythm and blues, Western swing and rock'n'roll. More genuine (i.e. tacky) in a funky way, is Delta 88 (332 Eighth Avenue, 212/924-3499). Decorated to look "country," the club hosts bands from Louisiana and Texas, and features a defiantly unsophisticated soul food menu.

A fusion of 90s sensibilities and 60s nostalgia, Wetlands (161 Hudson Street, 212/966-4225) is a curious place filled with psychedelic posters illuminated with black light, an ecological library and petitions to sign for the cause of the moment. The Age of Aquarius lives on. The Ritz (254 West 54th Street, 212/541-8900) started out in a beautiful, small theater in the East Village but moved a few years ago into a Theater District landmark, the building that used to house Studio 54. The limos do not line up as they did in the old days. Now, ordinary mortals can buy a ticket to these concerts and be let in without a fight.

Jazz and Piano Clubs

Jazz and New York have a special relationship; after all, the city's nickname of Big Apple was originally coined by jazz musicians. In the 20s and 30s, touring jazz musicians referred to the towns they played in as apples on a tree; New York was the biggest apple of all. In the 1930s, there was such a cluster of jazz clubs on West 52nd Street that it was christened *Swing Street*. Today, there are jazz clubs scattered all over town, certainly enough of them to allow everyone a bite of the Big Apple.

The Village Vanguard (178 7th Avenue South, 212/255-4037) is a dark room at the bottom of a flight of stairs with fairly uncomfortable chairs. But the music played here is of a caliber to enable one to forget the physical discomfort. Big names book here (as they have since 1935), so there is often a line out the door. Of equally high quality is the ebullient music at Sweet Basil (88 7th Avenue South, 212/2421785) and The Blue Note (131 West 3rd Street, 212/475-8592). The latter gets acts of the likes of jazz master Dizzy Gillespie; listeners are advised to book seats well in advance.

The more elegant Zinno (126 West 13th Street, 212/924-5182) is a tony Italian restaurant in a West Village brownstone. But they always book a jazz duo or trio, and music lovers can listen for the price of a couple of drinks. Bradley's (70 University Place, 212/473-9700) is well-known for its acoustics. Music simply sounds better in this dark, low-ceilinged

Right: The Charlie Bird Trio gives a performance of jazz, still one of New York's great musical attractions.

room, and there's an intimacy here loved by jazz pianists, bass players and listeners alike. Much less organized is The Knitting Factory (47 East Houston Street, 212/ 219-3055). It seems anyone can get up and play here. Whether jazz or rock is being played, it's usually experimental and raw.

The Village Gate (Bleecker and Thompson Streets, 212/475-5120) sometimes stages strange off-Broadway shows, but generally sticks to the jazz for which it's known. Applied to a club, S.O.B. is not a putdown, merely an abbreviation for *Sounds of Brazil* (204 Varick Street, 212/243-4940). Most nights, bands from Brazil, Africa or the Caribbean provide the intoxicating beat.

Cabarets

For an evening of intimate singing or witty repartee, there are a few sophisticated spots around town. Reclining on a banquette, sipping a martini and listening to a good torch song is not a bad way to see another side of New York.

The Upper East Side's stylish Hotel Carlyle (Madison Avenue at 76th Street, 212/570-7189) is home to two elegant musical venues. The dark leather Bemelman's Bar usually features a very expressive singer named Barbara Carroll; Cole Porter specialist Bobby Short generally performs in the mural-filled Café Carlyle. A legendary writers' hangout, the Algonquin hotel (59 West 44th Street, 212/840-6800) also has a cabaret room of note, the oak-paneled Oak Room. The acts change all the time, but they are chosen for their sophistication and wit.

The owner of the The Russian Tea Room (150 West 57th Street, 212/265-0947) noticed that cabarets elsewhere were doing good business, so she installed one in an unused room, which, since its inception in 1990, has been packing them in. Equally, popular is Rainbow & Stars (30 Rockefeller Plaza,

212/632-5000) next to the Rainbow Room, which draws big names to match its big view of New York.

Lower key in tone if not in quality is The Ballroom (253 West 28th Street, 212/2443005), an intimate space with wonderful acoustics. The legendary Miss Peggy Lee could have played anywhere in New York, but year after year she came back to The Ballroom. Michael's Pub (211 East 55th Street, 212/758-2272) also gets a celebrity visitor from time to time. When writer-director-comedian Woody Allen is in town and not working on a movie, he sits in on clarinet with the room's Dixieland band.

More casual – anyone might drop in and take the stage – is Eighty Eights (228 West 10th Street, 212/924-0088), a West Village cabaret. Most of the performers, and often customers as well, are young people working in the theater. Currently popular, and more esoteric, is a cabaret called The Nile (327 West 44th Street, 212/262-1111), decorated in the style of ancient Egypt.

Comedy Clubs

Due to the popularity of live, hip comedy shows on TV, comedy clubs have been in ascendence. Audiences willing to sit through a few uninspired acts by aspiring young comics may even get a special reward; established comedians like Eddie Murphy and Robin Williams have been known to drop in. The Improvization (358 West 44th Street, 212/765-8268) is the grand-daddy of this trend, a Theater District club that launched many well-known comedians. Catch a Rising Star (1487 First Avenue, 212/794-1906) and The Comic Strip (1568 Second Avenue, 212/861-9386), often get the same acts – sometimes, because of their close proximity, on the same night. Stand Up New York (236 West 78th Street, 212/595-0850) gets a few from TV. Caroline's at the South Street Seaport (Pier 17 at Fulton Street and East River, 212/233-4900) gets all kinds of aspirants, ranging from Wall Street yuppies who think they're funny to an occasional big name.

PERFORMING ARTS

"They say the neon lights are bright on Broadway..."

Throughout the entire country, New York's theater scene has the allure of a legend. "Broadway." – the word alone conjures up images of glamor and bright lights, after-theater dinners and stardom. No matter that the reality is, like the real Broadway, much larger and much dingier than it's usually depicted; no matter that aspiring young actors spend years waiting on tables and waiting for their big break. The city continues to draw hordes of young performers: dancers, singers, actors, instrumentalists from all over the world. And each of them comes for basically the same reason: New York is one of the world's great cultural capitals, one of the few places where the dream of superstardom still has a chance of coming true.

For audiences, of course, this makes New York a veritable theater Mecca. Whether one's in the market for Broadway tickets or an Off-Off-Broadway show in a Greenwich Village basement, one's assured of a memorable evening. Performances also take place in the parks, on the rooftops, in galleries, even in the streets. In fact, one of the biggest problems New York audiences face is what to see on any given evening.

Visitors to the city (and this includes former residents!) usually want to start with Broadway. No matter that some of the luster has tarnished with the years, that the 30-odd theaters clustered in the "Theater District" in the area around Times Square vie for space with nearby porn theaters and strip shows, or that critics charge theaters with running either sure-fire, glitzy hits or plays which have already been tried and found true in London (these two categories not, by any means, mutually exclusive). Despite everything, no other American theater center can hold a candle to Broadway.

The Theater District is commonly understood to denote the area between 41st and 53rd Streets, between Sixth and Eighth Avenue. This area, of course, includes Times Square, with its gigantic neon billboards, its lights and its TKTS Booth, where lines of would-be theatergoers wait patiently for discounted tickets for the evening's performance. It also includes Shubert Alley (between 44th and 45th Streets), the heart of the theater district, lined with theaters including, of course, the famous Shubert (one of the largest houses on Broadway, located at 225 West 44th Street, 239-6200). Here, in the surrounding theaters, such classic hits as *Oklahoma!*, *South Pacific*, and *Kiss me Kate* were premiered, establishing one of the United States' greatest and most enduring cultural traditions, the Broadway musical. The genre has continued to flourish with more recent arrivals on the scene: *Fiddler on the Roof*, *Evita* and *A Chorus Line*.

Production costs for a Broadway show, however, have risen so astronomically in the last decades that good theater has had to find other outlets. Thus, the term "Off-Broadway" has come to denote classy productions of dramatic integrity, rather than shows that weren't "good enough" for the big time. Indeed, Off-Broadway *is* the big time in New York these days, when one considers such superior venues as the Vivian Beaumont Theater in Lincoln Center, which has put on many award-winning plays. And tenacious organizations such as the Manhattan Theater Club (which performs at City Center, 131 West 55th St, 581-7907) put on a number of shows and revues big and small in the course of a season, with special rates for the members who help to keep the whole enterprise afloat. Another advantage that Off-Broadway has to offer is affordable ticket prices, nothing to sneeze at in an era when a ticket to a

Left: Carnegie Hall has maintained its high reputation for over a century now.

Uptown, Upstages

For those who like more music with their theater, the New York opera world has plenty to offer. Lincoln Center is a center indeed for the world's music-lovers, from young (such as the students of the Juilliard School nearby) to old. Its centerpiece is the Metropolitan Opera House. From the street, the building is striking; within, its modern staircases are as plushly red, its auditorium as studded with gold, and its performers as top-notch as any European theater.

On Saturday morning, aficionados line up for standing-room tickets for the week's performances; if Pavarotti is singing, your chances of getting in are slim, even in this enormous house (Tel: 362-2000). Next door, meanwhile, the New York City Opera holds forth in the New York State Theater (870-5570); its inclusion of a summer season makes it possible for opera buffs to get their fix in New York all year round. When the opera's not in season, the house is home to the New York City Ballet, while the Met is taken over by the American Ballet Theater.

Broadway show can easily cost $100. And don't think that "Off-Broadway" is a term only applicable to short-lived productions: the classic musical *The Fantasticks* has been running at Sullivan Street Playhouse (181 Sullivan Street at Bleeker Street 674-3838) for the last 32 years. It's still going strong.

Of course, it's hard to make hard-and-fast distinctions between theatrical genres; and it may seem slightly amusing that there's a line drawn between "Off-Broadway" and "Off-Off-Broadway." Roughly speaking, the distinction is between reputable smaller theaters and a real grab bag of performance happenings ranging from terrific to terrible. At an Off-Off-Broadway show, the unwitting audience member may find himself sitting in an almost totally empty house; but then again, he may have a once-in-a-lifetime experience.

Above: Ballet aficionados are always satisfied in New York. Right: One of Broadway's internationally famous productions.

But Lincoln Center also offers music *pur*, and plenty of it. Avery Fisher Hall, the third of the main edifices on the plaza, is home to the New York Philharmonic. Throughout the year, international soloists perform with the orchestra; often, tickets are available for the dress rehearsal in the morning (check newspapers for information; box office telephone is 875-5030). In July and August, the Mostly Mozart festival, now a city institution, is based in the hall, as well. For chamber-music fans, the smaller Alice Tully Hall across the street offers fare on a smaller scale, but of equal caliber (875-5050).

Still, neither of these venues can vie with the grand-daddy of New York concert stages, Carnegie Hall. Located on busy 57th Street, the majestic old building was recently spruced up in time for its

100th birthday in 1991. Some claim that the hall's renowned acoustics were damaged in the course of these extensive renovations; still, it remains a jewel among performance spaces – as well as one in the crown of any performer who's played there (247-7800).

New York's musical and operatic life doesn't stop with its famous stages. There's plenty going on in smaller venues. The Amato Opera Company (319 Bowery, at 2nd Street; 228-8200), for example, has been going for years, providing students and young singers with a real New York stage on which to test their mettle. Some of these distinctly home-grown productions are quite wonderful, and some of their stars have gone on to big careers. There's also the Village Light Opera Group, specializing in Gilbert and Sullivan operettas.

For concerts, meanwhile, there's the 92nd Street Y (the YMCA, that is, at Lexington Avenue and 92nd Street, 415-5440), which hosts wonderful evenings with performances by internationally-known instrumentalists, singers, and groups. Weill Recital Hall (formerly Carnegie Recital Hall) is a kind of "Carnegie Hall, Junior" for performers, offering recitals on a smaller scale. Town Hall hosts a wide variety of cultural events, and is a famous venue for New York recital debuts by young artists (143 W 43rd St, (212) 586-4680). And then there's CAMI Hall, across the street from Carnegie. If you get tired of just listening to all this music, go to CAMI Hall during their summer series, and join in one of their sing-alongs of works such as the Brahms or Verdi Requiem.

On Your Toes

From ballet to avant-garde; in New York, the word "dance" covers a variety of movements. Dance is an expensive business. Although dancers seem to have more difficulties making ends meet than any other performing artists, and the dance world has time and again been marked by the void left when yet another

157

company was forced to close up shop, the New York dance scene continues to forge ahead. New York has seen the birth of most of the major dance movements of the United States, from Balanchine's Classicism to Martha Graham.

Dance companies tend to have shorter seasons than operatic or musical ones. For instance, the American Ballet Theater, which appears at the Metropolitan Opera House, dances from late April to late June; New York City Ballet, also at Lincoln Center, also has a winter season, running from late November to February, when it performs, among other things, its famous *Nutcracker*. Both companies present repertory dances ranging from traditional story-ballets to Balanchine's abstractions. Then, there's the Joffrey, a well-respected ballet company which usually performs at City Center; and don't overlook the captivating Dance Theater of Harlem. New York being New

Above: The Metropolitan Opera is popular with spectators and the gossip columnists.

York, an average season will probably see guest appearances by anyone from the Paris Opera Ballet to the Kirov.

But all this is only the tip of the iceberg as far as New York dance is concerned. City Center is a major dance venue in Manhattan, and during the year, it may host performances by the Paul Taylor, Merce Cunningham, Trisha Brown, Eric Hawkins, or Alvin Ailey companies – all local names. Another theater to watch for is the Joyce (175 Eighth Avenue, 242-0800), home to the Eliot Feld Ballet Company, and host to a myriad others.

...and Beyond

After hearing a young woman perform some piano works, Noel Coward was asked whether he liked piano music. "No," replied Coward, "but I like *this*!"

Quite a few events that sneak into "Dance" or "Theater" listings in the city newspapers can't really be described as dance or theater. These are the works that fall into the "we don't know what it is, but we know it's performance" category. Many of them are on the cutting edge of what's happening in art today, such as pieces by performance artist Karen Finley, whose rejection for a National Endowment for the Arts grant on grounds of obscenity triggered a controversy.

If any single element could be said to characterize pieces in this general "performance" category, it would be that they're often by artists genuinely experimenting with the boundaries of what one's able to get across to an audience. Whether the piece is a play written and performed by an unknown dramatist or dance theater, it can be truly enlightening to watch what's going on in an artist's head, or to understand the process many performers go through before they make the big time. Of course, in many circles some of the places specializing in this category – such as the Kitchen (512 W 19th St, 255-5793) or **P.S. 122** (150 First Avenue, 477-5288) – are the big time, stages which have proved their mettle by consistently presenting intriguing experimental theater, dance and music.

Tickets, Please

Getting into the event of your choice isn't always as easy as it sounds. For most major shows, tickets can be ordered far in advance by calling one of the electronic reservation systems such as Ticketmaster, Teletron or Telecharge, which will book your seats for a surcharge of some dollars. Another option, of course, is to go directly to the box office.

If your show is reported sold out by these organizations, try a ticket broker. Union Tickets, N.Y. Tickets or Prestige Programs may be able to offer you seats. If you're really desparate, it may even be worth your while to pay double or triple the ticket's face value from Premiere Ticket Service.

Most people, however, like a bargain. And there are several ways to get Broad-

way tickets at great discounts. The most popular source for discount tickets is the TKTS Booth at Duffy Square in the Theater District. For cash or travelers checks, only – no credit cards – patrons can get tickets to a variety of Broadway and some Off-Broadway shows for half price plus a $1.50 surcharge. There is no phone, and no guarantee of availability, so hopefuls begin to congregate several hours before showtime to see what's to be had that day. Then it is a not-so-long wait in a lengthy, but efficiently fast-moving line for tickets. The booth has a branch location in the Wall Street area, at 2 World Trade Center.

Another great source of discount tickets, and one that does have a phone (212/3822323), is the Bryant Park Music and Dance Discount Ticket Booth, just west of the New York Public Library at 42nd Street. They sell tickets for performances at Lincoln Center, City Center, Carnegie Hall and a few nightclubs. Call to see when they're open and what tickets are currently available.

Anyone eager for a taste of the New York performing arts scene is advised to buy a local magazine or newspaper. *The New Yorker*, a city hallmark for decades, offers comprehensive listings of theater and music with brief descriptions of each event (it also, incidentally, has equally thorough listings of visual arts venues, museums, and films, and is a great aid in the course of any city visit, whether you're a tourist or a long-time resident). Another good source of information is the New York *Times*, particularly on Sunday. Weighing in at a good five pounds, the Sunday *Times* has comprehensive theater listings and reviews of current openings. Moreover, the *Times* is a quintessential after-theater reading, something to pick up on the way home from the theater so you can read about the show you saw on Saturday while sitting over coffee and a bagel bright and early on Sunday morning.

BROOKLYN

THE HEIGHTS
GREENPOINT/WILLIAMSBURG
BAY RIDGE
CONEY ISLAND

Across the river from Manhattan, linked to it by one of the great engineering feats of the 19th century, the Brooklyn Bridge, the vast borough of Brooklyn spreads out across one end of Long Island, reaching from the East River to the sea. Many Manhattanites never get around to exploring this part of their city, and the word "Brooklyn" is enough to make many taxi drivers discharge their fares. Their loss. Brooklyn pulses with its own life. A city unto itself, it has served as inspiration for generations of writers, artists, and filmmakers.

First-time visitors will discover that they already know Brooklyn. If they haven't read Thomas Wolfe *(Only the Dead know Brooklyn)* or Betty Smith (whose *A Tree Grows in Brooklyn* immortalized the neighborhood of Williamsburg), they'll have seen *Saturday Night Fever*, in which John Travolta danced out his nights in Bay Ridge discos; the **Bedford-Stuyvesant** race riot in Spike Lee's *Do The Right Thing*; or *Brighton Beach Memoirs*, Neil Simon's coming-of-age tale. Brooklyn has produced such classic pieces of Americana

Preceding pages: Jogging on Manhattan Bridge. The Brooklyn allegory at the Brooklyn Museum. Left: Many orthodox Jews have settled in the Williamsburg section.

as *Coney Island Red-Hots* (that's hot dogs to the uninitiated) and the Brooklyn Dodgers ("you can take the Dodgers out of Brooklyn, but you can't take Brooklyn out of the Dodgers").

Brooklyn is not a small place – far from it. Its population exceeds that of Philadelphia and Houston, to name just two major American cities. If Manhattanites nonetheless tend to label the borough "provincial," this is merely a reflection of its distinct character, on which it has kept a tenacious hold since its founding. From its ethnic neighborhoods to the distinct accents of its residents – "da goil on Toity-Toid" is a woman who lives on 33rd St – Brooklyn is rich in local color. Combining the urbanity of New York with the passionate hometown spirit of smaller cities, the borough retains more individuality, and more of a distinct neighborhood character, than any other in New York.

History

Before waves of Eastern Europeans, West Indians and Asians made Brooklyn a multi-ethnic wonderland, the borough was home to the Canarsee, a group of Algonquian Indians who farmed and hunted in villages throughout the territory of Manhattan and Long Island. By 1800, so

165

many Dutch had purchased Canarsee land that few of the natives remained. However, their legacy is still evident in Brooklyn, in the name of the neighborhood Canarsie, as well as Kings Highway, this area's main street, which was built on the site of the Indians' *Mechawanienk* trail.

By the mid-1600s, the Dutch had established several small towns in the area. Among these were *Breukelen*, from which the area took its current name; *Nieuw Amersfoort*, the present Flatlands district; *Boswijck*, later changed to Bushwick, which then included Greenpoint and Williamsburg. Gravesend was settled by colonists from England, led by Lady Deborah Moody.

It was in Brooklyn, in 1776, that the first major battle of the Revolutionary War occurred. The Battle of Brooklyn began when British forces landed at

Gravesend Bay, forcing the Americans to retreat to what is today's Brooklyn Heights. George Washington barely escaped capture by ferrying across the East River to Manhattan. A decade or so later, the ferries traveled the other way: many New Yorkers fled to Brooklyn to escape a 1790 yellow-fever epidemic.

By 1880, Brooklyn had become America's fourth largest industrial city. One reason for this was the Brooklyn Navy Yard, built in 1801, which would be easily flanked, some 100 years later, by the Williamsburg and Manhattan Bridges on either side. Still, even despite the borough's incorporation into New York City in 1898, Brooklynites continued to be regarded as provincial, a prejudice which persists, to a greater or lesser degree, to this day.

Large numbers of immigrants to New York settled in Brooklyn, establishing ethnic enclaves throughout the borough which have maintained their foothold. Around Bay Ridge, a Scandinavian community grew up near the docks where

Above: Townhouses in Brooklyn Heights, a pleasant alternative to the high rents in Manhattan. Right: Practicing curve ball.

166

ships from Denmark and Norway put in. Some blocks in Bensonhurst were replicas of specific towns in Sicily. In Fort Greene, Italians and blacks share the bucolic setting of 30-acre Fort Greene Park. Standing out in the crowd with their black coats and long beards, Hasidic Jews tend to keep to themselves: the Lubavicher sect's headquarters is in Crown Heights; the *Satmar* denomination is based mainly in Williamsburg; and the *Bobov* group can easily be found in Borough Park.

THE HEIGHTS

There's no better introduction to the borough of Brooklyn than to start by crossing the **Brooklyn Bridge** on foot. Moving along the pedestrian walkway between the two lanes of cars, you have a wonderful view of Manhattan and the shipping traffic on the East River. On the Brooklyn side, the walkway brings you to the green expanse of Cadman Plaza Park, and you're in **Brooklyn Heights**.

In 1965, this neighborhood became New York's first historic landmark district when 30 blocks containing many pre-Civil War buildings were saved from demolition. Several years earlier, the **Promenade**, which affords a splendid panoramic view of the skyline of lower Manhattan, had been built to allay local fears that the new **Brooklyn-Queens Expressway** would destroy the character of the neighborhood.

But its character has remained intact. Today, the Heights is a residential neighborhood growing ever more popular, and ever more expensive. Walking through its narrow, tree-lined streets with their rows of warm-colored brownstones, it's easy to understand why. Montague Street is the main shopping street, dotted with fun little boutiques and restaurants; in addition to other streets named for local luminaries (Remsen, Hicks, Middagh), there's a whole group of streets named for trees that were fashionable in the 19th century: Willow, Cranberry, Orange, Pineapple. Legend has it that some of the "luminar-

BROOKLYN

| 0 | 1 | 2 km |
| 0 | | 1 mile |

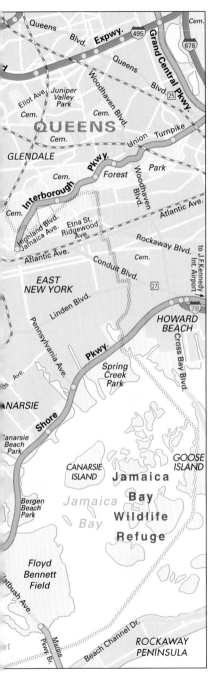

ies" were willing to do just about anything to ensure that certain of their rivals were not immortalized for posterity by having streets named after them.

On Orange Street, **Plymouth Church** dates from the 1800s, once a station on the Underground Railroad, a clandestine means for slaves to leave the South before the Civil War. Nearby, on Willow, is the oldest wooden house in the neighborhood, dating from 1824. And, if the splendid view of Manhattan from the Promenade appeals to you, make your way to the **River Café**, built on a pier at the foot of the bridge, which has food to match its spectacular scenery.

At the edge of the Heights are the borough's courthouses and municipal buildings, including the monumental **Borough Hall**. Following Clinton Street will bring you to **Carroll Gardens**, named after Charles Carroll, the only Roman Catholic signer of the Declaration of Independence. This neighborhood, which is also predominantly residential, was settled by Italian dock workers in the early 1900s.

Another influential ethnic group is the Arabs, both newcomers from Yemen and Morocco and old-timers whose Lebanese and Syrian forebears settled along **Atlantic Avenue** back in the 1940s. With the possible exception of Detroit, this area has the largest collection of Middle Eastern restaurants in the country, and rows of bakeries along the avenue produce tender phyllo confections and fresh pita bread and an appetizing aroma.

Atlantic Avenue continues on into the area of Flatbush, past Brooklyn's tallest skyscraper, the **Williamsburg Bank Building**, and its cultural center – and a major New York venue – the **Brooklyn Academy of Music** (31 Lafayette Avenue, Brooklyn, (718/636-4100). BAM, as it is fondly known, is host to performances of the finest in dance, opera, theater, and music, from symphony orchestras to Laurie Anderson.

Bedford-Stuyvesant

Nearby, the neighborhood of **Bedford-Stuyvesant** has, like Harlem, both a high population of black residents and some beautiful old residential buildings. Despite its inner-city appearance, "Bed-Stuy" still has some 17th-century wooden homes, and a remnant of the nineteenth-century Weeksville community, an early settlement of freed slaves.

Bedford-Stuyvesant is a visibly disadvantaged neighborhood. Crime and drugs are prevalent, and many fine blocks have decayed despite civic efforts to block the downward spiral. However, there are still beautiful brownstone areas, such as the **Stuyvesant Heights Historic District**, and **Restoration Plaza**, a $6-million, 300,000 square foot complex that includes the **Billie Holiday Theater**,

Above: The suburban brick look of Brooklyn. Right: The ethnic and cultural mix of Brooklyn is not always peaceful.

operating from 40 to 45 weeks a year, and an art gallery that is worth a visit.

Brownsville, not far away, contains an African-American cultural center, the **Brownsville Heritage House**, located on **Mother Gaston Boulevard**, named for the self-taught black historian and activist Rosetta Gaston. While Brownsville has changed since the earlier part of the century when it was predominantly Jewish, one neighborhood landmark has remained intact. The **Belmont Push Cart Market**, on **Belmont Avenue**, is one of the last open-air markets in the city, selling excellent fruit, fish and vegetables at wholesale prices.

GREENPOINT AND WILLIAMS-BURG

The tree that grew in Brooklyn in Betty Smith's novel grew along the border between **Greenpoint** and **Williamsburg** just north of the Heights. To see an actual specimen of the *Ailanthus* (imported to the area from China in the 1840s), you

don't need to journey here – the trees are all over Brooklyn – but the area still has something to offer.

In the mid-1800s, Greenpoint became a center for industrial activity. The Continental Iron Works produced the Union gunship *Continental*, which waged war with the Confederate *Merrimac* during the American Civil War. Today, both ships have been immortalized by a monument in Greenpoint's **Monsignor Mc-Goldrick Park**.

The Poles are the ethnic group most often associated with Greenpoint. There are some 30,000 of them in the neighborhood, largely situated around **St. Stanislaus Kostka Church**, on **Humboldt Street**. While there are numerous Polish eateries in the area, the best-known is probably the **White Eagle Bakery**, renowned for its *chruscik*, sugar-coated cookies boxed and sold all over the New York metropolitan area.

Greenpoint also has a sizable population of Russian Orthodox residents, who worship at the **Russian Orthodox Ca-thedral of the Transfiguration of Our Lord**, a magnificent landmark Byzantine-style sanctuary with five onion-shaped copper domes.

Like Greenpoint, Williamsburg has a few Eastern European-inspired religious sites, the difference being that Williamsburg's are Jewish. When the Williamsburg Bridge was built in 1903, Jews packed into the tenements of the Lower East Side poured across this new passageway to establish a place for themselves in Brooklyn. After World War II, the mystical *Satmar Hasidic* sect, so religious that they reject the state of Israel as sinful because it was founded by men and not the Jewish Messiah, arrived *en masse* from Hungary. Today, 50,000 of them maintain the red brick buildings and shops on **Lee Avenue**. The signs in these stores are frequently in Yiddish, a Jewish dialect from the Eastern European ghettoes that largely disappeared from Europe after World War Two.

But Puerto Ricans and Italians have also made their mark in Williamsburg.

For several Sundays in July, the latter group converts the area around the **Our Lady of Mount Carmel Church**, on **North Eighth Street**, into a replica of an Italian village, while 250 men carry a 65-foot sphere, or *giglio*, amid singing and dancing, as part of a 1500-year-old feast honoring St. Paulinus.

Hitting the Slope

Heading south again, Park Slope's most elegant section is located near **Prospect Park**, a rolling expanse of 526 acres laid out by none other than Olmsted and Vaux, famed as designers of Manhattan's Central Park. Few would dispute that it's this park, rather than the better-known one in Manhattan, that is their masterpiece. Prospect Park's attractions include a zoo, a skating rink, and the Lefferts Homestead, an 18th-century

Above: This plaque commemorates the viking Leiv Eiriksson. Right: Coney Island offers sun, sea and an amusement park.

dwelling. Nearby, the fabulous Brooklyn **Botanic Gardens** are an absolute must when the cherry trees are in blossom.

On Eastern Parkway, which runs into the park, you'll find the **Brooklyn Museum**, another of New York's hidden treasures. In addition to first-rate rotating exhibitions, the museum has an outstanding permanent collection including an Egyptian section that is one of the finest in the world.

The neighborhood known as **Park Slope** is located at the west side of the park. Around the park are reclaimed and refurbished brownstones, as well as turn-of-the-century tenements and former warehouses that have been converted into condominiums and lofts. Predictably, an abundance of trendy restaurants has also sprung up. Although the Hispanic population who used to dwell here has been displaced, to an extent, by the course of gentrification, numerous Caribbean and Spanish eateries still dot popular Fifth Avenue. Seventh Avenue is the local shopping street; while you'll find the Venetian-style edifice of the **Montauk Club** at 25 Eighth Avenue.

BAY RIDGE

John Travolta may have desperately tried to pull himself away from this neighborhood in *Saturday Night Fever*, but most residents would choose to live nowhere else. **Bay Ridge** is a safe, clean area of well-maintained one- and two-story houses on grassy lawns, located in the shadow of the **Verrazano Narrows Bridge**. The bridge, linking the borough with Staten Island, is named for Giovanni de Verrazano, the Italian explorer who ventured into New York Harbor in 1524. It is a source of great pride for the neighborhood's substantial Italian population, some of whom can trace their Bay Ridge roots five generations back.

Aside from the Italians, the descendants of Norwegian sailors who arrived

in the late 19th and early 20th centuries have also had a large impact on Bay Ridge. For years, this neighborhood had the only New York City high school to offer Norwegian courses. Local churches still hold services in the language. And every May, the city's Miss Norway is crowned in **Leiv Eiriksson Park**, near a statue of the 11th-century explorer which was donated by the Prince of Norway in 1939. The Danes, who came around the same time as their fellow Scandinavians, are also well represented; the Danish Soccer Club has competed in Eiriksson Park for the last 60 years.

The oldest historical attraction is **Fort Hamilton**, built between 1825 and 1831 to protect New York Harbor. Today, it is the only active army post in the city, and includes the **Harbor Defense Museum** for military aficionados.

CONEY ISLAND

When a small plane was forced to land on **Brighton Beach** several years ago, a local woman told the newspapers, "Just a typical day in the neighborhood." This statement is some indication of the quirkiness of this area, which was designed as a seaside resort centered around the amusement park of **Coney Island** and retains something of a carnival air. Combined, the two neighborhoods extend nearly three miles through the sand and boardwalk, which sees hardy strollers even on the coldest winter days.

It is believed that the area first gained its distinction as a vacation haven in the 1840s, when an entrepreneur opened a small hotel called the Coney Island House. Others were quick to follow his lead and, by the end of the Civil War, Coney Island had dozens of inns and clam chowder stands.

It was not long before a race track, gambling casinos and sports arenas were added. By 1897, Coney Island was the most spectacular place in New York. The lights from the ferris wheel in **Steeplechase Park** were seen on boats nearly 40 miles offshore.

173

In its glory days, Coney Island attracted newcomers and residents from all over the city. Such attractions as **The Cyclone**, the last remaining wooden roller coaster in the area, **Astroland Amusement Park** and **Nathan's Famous** hot dog stand have weathered some tough times, but are still open to welcome the current generation of New Yorkers unable to afford any other type of vacation. Meanwhile, the **New York Aquarium**, located right on the boardwalk, has everything from white Beluga whales to sea horses. And at **Gargiulo's** family-run Italian restaurant, the showmanship continues: Your meal is free if you can guess the number rolled on the waiter's dice.

While the neighborhood still has a flavor found nowhere else, it has contracted its share of urban diseases as well. A group of high-rise projects replacing derelict summer bungalows in the 1960s never attracted the middle- and lower-income families desired, becoming, instead, warehouses of drugs and crime.

In nearby **Brighton Beach**, however, an influx of Soviet immigrants has begun to stem the negative tide. In the late 1970s, the Soviet Union relaxed its emigration quotas and some 30,000 citizens, the majority of them Jews who said they wanted to go to Israel, took a detour to Brighton Beach. Most of them were from the port city of Odessa, and found in the sea and salt air reminders of the place they left behind. The area has become known as "Little Odessa by the Sea."

"The Russians," as they are called, stay in front of their homes and businesses until all hours of the night, deterring crime and reporting any wrongdoing to the police. At night clubs like **Odessa**, **Primorski** and **The National**, all on **Brighton Beach Avenue**, they drink vodka and dance to a curious mixture of Soviet tunes and American Top-40. Although their attempts to adopt American fashion can seem comical, all agree that their positive impact is good news.

Above: The Russian immigrants have no trouble understanding each other.

BROOKLYN
Access
New York City Transit Authority, buses and subways, Tel: 718/330-1234. **Long Island Rail Road**, Tel: 718/454-5477.

Accommodation
This borough is not noted for its hotels. Visitors mostly choose to stay in Manhattan. However, Brooklyn does have a number of relatively inexpensive small bed and breakfast inns, many of which are located in renovated historic buildings. Information on all types of accommodations at a range of prices: **Fund For Brooklyn**, Tel: 718/855-7882.

Restaurants
Almontstar, 218 Court Street, Tel: 718/624-9267, exotic Arab cuisine, exquisite food and atmosphere, Yemenite specialties like sautéed lamb, plus French dishes like frog's legs cooked in wine and lemon butter. **Atlantic Restaurant**, 514 Eighth Avenue, Tel: 718/438-9348, Norwegian delicacies. **Junior's**, 386 Flatbush Avenue, Tel: 718/852-5257, near the foot of Manhattan Bridge, a popular hangout for those involved in city politics. Hearty meals at reasonable prices until the early hours of the morning. Customers feast on hot pastrami sandwiches and Junior's well-known cheesecake.
Gargiulo's, 2911 West 15th Street, Tel: 718/266-4895, family-owned Italian restaurant where guessing the right number on the waiter's dice can win you a free meal. **Nathan's Famous**, Surf and Stillwell Avenues, Tel: 718/266-3161, a hot dog lover's heaven, where the "original Coney Island frank" was born.
Peter Luger Steak House, 178 Broadway, Tel: 718/387-7400, near the Williamsburg Bridge, a New York institution, attracting even snooty Manhattanites who rarely journey into Brooklyn. The steaks are excellent and the delicious sauces cannot be found anywhere else. Opened in 1887, Peter Luger's feels like a German beer hall, complete with waiters carrying the big steaks and baked Idaho potatoes to customers at bare wooden tables. **Polska Restauracja**, 136 Greenpoint Avenue, Tel: 718/389-8368, authentic Polish restaurant, reasonable prices, wonderful sour soup with sausage and mashed potatoes.
River Café, One Water Street, Tel: 718/522-5200, another restaurant that even the most elitist Manhattanites frequent, arguably the most romantic eatery in the city. Built on a barge beneath Brooklyn Bridge, the River Café provides a beautiful view of the Manhattan skyline, and "new wave" seafood. Salmon and duck are the big standouts. **Shang Chai**, 2189 Flatbush Avenue, Tel: 718/377-6100, kosher Chinese food. **Tommaso**, 1464 86th Street, Tel: 718/236-9883, on the 14th Street strip in Saturday Night Fever country, Bay Ridge, a pasta paradise. **Tripoli**, 156 Atlantic Avenue, Tel: 718/596-5800, Lebanese lamb dishes in the Arab quarter.

Ethnic Bakeries
ARAB: **Damascus Bakery**, 195 Atlantic Avenue, Tel: 718/855-1456.
ITALIAN: **Cammarei Brothers**, 502 Henry Street, Tel: 718/852-3606.
JEWISH (Eastern European): **Korn's**, 5004 16th Avenue, Tel: 718/851-0268. *JEWISH (Middle Eastern):* **Mansoura's Oriental Pastry**, 515 King's Highway, Tel: 718/645-7977.
POLISH: **White Eagle Bakery**, 600 Humboldt Street, Tel: 718/389-2214. **Polish and Slavic Credit Union Bakery**, 138 Greenpoint Avenue, Tel: 718/383-6268. *SCANDINAVIAN:* **Leske's Bakery**, 7612 Fifth Avenue, Tel: 718/680-2323. *WEST INDIAN:* **St. John's Bakery**, 1501 Fulton Street, Tel: 718/778-9341. **Taste of the Tropics**, 1249 Utica Avenue, Tel: 718/629-3582.

Festivals
Early June: *Welcome Back To Brooklyn*, Grand Army Plaza, Tel: 718/855-7882. First Monday in **September** (Labor Day): *West Indian American Day Parade*, the city's largest parade, extending two miles down Eastern Parkway, Tel: 718/625-1515. *Giglio* is Williamsburg's Italian festival, at Our Lady of Mount Carmel Church, 275 North Eighth Street, Tel: 718/278-1834.

Tours
The **Fund for Brooklyn** conducts culinary, architectural, historical and other tours, Tel: 718/278-1834 for information.

Culture / Leisure
Brooklyn Academy of Music, 30 Lafayette Street, Tel: 718/636-4100. **The Brooklyn Conservatory**, 58 Seventh Avenue, Tel: 718/622-3300. **Brooklyn Dance Consortium**, Tel: 718/797-3116. **Brooklyn Historical Society**, 128 Pierrepont Street, Tel: 718/624-0890.
The Brooklyn Museum, 200 Eastern Parkway, Tel: 718/638-5000.
Brownsville Heritage House, 581 Mother Gaston Boulevard, Tel: 718/385-1111.
Billie Holiday Theatre, 1368 Fulton Street, Tel: 718/636-7092.
New York City Transit Museum, Schermerhorn Street/Boerum Place, Tel: 718/330-3060.
New York Aquarium, Boardwalk and West Eighth Street, Coney Island, Tel: 718/265-3474.
Bargemusic, Fulton Ferry Landing, Tel: 718/624-4061. **Brooklyn Botanic Garden**, 1000 Washington Avenue, Tel: 718/624-4433.

BRONX

RIVERDALE
BELMONT
PELHAM BAY COAST

The Bronx, as neophytes all know, is a terribly dangerous place, where hoodlums and rats share space in vacant lots, where every house bears the mark of a fire, where junkies go to die, where lawlessness abides. In the minds of many, including no doubt some who live there, the Bronx is the last residence of desperados, the place people go to be forgotten. When the city needs money from the politicians, do they not visit the Bronx? Has not Rikers Island, with its infamously tough penitentiary been assigned to the Bronx, although it is physically closer to Queens?

And yet one looks in vain for signs on the Triborough, Whitestone or Throgs Neck Bridges advertising "Abandon all hope, ye who enter here." For what people say about the Bronx concerns a fairly small section in the south, specifically the area called Hunts Point. And it can be avoided fairly easily by staying on the Bruckner Expressway that bypasses Hunts Point.

For starters, the Bronx is the greenest borough in New York. An astounding 23 percent of it consists of parks. **Pelham Bay Park** alone is the largest in the entire city. Secondly, it has enough sights to

Left: Taking a jog in Van Cortlandt Park in the Bronx, New York's greenest borough.

keep anyone busy for days. Shopping enthusiasts will never get bored on **the Loop**, a strip of antique shops on **Bruckner Boulevard**, between **Alexander** and **Lincoln Avenues**. Once called "the borough of universities," the Bronx still houses eleven schools of higher learning.

History

Jacob Bronck gave the borough its name. He was a native of the Swedish province of Smaaland who later lived in Amsterdam and, it is believed, worked from there as a merchant sea captain. In 1639, he bought 500 acres of land from the Dutch Indies Company, and built a farm between Harlem and the river called *Aquehung* by the local Wiechquaesgeck Indians. He named his land Emmaus after the biblical town near Jerusalem. In time, the river became known as Bronck's River and the farm was colloquially referred to as Broncksland before it became the Bronx.

Today one-third of the people in the borough are African-Americans. But already in the 17th century the Bronx had a considerable black population working as slaves on the estate of one Richard Morris, a wealthy Welsh sugar merchant after whom the **Morrisania** neighborhood north of East 161st Street is named.

177

His grandson, the American statesman Gouverneur Morris (1752-1816), was to become one of the ardent opponents of slavery at the Constitutional Convention. He also tried to convince the gathering of founding fathers to make Morrisania the nation's capital, but he lost both cases.

The Morris family was the most influential clan in the borough until the 1850s, when 1920 acres of Morrisania were divied up and sold to different businessmen. Aside from the various streets and buildings named after the family, **Morris Avenue** is the best indicator of their onetime position in Bronx society: It passes through what was the Morris estate.

Many different ethnic groups established roots in the Bronx, partly because Manhattan was filled to the gills. **Grand Concourse** served as a kind of parade boulevard. Local Jewish residents used to

Above: The cottage where E. A. Poe lived is buried in the urban landscape. Right: The writing is on the wall for some of the Bronx.

use it for processions on the High Holidays. The 4.5-mile, tree-lined street was modeled after the Champs Elysées in Paris. With its Art Deco buildings, the largest collection of such structures in the world, wide courtyards and sculpted shrubberies, the Grand Concourse was the most majestic street in New York.

In the 1960s, crime, drugs and suburban migration put a major dent into the borough. When **Co-op City**, the largest (and by no means prettiest) apartment complex in the world, opened in the early 1970s, many neighborhoods in other parts of the Bronx literally emptied out and relocated into the buildings. The areas left behind became ghost towns of abandoned tenements and rubble-strewn lots. But there are positive initiatives. The destitute **Charlotte Street** strip was visited by both Jimmy Carter and Ronald Reagan during their presidential campaigns. While neither President did much for the neighborhood once he was elected, community activists continued fighting until the birth of **Charlotte Gar-**

dens, a collection of middle income private homes built on the site in 1986.

Most people see the Bronx from the Major Deegan Expressway that heads upstate. Where it begins at Port Morris is the **Mott Haven Historic District** (Alexander Avenue) with a number of solid houses dating back to the Civil War era and a library designed by Andrew Carnegie's personal architect. A little to the north, quite visible from the bumpy highway, is **Yankee Stadium**, where all the baseball legends appeared: Babe Ruth, Lou Gehrig, Joe DiMaggio, Mickey Mantle, and others. It is also the birthplace of that derisive flatulant sound mouthed at poor plays, known as the "Bronx Cheer."

The Major Deegan then passes by the **Bronx Community College** and the **Hall of Fame for Great Americans**. The latter consists of a colonnade of busts of 97 famous Americans, including Thomas Edison, George Washington Carver and Bronx resident Edgar Allan Poe. They surround three buildings on a bluff overlooking the Hudson and Harlem Rivers, the Cloisters and New Jersey's Palisades. The Hall of Fame underwent a three million dollar renovation in the 1980s, and now also has a full-time director.

RIVERDALE

In the northern part of the borough, there is **Riverdale**, overlooking the majestic green hills of New Jersey's Palisades, across the Hudson River, which is blue at times. This prosperous neighborhood is another shock to people who picture the Bronx as a collection of burned-out tenements and dangerous housing projects. Riverdale, which borders on the ultra-exclusive Westchester County, boasts some of the largest and most expensive homes in New York.

Parts of **Riverdale** have an agreeable country look to them, with grassy roadsides instead of asphalt sidewalks, and narrow, winding roads that snake into driveways or end abruptly. One can even encounter country churches in Riverdale.

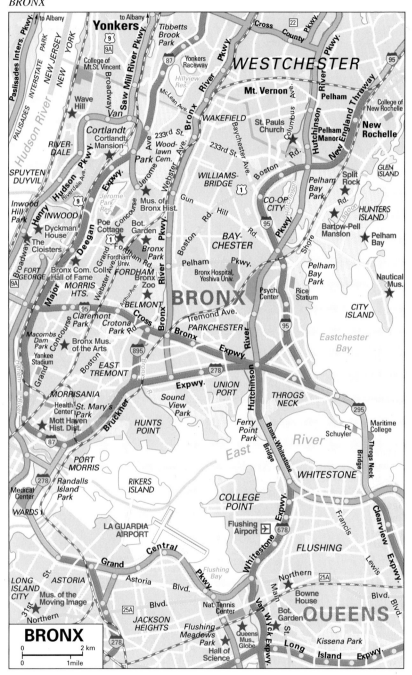

BRONX

0 ———— 2 km
0 ———— 1mile

Residents say they they enjoy the best of everything, homes as exquisite as any found anywhere, a breathtaking view of the Hudson River, and an address close to the energy and activity of Manhattan. Sports fans also like the fact that Riverdale is only ten minutes from Yankee Stadium. The large commercial streets like **Broadway**, **Mosholu** and **Riverdale Avenues**, provide a wide variety of restaurants with different tastes: German, Italian, Chinese, kosher.

Wave Hill is one of the highlights of the neighborhood: two mansions high above the Hudson River. Mark Twain and Arturo Toscanini both stayed at the 28-acre site, where tours are offered to the public. In addition to the sculpture garden and art shows, there are thousands of specimens of plants well cared for in pleasant greenhouses and wild and formal gardens. Frequently, musical performances enhance the scenery.

Residents of Riverdale who enjoy a round of golf do not have very far to go: to the east of Riverdale lies the green expanse of Van Cortlandt Park, which has the oldest municipal golf course in the country. The Van Cortlandt Mansion and Museum to the south of the park is a mid-18th century house, which once was used by George Washington. Today it holds remnants of pre-Revolutionary culture, including a beautiful collection of Delft.

South of the park lies what used to be the village of **Fordham** many decades ago. Its claims to fame are a university and Lehman College, and a gem of importance to the history of literature, the **Edgar Allan Poe Cottage**. Poe came to New York in 1844 seeking both the literary recognition and financial security he was unable to find elsewhere. He moved to the little cottage in Fordham in 1846, and there he wrote some of his finest works, including *Annabel Lee*, *Ulalume*, *The Bells* and *Eureka*. His wife died here too. Poe died in 1849, virtually unknown except to a small group of cognoscenti. In

1913, the city acquired the house and moved it to its present location in **Poe Park**. At one stage, the cottage had fallen into disrepair, but the Department of Parks and the Bronx Historical Society came up with the wherewithal to improve its appearance. Edgar Allan Poe Week is hosted at the house each April.

BELMONT

Belmont is an Italian enclave east of Fordham with great restaurants with bearable prices for fine fare, clean streets, neat houses. Italian-American residents of the Bronx insist their Little Italy offers more variety and character than the more famous one tucked away in Lower Manhattan, which is at any rate being swallowed by Chinatown. And no one here says "*Lasciate ogni speranza*," as one might imagine because it's the Bronx after all. On the contrary, the streets of Belmont are among the safest in the city.

The first Italians came to what was a fairly rural area in 1895; they were for the most part laborers on public works projects. Over the years they built up the neighborhood. In the 1950s, Italian teenagers from Belmont were partially responsible for creating the "doo wop" sound. The classic rock'n'roll hit songs *Runaround Sue* and *The Wanderer*, for example, were popularized by a local group called, quite appropriately, Dion and the Belmonts.

In the 1960s, the deterioration of the Bronx caused a major flight out to the suburbs. Belmont, nevertheless, held its ground as a solid Italian-American neighborhood.

The market on **Arthur Avenue** is considered by many people to be the best such neighborhood in New York. Family-owned shops and outdoor stalls offer a finger-licking bounty of pastries, cured meats, appetizers, pasta, fresh vegetables and fruit, garlic, wines. Neighborhood pride is reflected in murals of the Italian

flag painted around Belmont; one reads, "Little Italy in the Bronx, The Good Taste of Tradition." Another site, the **Enrico Fermi Cultural Center** (named after the great nuclear researcher and one of the fathers ofthe A-bomb), is the first library in the nation with some 2,500 Italian-language books on literature, history, biography and science, and with an Italian-speaking staff to help you find what you are looking for.

The **Belmont Italian-American Playhouse**, the only Actor's Equity Showcase theater in the Bronx, was recently opened on **Arthur Avenue** to raise awareness of the artistic contributions of Italians. Among the productions the theater has seen is *Italian American Reconciliation*, by author John Patrick Shanley.

Belmont is next to a zoo. The **Bronx Zoo** is the largest American urban zoo, with about 4000 wild animals. It is lo-

Above: Belmont in the Bronx is by all accounts New York's genuine Little Italy. Right: The Bronx Zoo, one of the finest in the USA.

cated in the Bronx Park. They say a person would have to travel some 31,000 miles in order to see the variety of animals that can be seen at the Bronx Zoo in a single day. Unlike other zoos, which keep the creatures in cages with concrete scenery in the background, the Bronx Zoo tries its best to show the animals in very natural surroundings. In fact, it sometimes seems that the humans are the ones in cages as they observe the animals wandering through 265 acres of park lands, woods, streams and ponds.

Visitors can explore the zoo any number of ways: by foot, aboard the **Safari Train** running through the facility or via the aerial tramway called the **Skyfari Ride**. **Jungle World** is an indoor section of the facility modeled after a rain forest for such tropical Asian wildlife as hornbills, gibbons, tapirs and gharials. In the **Himalayan Highlands** portion of the zoo, there are rare breeds like graceful white-naped cranes, an Asian symbol of fidelity, red pandas and snow leopards. **Wild Asia** is a replica of the forests and

open meadows of Asia. The **Bengali Express** monorail train rides by unique sitka deer, antelope, Siberian tigers.

The **World of Birds** is a reproduction of a rain forest, complete with a thunderstorm every day at 2 p.m. sharp. The specimens on display include the nearly extinct pink pigeon, Guam kingfishers, rollers and birds of paradise. The **World of Darkness** is a duplicate of the night for nocturnal animals like bats, sugar gliders and bush babies. And rare crocodiles, fluorescent green tree frogs and pythons are found in the **Reptile House**.

The Children's Zoo is a place where youngsters can learn about the creatures by acting as the animals do: climbing spider webs, crawling through prairie dog tunnels, scampering down hollow trees like a lizard. There are also domestic animals for the children to pet and feed.

PELHAM BAY COAST

The Bronx and Pelham and the Hutchinson River Parkway leads out to one of the most pleasant sections of New York: **Pelham Bay Park**. This is the city's largest green space, with a total area of 2764 acres. It is not just the presence of some vegetation that makes the park so attractive. **Rice Stadium** is at the southern entrance, a popular place for sporting meets. Two golf courses are situated in the park. One is near **Split Rock**, which, according to geologists, broke in half about 10,000 years ago. It is also the spot where the settler Anne Hutchinson, for whom the Hutchinson River was named, was murdered by Indians.

The **Bartow-Pell Mansion and Museum** was built by Robert Bartow a descendant of Thomas Pell, the man who originally purchased **Pelham Bay** in the 1830s and ultimately gave its name. Inside, the style is ornate Greek Revival, while the exterior was constructed with local stone in the sober Federal style. **Glover's Rock** was the site of the 1776 battle in which American rebel Colonel John Glover held off British forces long enough for General George Washington

to reach White Plains in Westchester County for supplies and reinforcements.

Pelham Bay Park's most boisterous attraction, however, is **Orchard Beach**, a mile-long, 115-acre sand beach that overheated New Yorkers have enjoyed since the 1930s. It was the brainchild of the city's "megadeveloper" Robert Moses and was made of sand barged in from the Rockaway Beach area in Queens, among other sites. Fast food and drinks concessions, a central pavilion and facilities for handball, paddleball and basketball line the beach promenade. Nearby, space has been provided for tennis. Ten courts were recently renovated. There are fields for baseball, softball and football, and there is also a 440-yard running track.

A narrow causeway to the east of the park leads to a place that seems to have landed by accident next to the teeming megalopolis. **City Island** resembles an old New England town, with clapboard

Above: The idyllic City Island is part of the Bronx, as unbelievable as it might seem.

houses, fishing boats, sail boats, coffee shops with original names, seafood restaurants, antique shops, crafts stores, chandleries, shipyards and marinas, seaman's taverns and the like. The sailing and ship-building tradition is alive and well here: The *Columbia*, a yacht that won the America's Cup, was built here in City Island.

The most surprising aspect of City Island is its magic ability to remain the same in spite of the visits by frenzied New Yorkers. It is as if the residents who have nothing in common with New Yorkers except the area code held the secret to eternal youth, or in this case eternal sameness. Even during the upheavals of the 1960s, the "islanders" proceeded with their daily routines as if nothing were happening.

City Island Avenue is the main street running the length of the island. Its end offers a wide view of the Long Island Sound. To the right is the Throgs Neck Bridge that connects the Bronx to Queens.

184

BRONX
Access
Metropolitan Transportation Authority, subways and buses, Tel: 718/330-1324. **Liberty Lines Express**, bus service between Manhattan and the Bronx, Tel: 212/652-8400.

Accommodation
Visitors rarely stay overnight in the Bronx unless they are visiting the home of a friend or relative.

Restaurants
CHINESE: **Twin Dragon**, 2184 White Plains Road, Tel: 212/824-3050, Szechuan, Mandarin and Cantonese. **Yu Yang Garden**, 3717 Riverdale Avenue, Tel: 212/884-1077, Szechuan- and Hunan-style dishes seven days a week.

GERMAN: **Charlie's Inn**, 2711 Harding Avenue, Tel: 212/931-9727, garden dining with a German *Biergarten* atmosphere in warm weather and an indoor fireplace blazing in winter. In appreciation of the borough's multi-ethnic composition, there is Irish music here once a week. **Ehring's Tavern**, 228 West 231st Street, Tel: 212/549-6750, this picturesque place, bedecked with old beer steins, guns and cuckoo clocks, is a standout restaurant in upscale Riverdale.

ITALIAN: **Café D'Oro**, 4359 White Plains Road, Tel: 212/994-0950, Italian-American music, dining until 4 am, great cappucino, espresso and pastries. **Dominick's**, 2335 Arthur Avenue, Tel: 212/733-2807, no menu, as each dish is prepared as the specialty of the day. The restaurant's motto: "Welcome to our home, our family." **Mario's**, 2342 Arthur Avenue, Tel: 212/584-1188, hearty Neapolitan cuisine.

JEWISH: **B & G Kosher Deli**, 772 Allerton Avenue, Tel: 212/655-9044, traditional New York Jewish deli, delicious corned beef and pastrami sandwiches, knishes and chicken soup. **Schweller's Kosher Gourmet Restaurant**, 3411 Jerome Avenue, Tel: 212/655-8649, the oldest delicatessen in the Bronx, kosher gourmet specialties such as Hungarian goulash, stuffed cabbage and stuffed derma.

SEAFOOD: **Boat's Inn**, 601 Bridge Street, Tel: 212/885-9800, a favorite on City Island because patrons can dock at the restaurant's marina before sampling the Italian seafood, veal and pasta dishes. **The Neptune**, 35 City Island Avenue, Tel: 212/885-1168, on City Island, Spanish seafood, paella, lobster and shrimp. **Thwaite's Inn**, 536 City Island Avenue, Tel: 212/885-1023, choice seafood, steak and duck.

Sports
Yankee Stadium, the historic home of baseball's New York Yankees, is located on River Avenue and East 161st Street, Tel: 212/293-4300.

Leisure
The Bronx Zoo, Bronx River Parkway and Fordham Road, Tel: 212/367-1010. **Crotona Park**, Claremont Parkway and Crotona Avenue, Tel: 212/589-4683. **Ferry Point Park**, adjacent to the Bronx-Whitestone Bridge service road, Tel: 212/822-4288. **The New York Botanical Garden**, Southern Boulevard, north of Fordham Road, Tel: 212/220-8700. **Pelham Bay Park**, the city's largest park, Tel: 212/430-1890. **Orchard Beach**, in Pelham Bay Park, on Long Island Sound, Tel: 212/885-1828. **Roberto Clemente State Park**, West Tremont Avenue and Mathewson Road, Tel: 212/299-8750. **Van Cortlandt Park**, on two square miles in the northern Bronx, Tel: 212/430-1810.

Special Events
June: Each year, the Bronx launches a week-long celebration, *Bronx Week*, honoring the borough's various ethnic groups and organizations with shows, parades, seminars and other programs, information Tel: 212/590-3199.

Cultural and Historic Sites
Bartow-Pell Mansion, Shore Road in Pelham Bay Park, Tel: 212/885-1461. **Belmont Italian-American Playhouse**, 2385 Arthur Avenue, Tel: 212/364-4700. **Bronx Historical Society**, 3309 Bainbridge Avenue, Tel: 212/881-8900. **Bronx Museum of the Arts**, 1040 Grand Concourse, Tel: 212/681-6001. **Museum of Bronx History**, Bainbridge Avenue and 208th Street, Tel: 212/881-8900.
Hall of Fame for Great Americans at Bronx Community College, University Avenue at 181st Street, Tel: 212/220-6312. **Enrico Fermi Cultural Center**, East 186th Street and Hughes Avenue, Tel: 212/933-6410. **Edgar Allen Poe Cottage**, Grand Concourse and Kingsbridge Road, Tel: 212/881-8900. **Van Cortlandt Mansion**, Broadway and 246th Street, Tel: 212/543-3344. **Wave Hill**, Independence Avenue at 249th Street, Tel: 212/549-2055. **Woodlawn Cemetery**, Jerome and Bainbridge Avenues, Tel: 212/652-2100.

Safety in the Bronx
The Bronx has long been burdened with a reputation for its criminal element. However, this mainly applies to a fairly small section in the south, specifically the area called Hunts Point. While one must certainly be careful when walking the streets, the visitor should also realize that the Bronx is a many-faceted borough, and, incidentally, the greenest borough in New York. According to a recent study, people in the Bronx generally have higher moral standards than those in Beverly Hills, California.

QUEENS

WOODSIDE

ASTORIA

FLUSHING

JAMAICA

To those in Manhattan who fancy themselves sophisticates, an address in Queens is a social liability. While Manhattan is seen as the playground of the rich and famous, Queens is the place to which the city's police, fire fighters, taxi drivers and secretaries return after work.

Nevertheless, the natives of this borough consider Queens to be the true heart and soul of New York. This is a borough of stable neighborhoods, where people know each other's business and keep the streets safe. Queens is also a multi-cultural experience: no less than 75 languages are spoken within the borough. Here you'll find everything from Irish dancing in Woodside to German beer in Glendale; while Flushing has the largest Korean population on the East Coast.

Queens is the first piece of America an international traveler glimpses as he steps off the airplane: It's here that New York's two main airports, **John F. Kennedy International** and **LaGuardia**, are situated. Baseball fans associate the borough with **Shea Stadium**, the home of the New York Mets, and plans are in the works to build a Sheraton hotel in the heart of Flushing to accommodate visi-

Preceding pages: Queensborough Bridge from Manhattan. Left: Throg's Neck Bridge from the Bronx.

tors to the U.S. Open Tennis Tournament. And, despite Manhattan's tendency to look down its nose at this country cousin, rising prices have driven more and more former Manhattanites across the river to settle in, discover, and enjoy this interesting and attractive borough.

History

Originally settled by the Dutch, Queens gained a reputation for being one of the most tolerant sections of the New World. The borough's first residents included many who were excluded from communities elsewhere – setting a precedent for the many immigrant groups who have since found shelter here. In 1657, supporters of John Bowne drafted The Flushing Remonstrance, a document guaranteeing religious freedom for all creeds, one of the inspirations for the First Amendment of the United States Constitution. When Bowne, in 1661, built a house of worship for Quakers, he was deported to Holland; there, however, he was acquitted and granted the right to return to New York. The Bowne House and Friends Meeting House, constructed in 1694, still stand as symbols of defiance against bigotry.

The eponymous "Queen" of this borough, one of New York's ten original

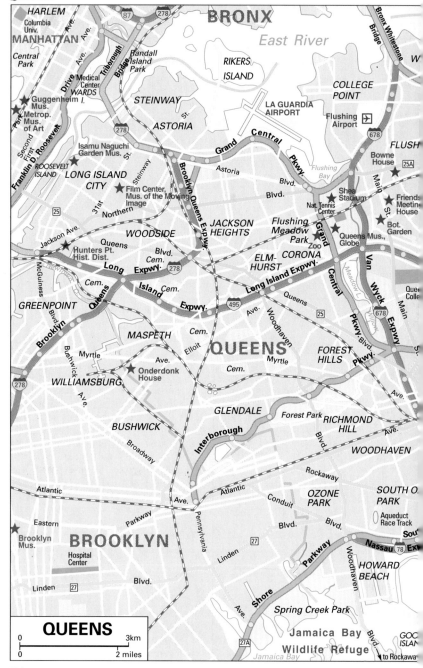

QUEENS

0   3km

0   2 miles

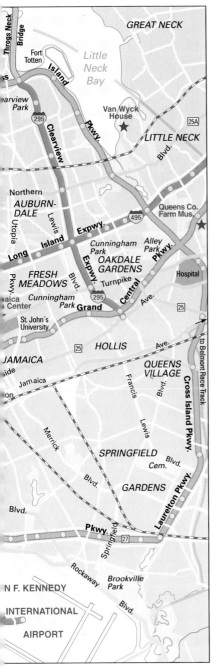

counties, was Queen Catherine of Braganza, Portugal (1638-1705), wife of Britain's King Charles II. She was less than popular in England because of her Catholic faith; like so many others misunderstood abroad, Catherine was better appreciated in Queens.

A Dutch tulip, the red rose of the English House of York, and the *wampum* beads worn by the Matinecock Indians of the Algonquin nation, the original inhabitants of the borough, are all part of the official symbol of Queens. This emblem was created in 1898, the year the individual towns of Queens County – among them **Jamaica**, **Long Island City** and Flushing – were incorporated into New York City.

Both the construction of the **Queensborough Bridge,** also called the 59th Street Bridge, and the introduction of a subway service linking the borough with Manhattan in the early part of this century contributed to an increase in Queens's population. Still, a good deal of Queens – with the notable exception of Long Island City, an industrial area occupying the northwestern portion of the borough – remained rural until the building boom that followed the end of World War Two. At that time, German and Norwegian neighborhoods were displaced by an influx of Irish, Italians, Greeks and Jews. After a few more years, these areas became Hispanic or Asian. With each new wave of immigrants came visible changes in the various neighborhoods, from architecture to restaurants, ambiance to street culture. Today, Queens is still in an exciting period of transition, as former residents of the Caribbean, Soviet Union and Afghanistan stake out their territory in New York's largest, and some would say most welcoming, borough.

WOODSIDE

Woodside was and is a starting point for hundreds of young Irish seeking to

escape the unemployment in their homeland. Although one sometimes hears disparaging talk of the "Woodside Irish" as being clannish and closed to their new nation, the area is as colorful a link to Erin as anywhere in America. Guinness stout flows out of the taps at the pubs here, while Uillean pipers, fiddlers and tin whistles play heartily at so-called *seisuns*, (Gaelic for "sessions").

One of the most atmospheric Irish bars in the city is situated in nearby **Jackson Heights**. Entry into **Gibbons' Pocheen Still Pub** (named for a strong brew of illicit alcohol from County Galway) is a journey into Old Ireland. Along with Irish music and liquor, there is a shop selling Irish food, crafts and newspapers. Not that the pub observes an Irish-only policy: it is not uncommon to see Puerto Ricans and Chinese residents trying the Irish jig on the dance floor.

Above: Steinway and Sons, makers of fine pianos, are among New York's largest manufacturers with about 400 employees.

ASTORIA

Just minutes by subway from Manhattan, **Astoria** is known for inexpensive housing, safe streets and Greek heritage. It has been said that only in Athens are there more Greeks than in Astoria. Just about every region of Greece is represented in the neighborhood, as well as Cypriot immigrants of Greek ancestry. The culture is responsible for the neighborhood's sidewalk cafes, affordable restaurants, pastry shops and *glenti* (Greek street celebrations).

Once, the Steinway Piano manufacturer was Astoria's main employer; hence the name of the main thoroughfare in the neighborhood, **Steinway Street**. William Steinway converted 400 acres of wooded land into a company town, building the **Steinway Mansion**, **Steinway Factory Building** and **Steinway Row Houses**.

Although film production companies periodically threaten to boycott New York due to high union costs, the Big Apple is still irresistible to movie makers, and the **Kaufman-Astoria Motion Picture and Television Center** serves their purposes well. **The Museum of the Moving Image** at the facility reinforces Astorians' belief that the neighborhood is indeed the Hollywood of the East.

FLUSHING

Longtime Flushing residents debate exactly when the neighborhood became international rather than an area where many residents in the Victorian-style houses could trace their ancestry back to the American Revolutionary War.

Largely responsible, no doubt, were the two New York World's Fairs, held in **Flushing Meadow Park** in 1939 and 1964-5. Since the more recent of these international extravaganzas lasted for two years, representatives from various nations opted to purchase private homes in Flushing and send their children to local public schools. As a result of this, blocks which had been primarily German and Irish suddenly had Moroccan, Sudanese and Thai influences.

Just as Quakers initially sought freedom of religion in this neighborhood, so, in recent years, have Hindus, Muslims and Buddhists. While a degree of prejudice is perhaps inevitable, many locals are fond of their new neighbors. The Asian Flushingites are mainly industrious people who have made the area so vibrant that it is one of the few sections of New York City that was able to weather the recent recession in reasonable economic health.

The World's Fair buildings themselves still stand in the park, curious-looking edifices which offer the visitor such noteworthy sights as the **Queens Museum**, the **Hall of Science**, and the gigantic **globe of the world** (the latter visible from afar, a familiar landmark to commuters caught in rush-hour traffic on the Brooklyn-Queens expressway). On the park's rolling green lawns are also the National Tennis Center (home to the U.S. Open), a botanic garden, and a zoo; as well as armies of picnickers and frisbee players when the weather is accommodating. A frequent background noise is the roar of the crowd from nearby **Shea Stadium**.

JAMAICA

Jamaica, the largest shopping center in the borough, was the home of Rufus King, a senator, ambassador and one of the signers of the American Declaration of Independence. Today, his home on **Jamaica Avenue**, the **King Mansion Museum**, is open to the public. Real history buffs might want to make the short pilgrimage to his grave at the **Grace Episcopal Church** a few blocks away.

A substantial percentage of Queens' 350,000 African-Americans live in Jamaica. Black cultural hubs in the area include the **Roy Wilkins Community Center**, **African Poetry Theatre** and **Laurelton Theatre of Performing Arts**.

Unfortunately, when the crack/cocaine epidemic hit New York in the 1980s, Jamaica was hit particularly hard. Because of the criminality that tends to spring up in areas where these drugs are heavily used, it's wise to be on one's guard against purse-snatchers and other dangerous characters, although the shopping bargains and sights in the neighborhood are certainly worth pursuing.

Long Island City

Once seen only as a manufacturing region at the foot of the 59th Street Bridge, **Long Island City** is now something of an artist's colony. A lot of painters, photographers and sculptors, fleeing Manhattan's pretensions and its high rents, have settled in the spacious lofts of one-time factory buildings. Some of these artists do not even have to go to Manhattan to do business.

The **International Design Center of New York**, housing the world's top furniture, fashion and interior design firms, is located on the site of a former railroad loading dock. A former bread factory is now **Silvercup Studios**, a film and video center facing the bridge. What was a public school has become the **P.S. 1 Museum**, showcasing emerging artists from throughout the world. Near the waterfront are the famed **Isamu Noguchi Garden Museum**, featuring three-dimensional art, and the **Socrates Sculpture Park**, overlooking the breathtaking skyline of Manhattan.

The Rockaways

As recently as the 1970s, people who lived as close as Brooklyn would take off for the summer to vacation in **the Rockaways**, a ten-mile strip of beach on a peninsula not far from the upper middle

Above: Taking a stroll along Rufus King Park in the lively area of Jamaica, Queens.

class **Howard Beach** neighborhood and **Jamaica Bay Wildlife Refuge**. While some of the old summer houses and bungalows are in disrepair, and crime centered around the public housing in the Rockaways has made the area less desirable than in times past, the beaches at the end of the subway line are still viewed by many as a summer haven.

On the western part of the peninsula, **Breezy Point Park** is a nature preserve where middle-class people can still afford homes along the seashore. Nearby, the amenities at **Jacob Riis Park**, named for an enterprising journalist who forced people to confront the ugly reality of poverty in the city nearly 100 years ago, include beaches, miniature golf course, handball courts and a boardwalk.

Of all the ethnic groups that flocked to the Rockaways in their heyday, the Irish had the most visible influence and remain an integral part of the area. The thousands of Irish relocating to New York during the past decade have added spirit to the Irish Festival held each July.

QUEENS
Access
John F. Kennedy International Airport, Tel: 718/656-4444. **LaGuardia Airport**, Tel: 718/476-5000. **New York City Transit Authority**, buses and subways, Tel: 718/330-1234. **Long Island Railroad**, Tel: 718/454-5477.

Accommodation
LUXURY: **JFK Plaza Hotel**, 135-30 140th Street, Jamaica, 11436, Tel: 718/659- 6000, close to John F. Kennedy Airport. **Sheraton LaGuardia East**, Main Street and 39th Avenue, Flushing, Tel: 718/460-6666.

MODERATE TO BUDGET: **Adria Motor Inn and Conference Center**, 220-33 Northern Boulevard, Bayside, 11361, Tel: 718/631-5900. **City View Motor Inn**, 33-17 Greenpoint Avenue, Long Island City, 11101, Tel: 718/392-8400. **Days Hotel LaGuardia Airport**, 100-15 Ditmars Boulevard, East Elmhurst, 11369, Tel: 718/898-1225.

Restaurants
CHINESE: **Stony Wok**, 137-40 Northern Boulevard, Flushing, Tel: 718/445-8535. *FRENCH:* **Le Triomphe**, 21-50 44th Drive, Long Island City, Tel: 718/706-0033. Elegant dining: **Water's Edge**, 44th Drive at the East River, Long Island City, Tel: 718/482-0033. *GERMAN:* **Niederstein's,** 69-16 Metropolitan Avenue, Middle Village, Tel: 718/326-0717. **Triangle Hofbrau**, 117-13 Jamaica Avenue, Richmond Hill, Tel: 718/849-1400.

GREEK: **Taverna Astoria Park**, 19-06 Ditmars Boulevard, Astoria, Tel: 718/626-9035. *INDIAN:* **Tandoor Restaurant**, 95-25 Queens Boulevard, Rego Park, Tel: 718/997-6800. *ITALIAN:* **Altadonna Restaurant**, 137-03 Cross Bay Boulevard, Ozone Park, Tel: 718/848-6895. **Bacigalup's**, 41-42 Main Street, Flushing, Tel: 718/358-6666. *ISRAELI:* **Café Baba of Israel**, 91-33 63rd Drive, Forest Hills, Tel: 718/275-2660. *KOREAN:* **New Seoul Restaurant**, 108-01 Northern Boulevard, Flushing, Tel: 718/426-6660. *SPANISH:* **Marbella**, 220-33 Northern Boulevard, Bayside. **El Inca**, 85-01 Roosevelt Avenue, Jackson Heights.

Special Events
Spring: *Greek Easter Pascha Parade*, Astoria, Tel: 718/291-1100.

Late May: *Richmond Hill Colonial Weekend Encampment and National Muster*, Forest Park at Park Lane South and Myrtle Avenue, Richmond Hill, celebrations on Memorial Day Weekend, Tel: 718/291-1100.

Czechoslovak Festival, Bohemian Hall, Astoria, Memorial Day Weekend, Tel: 718/274-4925.

In Summer: *Art on the Beach*, Avant-Garde Arts Festival, 55th Avenue and 2nd Street, Hunter's Point, Long Island City, July-September, Tel: 718/619-1100. *Irish Festival*, 116th Street, Rockaway, in July, Tel: 718/291-1100. *Thunderbird American Indian Dancers Midsummer Pow Wow*, Queens County Farm Museum, Floral Park, late July, Tel: 718/347-FARM.

September: *Hispanic Day Parade of Queens*, 37th Avenue, Jackson Heights.

Korean Harvest and Folklore Festival, Flushing Meadow Park, Tel: 718/507-3123. *Agricultural Fair*, Queens County Farm Museum.

Queens Ethnic Music and Dance Festival, Bohemian Hall, Astoria, Tel: 718/691-9510.

US Open Tennis Championships, Flushing Meadow Park, Tel: 718/592-8000.

December: *Kwanzaa African American Harvest Festival*, various locations, Tel: 718/523-3312.

Cultural and Historic Sites
International Design Center of New York, 29-10 Thomson Avenue, Long Island City, Tel: 718/937-7474. **Isamu Noguchi Garden Museum**, 32-37 Vernon Boulevard, Long Island City, Tel: 718/204-7088. **King Mansion Museum**, 150th to 153rd Streets on Jamaica Avenue, Jamaica. **Queens Museum**, New York City Building, Flushing Meadow Park, Flushing, Tel: 718/592-555. **Queens County Farm Museum**, 73-50 Little Neck Parkway, Floral Park, Tel: 718/347-FARM.

African Poetry Theater, 176-03 Jamaica Avenue, Jamaica, Tel: 718/523-3312. **Colden Center for the Performing Arts**, Queens College, Flushing, Tel: 718/793-8080. **Laurelton Theater of Performing and Visual Arts**, 228-05 Merrick Boulevard, Laurelton, Tel: 718/723-9177. **Thalia Spanish Theater**, 41-17 Greenpoint Avenue, Sunnyside, Tel: 718/729-3880. **Bowne House**, 37-01 Bowne Street, Flushing, Tel: 718/359-0528.

Greater Ridgewood Historical Society, 1820 Flushing Avenue, Ridgewood, Tel: 718/456-1776. **Queens Historical Society** (promotes tours of the borough), 143-35 37th Avenue, Flushing, Tel: 718/939-0647. **New York Hall of Science**, 47-01 111th Street, Flushing, Tel: 718/699-0005. **Queens Botanical Garden**, 43-50 Main Street, Flushing, Tel: 718/886-3800.

Sports
Shea Stadium, 125th Street and Roosevelt Avenue, Flushing, Tel: 718/507-TIXX. **National Tennis Center** (US Open), Flushing Meadow Park, Tel: 718/592-8000. **Aqueduct Racetrack**, Rockaway Boulevard and 108th Street, Ozone Park, Tel: 718/641-4700.

STATEN ISLAND

ROSEBANK
THE GREENBELT
RICHMONDTOWN

Staten Island is New York's forgotten borough. Though connected to the rest of the city by the **Verrazano-Narrows Bridge**, built in 1964, it is still outside the subway system. Direct access to Manhattan is by ferry to Battery Park.

This isolation from the turmoil of the other four boroughs has not bothered the islanders, who frequently think aloud about the possibility of secession. For one, they pay high taxes and have to serve as a landfill. Secondly, they are geographically closer to New Jersey. Thirdly, islanders are different: They have more traditional, middle-class family values, they have the only Republican in the City Council, they read the *Staten Island Advance*, not the *New York Times*, the *Post* or the *News*, they mind their own business. They have all they need on the island, green space, museums, entertainment and a quickly growing tax base. They do not need the city.

History

Italian Staten Islanders are proudly willing to believe that it was Giovanni da Verrazano, flying a French flag, who

Left: Richmondtown Restoration vividly recalls the halcyon days of Staten Island.

"discovered" Staten Island in 1524. The great explorer was blown ashore somewhere in the region, but nobody was there to tell him where he was, so he sailed on. At the time Staten Island was the domain of the Aquehonga tribe of the Raritan Indians. The Dutch established the first Staten Island settlement in 1630, eventually relinquishing control to the English in 1664.

During the Revolution, the British maintained 30,000 troops here. In 1776, American patriots Benjamin Franklin, John Adams and Edward Rutledge traveled to the county of Richmond, as it was called, to meet with Lord Howe to discuss peace. The outcome was unsatisfactory, but the **Conference House** at the southern tip of the island where they met remains a local landmark.

By the 1860s, Richmond County had its own steam railroad and ferry service to and from Manhattan. Although it was incorporated into New York City in 1898, Staten Islanders had better access to New Jersey over three short bridges built between 1928 and 1930.

Nothing affected the island more than the building of the Verrazano-Narrows Bridge, however. The name Staten Island became official, replacing Borough of Richmond. Overnight, entire neighborhoods changed or sprang up out of nowhere. The population grew in leaps and bounds, from 250,000 in 1964 to 380,000 in 1981, to nearly 500,000 in 1990.

Bay Street Village used to consist of not-so-attractive warehouses until young, dynamic professionals with enough cash and a willingness to invest turned them into a cooperative complex. For someone working in Manhattan, this is a perfect address. The apartments generally face the waterfront, and the Staten Island Ferry to Manhattan is a five-minute walk from the Village.

A number of well-known soap opera stars insist that the secret to success lies in living on Staten Island. After laboring amid the stress and egos of the Manhattan television industry, they say they are revived by taking the ferry home to their quiet and friendly neighborhoods.

The typical ethnic jumble of New York is absent on the island. There is a small Orthodox Jewish community and an Irish community. It is the Italians, however, who make up the largest single ethnic group on Staten Island. Many were here "before the bridge," others arrived later, fleeing the deteriorating sections of Brooklyn and the Bronx. They live for the most part in the **Rosebank** section a little south of the ferry.

ROSEBANK

One source of great pride in Rosebank is the **Garibaldi Meucci Memorial Museum**, a source of local Italian-American pride. The building itself is a fine example of neo-Gothic architecture of the kind common around the 1840s. It was purchased in 1850 by a gentleman named Antonio Meucci, born in Florence. He opened a candle factory, but was already toying with electricity. He was indeed a skilful inventor, who, by the year 1857, had developed a gadget called the *telettrophono*, which was to all intents and purposes a telephone. Alexander Graham Bell applied for a patent for his telephone

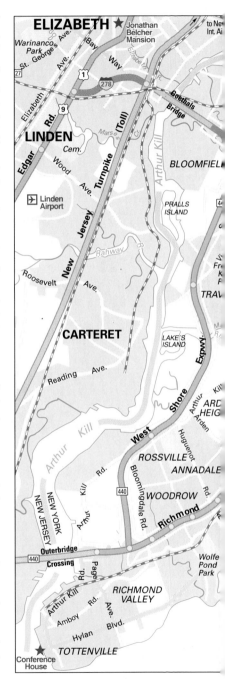

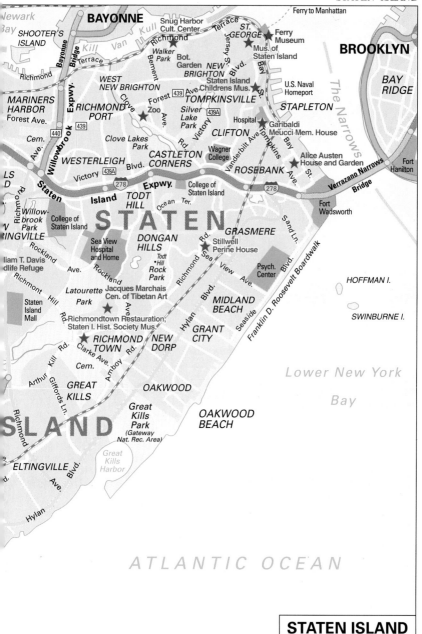

Ferry to Manhattan

BAYONNE

SHOOTER'S ISLAND

Newark Bay

Snug Harbor Cult. Center

ST. GEORGE

Ferry Museum

Mus. of Staten Island

BROOKLYN

BAY RIDGE

Richmond Terrace

Van Kull

Kill

Bayonne Bridge

Terrace

Walker Park

Bot. Garden

NEW BRIGHTON

Staten Island Childrens Mus.

The Narrows

MARINERS HARBOR

Forest Ave.

WEST NEW BRIGHTON

RICHMOND PORT

Forest Zoo

439 Ave.

TOMPKINSVILLE

U.S. Naval Homeport

STAPLETON

Richmond

Willowbrook Expwy.

Clove Ave.

Silver Lake Park

439A

Hospital

Garibaldi Meucci Mem. House

Cem.

440

439

Clove Lakes Park

Victory Rd.

CLIFTON

WESTERLEIGH

CASTLETON CORNERS

Wagner College

Vanderbilt Ave.

Tompkins Ave.

Alice Austen House and Garden

St.

Fort Hamilton

LS D

Victory

439A

Blvd.

ROSEBANK

Verrazano Narrows Bridge

Staten Island Expwy.

278

College of Staten Island

278

Willowbrook Park

College of Staten Island

TODT HILL

Ocean Ter.

Fort Wadsworth

INGVILLE

STATEN

Rockland

Sea View Hospital and Home

DONGAN HILLS

Richmond Rd.

GRASMERE

Sand Ln.

HOFFMAN I.

liam T. Davis dlife Refuge

Richmont

Todt Hill Rock Park

Stillwell Perine House

Sea View Ave.

Psych. Center

Roosevelt Blvd.

SWINBURNE I.

Rockland Ave.

Latourette Park

Jacques Marchais Cen. of Tibetan Art

Blvd.

MIDLAND BEACH

Franklin D. Roosevelt Boardwalk

Staten Island Mall

Richmondtown Restauration; Staten I. Hist. Society Mus.

Hylan Blvd.

Seaside

Lower New York

RICHMOND TOWN

NEW DORP

GRANT CITY

Bay

Clarke Ave.

Amboy Rd.

Cem.

Kill Rd.

GREAT KILLS

OAKWOOD

OAKWOOD BEACH

Arthur

Giffords Ln.

ISLAND

Great Kills Park (Gateway Nat. Rec. Area)

Richmond

ELTINGVILLE

Blvd.

Great Kills Harbor

Ave.

Hylan

ATLANTIC OCEAN

STATEN ISLAND

0 _____ 3 km

0 _____ 1 _____ 2 miles

199

19 years later. When the Italian revolutionary commander Garibaldi took refuge in the United States after the failed revolution of 1848 against Austrian domination, he stayed with his friend Meucci. He whiled away the time hunting and investigating the candle factory until 1854, when he returned to continue the struggle to unify Italy, this time with success.

The life and times of these two great Italians, one famous, the other less so, are exhibited in the house. The grounds of the estate show some of the other skills performed by Italian immigrants, such as papermaking, dyeing and brewing. A visit to the Meucci homestead should also include the **Manteo Family Sicilian Marionette Theatre**, which gives performances with southern Italian puppets.

The neighboring **Stapleton** section has been upgraded as a result of the prox-

Above: The Verrazano Narrows Bridge to Staten Island was made famous in "Saturday Night Fever." Right: The Children's Museum in the Snug Harbor Project.

imity of the **U.S. Naval Homeport** being in the area. Many of the Victorian homes of a much earlier period of Staten Island history stand amidst more generic developments. Another important development here is the **Snug Harbor Cultural Center,** which presents dramatic performances and provides space for local artists to use as they please. In 1801, **Snug Harbor** was chosen as the location for the first hospital and retirement home for sailors of the United States Navy. The home was built in the Classical style of the period. Considered New York City's fastest-growing center of the arts, this 80-acre National Landmark District park currently comprises 26 restored and converted historic buildings. In warmer months, the park becomes the site of the Summer Sculpture Festival, complemented by outdoor concerts and the contemporary art in the **New House Center**.

Two other centers of activity should be mentioned here. The first is the **Banks Street Art Center** located in the commercial **New Brighton** neighborhood. It

contains three art galleries, in addition to a frame shop, video center, poetry performance area and a 75-seat theater. Contemporary art is the specialty of the month-long exhibits and artist's workshops.

THE GREENBELT

As one heads southward, Staten Island begins to show its most natural side. The Seaside Boulevard runs parallel to the Atlantic Ocean, passing by **South Beach**. The view of the Verrazano-Narrows Bridge and Lower New York Bay is particularly impressive from here. On hot days it is an ideal place for some swimming, fishing, or just a pleasant walk on the 2.5 mile **Franklin D. Roosevelt Boardwalk**, the fourth largest in the world.

The largest spot of non-developed land is the Greenbelt, however, a godsend to those who need a little rest and recuperation from the city. This 2500-acre park includes two major trails. The 8.5-mile

Blue Trail starts at the **College of Staten Island** and winds through **High Rock Park** and **Latourette Park**. It crosses **Todt Hill**, which, as unlikely as it may seem, is the highest point of land along the entire eastern seaboard. **Ocean Terrace**, also on the way, was a look-out point for the British during the Revolutionary War. The **White Trail** runs from **Willowbrook Park** to **Great Kills Park**. At the 260-acre **William T. Davis Wildlife Preserve**, the woodland and salt marsh have been maintained for the study and appreciation of nature. Several groups organize hiking, bird watching and cross-country skiing in this area.

RICHMONDTOWN

The **Richmondtown Restoration** beside Latourette Park, offers a glimpse into the Staten Island of the distant past, a restored pre-Revolutionary War version of **Richmondtown**, the county seat before the borough joined New York City. The **Richmondtown Restoration** is an ongo-

ing project sponsored by both the city's Department of Cultural Affairs and the Staten Island Historical Society. It provides a comprehensive glimpse into the past ages of the island and America in general. It currently consists of about 40 specific sites that have been renovated. Aside from a museum, there is a carpentry shop, general store, carriage house and county court building, in addition to the British fortifications from the War of Independence on **Richmond Hill**. **The Tavern** at Richmondtown Restoration is a recreation of a typical 19th-century tavern, serving beer and hot cider prepared on a wood-burning stove. At concerts in the Tavern, visitors bask in the glow of candle-light, listening to ethnic and folk music.

The **Staten Island Zoo** near Silver Lake Park is known for its collection of reptiles. Here is found the **Jacques Marchais Center of Tibetan Art,** which was founded in 1945 by Jacques Marchais, the professional name of Jacqueline Klauber, a female art dealer who used a male name to get along better in the business. Her collections can be found in two stone buildings constructed on a hillside. The brass, bronze and copper objects in the museum, mainly figurines of Buddhas and deities, come from Tibet, India, Nepal and China, and date from the seventeenth to twentieth centuries. One of the buildings is designed like a Tibetan Buddhist mountain temple, with terraced gardens, a lily pond and views of lower New York Bay.

Another fine example of nature conservation on Staten Island is **Gateway National Recreation Area**, or Great Kills Park, a few miles further along the coast. which is not only ideal for fishing and beach swimming, but also for forest study. Park rangers lead tours focusing on the area's history and local plant and animal life. There are also sports fields, picnic areas, a pleasant marina and a large indoor ice rink.

Above: Continuing the work on the Richmondtown Restoration is a painstaking job.

STATEN ISLAND

Access

Staten Island Rapid Transit trains operate 24 hours a day, and there is express service between Great Kills and St. George, Tel: 718/447-8601.
New York City Transit Authority buses only run on Staten Island, Tel: 718/330-1234. There is no subway service.
The **Staten Island Ferry** links the borough to Manhattan. This is one of the most enjoyable rides in New York, affording views of the Statue of Liberty and the New York City skyline. Commuters fill the boats by day, but the night time views are particularly spectacular and the ferry is also a traditional cheap date for the romantically inclined, Tel: 212/806-6940.

Accommodation

MODERATE TO BUDGET: **Cosmopolitan Hotel**, 1274 Hylan Boulevard, 10305, Tel: 718/979-7000. **Holiday Inn,** 1415 Richmond Avenue, 10314, Tel: 718/698-5000.
West Shore Hotel, 2600 Veterans Road West, 10314, Tel: 718/967-4800.

Restaurants

AMERICAN: **Clove Lakes Café**, Clove Lakes Boat House, Tel: 718/442-7451. **Sleepy Hollow**, 514 Bloomingdale Road, Tel: 718/984-0700.
CHINESE: **Chinatown**, 366 New Dorp Lane, Tel: 718/987-1414.
CONTINENTAL: **Esquire Club**, 461 Clove Road, Tel: 718/447-9186. **Li Greci's Staaten**, 697 Forest Avenue, Tel: 718/448-6000. **Marina Café,** 154 Mansion Avenue, Tel: 718/967-3077.
ITALIAN: **Basilio Inn**, 6 Galesville Court, Tel: 718/447-9292. **La Fontana**, 2879 Amboy Road, Tel: 718/667-4343. **Roberto's**, 981 Bay Street, Tel: 718/447-7885.
SPANISH: **Carmen's**, 750 Barclay Avenue, Tel: 718/948-9503. **Real Madrid**, 2073 Forest Avenue, Tel: 718/447-7885.

Special Events

A number of happenings take place in the borough's parks each year, including concerts and seasonal festivals. Information: **City of New York Parks and Recreation Public Information Office**, Tel: 212/360-1350.

Parks / Leisure / Golf

Cloves Lake Park, Tel: 718/390-8000. **Gateway National Recreation Area**, Tel: 718/351-8700. **Walker Park and Tennis Club**, Tel: 718/442-9696. **Willowbrook Park**, Tel: 718/698-2186. **Wolfe's Pond Park and Beach**, Tel: 718/984-8266. **Staten Island Zoo**, commonly referred to as "New York's biggest little zoo," Martling Avenue between Clove Road and Broadway, Tel: 718/442-3101.

GOLF: **Latourette Park and Golf Course**, Tel: 718/351-1840. **Silver Lake Golf Course**, Tel: 718/447-5686. **South Shore Golf Course**, Tel: 718/984-0101.

Reserves / Tours

The Greenbelt, Tel: 718/987-6233. **Clay Pit Ponds**, Tel: 718/967-1976.
The Urban Park Rangers offer tours of the Greenbelt, Tel: 718/667-2165. Information about treks through other spots on Staten Island from the **Staten Island Cultural and Information Center**, Tel: 718/809-4444 or from **Staten Island Historical Society**, Tel: 718/351-1611.

Museums / Culture

Art/Network at the Banks Street Art Center, 15,500 square feet of galleries and theaters, 15 Banks Street, Tel: 718/442-0005. **Jacques Marchais Center of Tibetan Art**, a rare collection of Tibetan and other Buddhist artifacts, 338 Lighthouse Avenue, Tel: 718/987-3478. **Garibaldi Meucci Memorial Museum**, home to the original inventor of the telephone, Antonio Meucci, and Italian patriot Giuseppe Garibaldi, 420 Tompkins Avenue, Tel: 718/442-1608. **John A. Noble Center**, a study center for maritime art and history, 270 Richmond Terrace, Tel: 718/447-6490. **Manteo Family Sicilian Marionette Theater**, a fascinating shrine to the art of marionette performance. No walk-ins allowed, appointments only, Tel: 718/727-1135.
Staten Island Ferry and Ferry Museum, with display of older ferry boats at the St. George terminal; at the foot of Bay Street, Tel: 212/806-6940. **Museum of Staten Island**, the oldest cultural institution on Staten Island (opened in 1881), specializing in science, art and history, 75 Stuyvesant Place, Tel: 718/727-1135.
Snug Harbor Cultural Center, a designated historic district including the **Newhouse Center for the Arts**, **Staten Island Botanical Garden** and the **Staten Island Children's Museum**, 1000 Richmond Terrace, Tel: 718/448-2500.

Historic Sites

Alice Austen House, home of the famous photographer who documented life in a changing America from 1884 to 1934, 2 Hylan Boulevard, Tel: 718/816-4506.
Conference House, where American patriots failed to secure a peace treaty during a 1776 meeting with the British; at the foot of Hylan Boulevard in Tottenville, Tel: 718/984-2086.
Richmondtown Restoration, a carefully preserved replica of the Staten Island of years past, 441 Clark Avenue, Tel: 718/351-1611.
Staten Island Homeport, home to the *USS Iowa*, Stapleton waterfront, Tel: 718/643-4444.

LONG ISLAND

OYSTER BAY
FIRE ISLAND
THE HAMPTONS

In 1947, when a contractor in the Long Island town of Island Trees bought a few potato fields and announced that he was going to build 2000 rental houses, nobody realized that William J. Levitt would alter the way America looked. World War Two veterans were soon fleeing the crowded conditions of New York City and flocking to the homes, which only cost $60 a month. Levittown was to grow to 17,000 homes and 83,000 people; but, more importantly, it became the prototype for suburban America.

Measuring approximately 100 miles from the Queens-Nassau border to the lighthouse built in 1795 at the tip of Montauk Point, Long Island supports a wide variety of communities. Within commuting distance of the city are many of the suburban enclaves Long Island invented, with their rows of look-alike houses and concrete shopping malls; but the rural North Fork at the island's eastern tip is lined with lovely old houses – some of the oldest in New York – tree-shaded streets, and truck farms selling fresh produce (visitors can pick their own berries). Summer is Long Island's most active season: celebrities (and voyeurs) flock to the

Preceding pages: Pumpkin season brings out the best in people. Left: A windmill on Long Island, a touch of Dutch.

Hamptons; artists congregate on Fire Island; families splash off the beaches near Sag Harbor. Far from being merely suburbia, Long Island is a veritable vacationland within easy reach of New York City.

History

Because of the island's fish-like shape, with a mouth in Queens' Jamaica Bay and tail at Montauk and Orient Points, the Indian name for Long Island was *Paumonok*: fish. Later, the Dutch would rechristen it *Lange Eylandt*, a name subsequently translated by the English.

Today's suburban communities are named for some of the Indian tribes who originally inhabited the land: Massapequa, Mattituck, Wyandanch, Manhasset, Setauket, Matinecock, Rekonkoma. The Shinnecock and Poosepatuck tribes still dwell in two Indian reservations in Suffolk County. A European influx began with Henry Hudson, who landed on the western portion in 1609, and Dutch trader-explorer Adrian Block, who went ashore at Easterly Montauk Point, in 1614. Long-term settlers followed; in 1636, the first English community was established in the North Fork town of Southold.

Both Long Island's proximity to New York and its sheer physical length in-

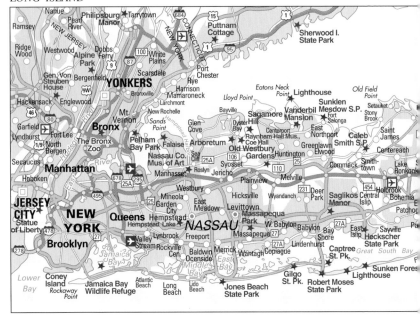

fluenced its population almost from the beginning. The areas nearer the city were the province of wealthy urban families seeking country retreats on their large estates, while the bays, harbors and fields to the east were centers for fishermen and farmers. Most of the island remained the domain of these latter two groups until after World War Two, when the suburban housing boom began. In the decade from 1950 to 1960, Nassau County's population jumped from just above 670,000 to over 1,300,000.

Although some consider Long Island a commuter's haven, only 24 percent of residents work in New York City. With growth came industries to support the locals: electronics, aircraft and pharmaceuticals, among others. The Grumman company, whose manufacture of airplane parts was both lucrative and essential during World War Two, is one of the area's major employers. Today, the standard of living of many Long Islanders is high, and the unemployment rate is one of the lowest in the entire nation.

Cars on Long Island sport bumper stickers with slogans like "When the going gets tough, the tough go shopping." Hence malls abound: in **Roosevelt Field**, **Garden City**, **Huntington, Green Acres**, and **Valley Stream**, to name a few. So beloved is shopping among local residents that there are whole villages designed specifically to lure consumers. **Sea Cliff** is a scenic community that resembles its name. **Hempstead Harbor** extends below the winding hills of the town. While taking in the scenery, there is also plenty of browsing to be done at the shops along **Sea Cliff Avenue**. One of the most scenic shopping districts on Long Island, Bellport is filled with Victorian homes, visible reminders of the area's first English settlers.

OYSTER BAY

At once a suburban community and vacation retreat, Oyster Bay offers something of everything: classical music festivals and a wildlife preserve, a marina and

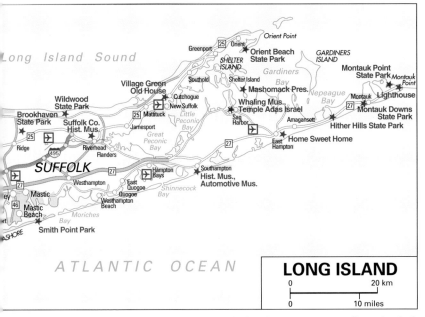

national parks. Early in this century, influential politicians and industrialists built estates on the protected bay; some of these dwellings can be visited today.

Notable among these residents was Theodore Roosevelt, whose Victorian mansion has been re-christened the **Sagamore Hill National Historic Site**. Completed for the future president in 1885, the building became the Summer White House from 1901 to 1909. The 23-mansion estate has been well-maintained for tourists, who get to see exhibits and an audio-visual program about the feisty president when they tour the grounds. His and his wife's simple grave is in the cemetery a few miles away.

Not far away is another piece of history: **Raynham Hall Museum**, a 22-room house inhabited since 1738 by one of the town's most prominent families, the Townsends, and occupied by British troops during the American Revolutionary War. The planting fields at **Coe Hall**, a Tudor Revival mansion nearby, feature extensive greenhouse displays and horticultural programs, as well as classical, jazz and folk music during its annual summer festival.

The Gold Coast

Coe Hall is an example of the monumental homes which sprang up in the 1920s along what became dubbed Long Island's "**Gold Coast**." These were showplaces built in the countryside along **Long Island Sound** by industrialists with names like Vanderbilt, Chrysler, Guggenheim, Woolworth and Phipps, people who lived in an elegant and indulgent world of fox hunts, squash games, polo matches and, naturally, scandal.

It was this world that F. Scott Fitzgerald chronicled in his seminal novel *The Great Gatsby*, and a taste of it can be had by visiting the mansions still standing from that era. The Phipps estate, **Old Westbury Gardens**, is a Georgian mansion surrounded by tree-lined avenues and formal gardens. Containing Chinese porcelains and priceless Gainsboroughs,

In posh Roslyn, the **Nassau County Museum of Art** stands in the renovated Georgian mansion that once belonged to Childs Frick, son of US Steel co-founder Henry Clay Frick. Now, ten galleries and sculpture displays occupy the 145-acre grounds. Also on the Gold Coast is an estate associated with another time in history: **Sagtikos Manor**, in **West Bay Shore**, a 42-room mansion built in 1692. One of many Colonial houses which can make the boast "George Washington slept here" (in 1790), the building also served as headquarters for his British adversaries in the Revolutionary War.

FIRE ISLAND

Located near Jones Beach, which draws bathers from all over New York City and Nassau County, **Fire Island** is a long, narrow strip of land which extends 32 miles along the Long Island shore, from **Smith Point Park** in the West to **Robert Moses State Park** in the East. In between are small resort communities which heat up when the weather does. Although the two parks can be reached by car, the other areas are accessible only by ferry.

the mansion has been used by film makers wishing to recreate the kind of excessive splendor enjoyed by the privileged classes in the18th and 19th centuries. In **Centerport**, the architecture of the stunning **Vanderbilt Mansion** hearkens back to Spanish-Moroccan influences. Today, the house and grounds have become the **Vanderbilt Museum;** an interesting amenity is the Planetarium, one of the largest in the country.

In **Sand's Point**, on a hill overlooking Long Island Sound, is the **Falaise**, Harry F. Guggenheim's Normanesque estate of 1923, where Charles Lindbergh (who, incidentally, began his historic trans-Atlantic journey at **Mitchell Field**, near the Nassau Coliseum) wrote his memoirs. Even in this affluent enclave this manor, a beautiful medieval-style hacienda with ivy-covered walls, outshines the dwellings around it.

Above: The final resting place of Theodore Roosevelt in Sagamore, Long Island. Right: Fishing for bass at Montauk Point.

While some of the communities are quiet, others draw a rambunctious element. Fire Island is famous as a summer retreat for young, liberal New Yorkers, who rent shares in the large beach houses and set out to enjoy themselves with a vengeance. This summer crowd includes an active gay community. Nude beaches on the island are popular with these vacationers; frequently, revels begun on the beach are continued at a nightclub until the wee hours of the morning.

But Fire Island's attraction lies in its natural beauties. The **Fire Island National Seashore** has been preserved by the National Parks Service. Hidden throughout this wilderness area are hardwood groves, wild geese, herons and deer. **Sunken Forest,** located below the

dunes, is one of the more intriguing sites. East of Robert Moses State Park, the **Fire Island Lighthouse** was built in 1858. The classic, beehive-shaped structure, which projects a beam of light for 21 miles, has been illuminated by an automatic light since 1974. The keeper's quarters have been transformed into a museum and gift shop.

THE HAMPTONS

The South Fork of Long Island has been nicknamed the "New York Riviera." Notable for its miles of white dunes and beaches washed by the breakers of the Atlantic Ocean and its quaint, Colonial-style towns, the Hamptons have become the place for New York society to vacation. Pretentious or no, the area is undeniably a wonderful spot for beach-going or browsing in the boutiques and restaurants that fill the white clapboard buildings of the villages.

Since the beginning of the century, the Hamptons have had a reputation for attracting the city's monied classes. **Southampton** – which also claims to be Long Island's oldest settlement – and **East Hampton** are where most of the jet-setters go: Dune Road, in Southampton, boasts some of the most luxurious modern homes in the state. These glass and wood structures seem to have been built by people anxious to impress outsiders or to throw huge parties. East Hampton is equally grand, but has a different style: older and more sedate in appearance, it features well-preserved buildings dating back to the 1600s along streets lined with majestic elm trees. A different crowd gravitates toward **Hampton Bays** and **Quogue** – more outdoorsy types who genuinely appreciate nature.

With its yacht clubs, begonias, pine shrubs and lighthouse, **Montauk Point** remains perhaps the most alluring spot on Long Island. Fishermen and summer yachtsmen occupy its harbor, while its signature lighthouse, commissioned by George Washington in 1797, dominates the scene from its point of land. The

Montauk Downs State Park and the **Montauk Point State Park** are the place for long beach walks or a visit to the museum located on the grounds.

Sag Harbor and Shelter Island

Despite new buildings and a new tourist population Sag Harbor maintains the flavor of its rich historical past. The town reflects the influence of the British troops who occupied it during the Revolutionary War; some houses they built still stand.

Another side of Sag Harbor is its whaling history. By 1845, the harbor was the fourth largest whaling port in the world. This era is documented and to an extent preserved in the **Whaling Museum**, a Greek Revival mansion stocked with log books, whaling equipment, models of vessels and memorabilia.

Jewish culture also played a major role in Sag Harbor history. The town's largest

Above: Agriculture is the mainstay of a number of inland Long Islanders.

employer in the 1890s was a watch-casing factory; many Jewish laborers were included in its workforce. **Temple Adas Israel**, a Gothic, stained glass sanctuary built in 1898, is the oldest synagogue on Long Island.

A ferry ride across the bay brings you to **Shelter Island**, an exclusive enclave which has managed to stay "sheltered" from some of the overt commercialism found in other Long Island beach communities. Island features are striking white beaches and wooded, rolling hills; Mashomack Preserve maintains the natural character of a part of the island.

North Fork

More "undiscovered" than the bustling Hamptons, the rural fork of eastern Long Island preserves the flavor of small-town America. A drive along Route 25 from Riverhead to Orient takes you past lovely colonial houses; towns give way to small fields with roadside farm stands where you can buy fresh raspberries or home-made peach pies, depending on the season. Unselfconsciously historical, the area preserves its heritage in places such as Cutchogue's **Village Green**, where the **Old House** which still stands was built in 1649. Also in Cutchogue, Wikham's Fruit Farm is modeled on an 18th-century facility. In Greenport, you can take boat trips through the harbor or browse in antique ships for another glimpse into the past. In Riverhead, the **Suffolk County Historical Museum** contains a wealth of information about the area.

The past decade has seen over 50 vineyards and fourteen wineries spring up in the area. The wines produced – Sauvignon Blanc, Riesling, and Chardonnay among them – have received high ratings from experts. Ground-breaker in this area was Cutchogue's Hargrave Vineyard. Today, **Palmer Vineyards** and **Mattituck Hills** are among the wineries offering tours of their facilities and wine tastings.

LONG ISLAND
Access

Long Island's **MacArthur Airport**, 100 Arrival Avenue, Ronkonkoma, Tel: 516/588-8062. **East Hampton Airport**, Tel: 516/537-1130. **Suffolk County Airport**, Westhampton Beach, Tel: 516/288-3600. **Long Island Railroad**, Tel: 516/217-LIRR. The railroad provides service to the Hamptons, as well as commuter service and "one day getaways" to various Long Island landmarks. **Metropolitan Suburban Bus Authority**: In Nassau, Tel: 516/222-1000. In Suffolk, Tel: 516/360-5700. During the summer, there are buses from all parts of Nassau to Jones Beach.

Accommodation

LUXURY: **Long Island Marriott**, 101 James Doolittle Road, Uniondale, 11553, Tel: 516/794-3800, within walking distance of the Nassau Coliseum, Jones Beach and the Roosevelt Field mall, with nightclub, health club, restaurants, indoor pool and plush rooms.

Montauk Yacht Club Resort Marina, Star Island Road, Montauk, 11954, Tel: 516/668-3100. Built around a lighthouse, this unique resort offers tennis, a marina and, naturally, the white Hamptons sands.

Southampton Inn, 97 Hill Street at First Neck Lane, Southampton, 11968, Tel: 516/283-6500, hotel and convention center in walking distance of the village of Southampton, outdoor pool, two tennis courts, comedy club and exciting "murder mystery" weekends.

MODERATE TO BUDGET: **Avalon Indian Ridge Lakefront Resort**, Box 89L, Second House Road, Montauk, 11954, Tel: 516/668-5960. More geared for the sportsman than the scene-setter, with freshwater fishing, free rowing- and paddleboats, and a mini farm.

Dutchess Chateau Bed and Breakfast, 2900 Boisseau Avenue, Southold, 11971, Tel: 516/765-2900, breakfast is served on the porch in this countrified spot near wineries and beaches.

Freeport Motor Inn and Boatel, 445 South Main Street, Freeport, 11520, Tel: 516/623-9100, directly on the water with a marina and docking facilities, close to the town's great seafood restaurants and "Nautical Mile."

Restaurants

Bay Mist, on Great South Bay, in Patchogue, Tel: 516/475-1606, a combination of culinary and nautical adventure, Long Island's top dinner cruise ship, reservations required.

Ben's Kosher, 135 Alexander Avenue, Lake Grove, Tel: 516/979-8770, gourmet delicatessen food. **Buonasera**, 730 Montauk Highway, Lindenhurst, Tel: 516/226-9868, seafood imported from Italy. **Café Continental Restaurant**, 1538 Northern Boulevard, Manhasset, Tel: 516/627-4269, serves outstanding, classic Italian and delicious Continental cuisine. **Gurney's Inn Resort and Spa**, Old Montauk Highway, Montauk, Tel: 516/668-2345, next to the beach, spa cuisine along with a beautiful view of the ocean. **Piping Rock**, 130 Post Avenue, Westbury, Tel: 516/333-5555. The speciality here is atmosphere: Each of the five rooms has its own theme. For example, the Royal Room has high-backed chairs and regal decor, while the Balcony Room evokes images of the Roaring 20s. Continental, American and Italian menus. **Plattdeutsche Park Restaurant**, 1132 Hempstead Turnpike, Franklin Square, Tel: 516/354-3131, for lovers of Old World German cooking, restaurant with seven banquet rooms. **Seashore Inn**, Watch Hill Marina at Watch Hill, Fire Island, Tel: 516/597-6655, fine Continental restaurant with picturesque views.

Sports

Car/Motorcycle Racing: **Bridgehampton Raceway,** sports car, formula car and motorcycle racing, from April through November, Tel: 516/725-0888.

Stock Car Racing: At **Riverhead Raceway**, May until September, Tel: 516/727-0010.

Thoroughbred Racing: **Belmont Park** in Belmont, from May to October, Tel: 718/641-4700.

Professional Hockey: The New York Islanders play home games at the **Nassau Coliseum,** in Uniondale, Tel: 516/794-9300.

Winery tours

Mattituck Hills, Bergen and Sound Avenues, North Fork, Tel: 516/298-9150.

Palmer Vineyards, Riverhead, Tel: 516/722-WINE.

Museums / Historic Sites

Long Island Cultural History Laboratory and Museum, Stony Brook, Tel: 516/929-8725.

Nassau County Museum of Art (the former Frick Mansion), 346 #1 Museum Drive, Roslyn, Tel: 516/484-9337. **Raynham Hall Museum**, 20 West Main Street, Oyster Bay, Tel: 516/922-6808. **Sag Harbor Whaling and Historical Museum**, Sag Harbor, Tel: 516/725-0770. **Vanderbilt Museum and Planetarium**, 180 Little Neck Road, Centerport, Tel: 516/262-7888. **Coe Hall**, Oyster Bay, Tel: 516/922-0479. **Fire Island Lighthouse Preservation Society**, Lighthouse Road, Babylon, Tel: 516/321-7028.

Old Westbury Gardens, Old Westbury, Tel: 516/333-0048. **Sagamore Hill National Historic Site**, 20 Sagamore Hill Road, Oyster Bay, Tel: 516/922-4447.

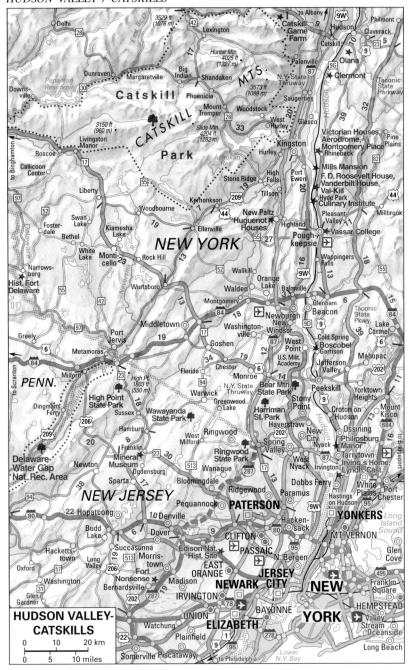

HUDSON VALLEY-
CATSKILLS

0   10   20 km

0   5   10 miles

HUDSON VALLEY

WESTCHESTER COUNTY
HUDSON HIGHLANDS
CATSKILLS

Many visitors arrive in New York with the prejudice that the name is synonymous with noise, crime, and dirt. Anyone who takes the time to look around a bit finds out that New York is much more than just that. Just as there's more to the city than its pollution, so is there much more to "New York" than just the city: a whole huge state, in fact, with some of the most beautiful landscapes in America. And some of that beautiful landscape is within one to two hours' drive of the city. Following the New York State Thruway, the Taconic State Parkway, or several other state roads to the Hudson Valley and the Catskills, the traveler weary of urban life will find clean air, lovely views, historic sights and a plethora of country inns and restaurants.

To those in the know, the Hudson River Valley has always been popular. Ever since its eponymous "discoverer" Henry Hudson first sailed up the river in 1609, travelers upriver have been impressed by the beauties of what they saw. A group of landscape painters in the 1800s were so overwhelmed by the landscape that they became known as the Hudson River School. Of somewhat later vintage, the many sumptuous mansions overlooking the **Hudson River** are indicative of the popularity of this region with the wealthy over the years, and ex-

plain why this river has been called America's Rhine.

WESTCHESTER COUNTY

Visitors driving up the winding **Saw Mill River Parkway** will pass right by the old towns of the **Lower Hudson Valley** in **Westchester County.** While many of the Westchester towns nearest to New York are developed, industrial, or suburban places, the area becomes increasingly picturesque as one moves north. For a more scenic route, leave the highway at Hastings-on-Hudson for the smaller **Route 9** and travel north to **Irvington**. Earlier this century, around World War One, Irvington was the richest suburb of New York City. The Director of the New York Central Railroad lived here, as did Louis Tiffany, of the Tiffany glass fame, and many other luminaries.

Not commerce, but art, distinguishes nearby **Sunnyside**, once home to the celebrated American writer Washington Irving, the man who brought to life the characters of *Rip Van Winkle* and the Headless Horseman of *The Legend of Sleepy Hollow*. Irving's home was a meeting-place for notables of the 19th century after Irving settled there in 1835. Today, guides in period costumes lead visitors through the house, restored in

215

detail to the condition in which Irving and his guests knew it.

Nearby, about a mile away, commerce is again the order of the day at **Lyndhurst**, the Gothic castle of railroad robber baron Jay Gould. Gould was not the first owner of this spectacular house when he moved in in 1880, but he expanded it in a gaudy style suitable to the era. Today open to the public and complete with its original furnishings, the house also hosts special shows, featuring antique cars, furnishings, and crafts, throughout the year.

Several miles north of Lyndhurst is **Philipsburg Manor**, the reconstruction of a house which was very important during the seventeenth century. Originally the manor house of a 52,000-acre estate owned by the prominent Philips family, the house left the family's possession after the Revolutionary War because

the head of the family had sided with the British. It was maintained as a private residence until 1969, when a local son – John D. Rockefeller Jr., whose family maintains a mansion in nearby **Pocantico Hills** – stepped in and bought it. The manor house, mill, dam, granary, wharf and mill pond were restored and opened to the public.

Over the **Tappan Zee Bridge**, on the other side of the river, is the Victorian village of **Nyack**, which has, over the years, attracted artists able to appreciate the quaint old houses and views of the river. Now it is popular with antique collectors, who comb the shops on **South Broadway** selling early American antiques. It is easy to make a brief detour over to Nyack, see the village, and then cross back to the east bank of the river to continue the Hudson Valley drive northward.

HUDSON HIGHLANDS

North of **Peekskill**, travelers enter the scenic stretch known as the **Hudson**

Above: The Hudson River just north of New York City. Right: West Point, a world-famous institution for military education.

Highlands, where craggy mountainsides contrast dramatically with spectacular views of the river. As marvelous as the scenery is, the region is famed more for its military importance. During the Revolutionary War, in 1776 and 1777, British soldiers and the American army skirmished all over this territory. Although the British often maintained the upper hand, they did suffer some decisive setbacks. One was in 1780, when Benedict Arnold, the commander of the American fort of West Point, was prevented from handing his fort over to a British general. Arnold has gone down in history as America's most famous traitor.

His former command post, meanwhile, has become renowned as the country's leading military academy. On the west side of the Hudson, north of **Bear Mountain State Park**, a somewhat over-developed site popular with day-tripping hikers, is the **United States Military Academy**, known by the name of the rocky promontory on which it stands: **West Point**. Cadets began to train here

for military service as early as 1794. During the Revolutionary War, it was the patriots' most strategic fortification; every ship that sailed up or down the Hudson passed by West Point's guns. Today, West Point is a college for the U.S. Army – students are admitted only at the nomination of a U.S. Congressman – and is open to the public. Some of the Academy's more renowned graduates include Presidents Ulysses S. Grant and Dwight D. Eisenhower, Generals Robert E. Lee, Patton and MacArthur.

Back on the east bank of the Hudson, **Route 9D** sticks close to the river as it winds its way north. At **Garrison-on-Hudson**, it passes **Boscobel**, a sumptuous palace built in 1806 and filled with priceless furniture and paintings. In fact, the mansion was not actually built here: its original location was 15 miles south, but it was moved when a veterans' hospital took over its land. North of Boscobel is the charming nineteenth-century village of **Cold Spring**, a town known, like Nyack, for its vintage houses, views of

the river, and antique shops filled with Americana. Be forewarned: if you arrive on a Sunday, you may not see the charm for the crowds. Since the town is a quick, easy train ride from Manhattan, many urban weekenders head straight for it.

North of Cold Spring is **Poughkeepsie**, a former industrial town known now primarily as the home of reputable **Vassar College**. A better place to visit in this area is **New Paltz**, on the other side of the river, accessible via the Mid-Hudson Bridge. New Paltz was settled by French Protestants forced by religious intolerance to leave Europe in the mid-1600s. They settled here in 1692; many of the stone houses they built still stand today. **Huguenot Street**, the oldest street in America, contains only its original houses, most of which contain original furnishings as well.

Above: Franklin Delano Roosevelt, Hyde Park's most renowned son. Right: Vanderbilt's pompous mansion overlooks the Hudson Valley.

Back on the east bank of the Hudson, north of Poughkeepsie, the mid-Hudson region begins. The scenery here is among the most beautiful you'll find in the area, with views of the Catskills and the Hudson opening out to the west. Such views must have been one of the enticements which led so many aristocratic families to erect elaborate mansions in this area. Many of these are open to the public and definitely worth a visit.

North on Route 9, the town of **Hyde Park** inherited its aristocratic-sounding name from Edward Hyde, Viscount Cornbury and English governor of New York, who settled here in 1741. Cornbury may have been the state's most visible cross-dresser since he seems to have had a confusing habit of wearing dresses in public. This fact, however, did not prevent city fathers from naming the town in his honor.

An impressive red-brick building on Route 9 in Hyde Park, once a Jesuit seminary, has become one of the greatest training centers for chefs in the world. Many graduates of the **Culinary Institute of America** (or CIA, as its students, rather confusingly, call it) have gone on to fine restaurants around the world. Others, to the locals' delight, have stayed in the area and opened their own restaurants. To sample the products of the students' labors, dine in one of the school's four restaurants: **American Bounty**, an elegant restaurant featuring American cuisine; **Escoffier**, a bastion of classical French; the **Caterina de Medici Dining Room**, with regional Italian food; or **St. Andrew's Café**.

Presidential Material

Continuing north, one comes upon a 16-mile-long stretch of riverfront estates. The first of these, **Springwood,** is also known as the **Franklin D. Roosevelt Historic Site**. FDR was born and raised in this elegant mansion, and returned to it

frequently during his adult years; it has been preserved in exactly the same condition it was in when the President died in 1945. Its luxurious furnishings give visitors a feel for the kind of country gentry of which the Roosevelts were undeniably a part; still, compared to the ostentation of many other estates, Springwood is relatively down-to-earth. Also on the grounds are a rose garden with the graves of the President, Mrs. Roosevelt and their beloved dog Fala, and the **Franklin D. Roosevelt Library Museum**, which displays Roosevelt family memorabilia and mementos of various visitors to the house, including King George, Queen Elizabeth and Winston Churchill.

As so often happens in families, there were definite tensions between FDR's mother Sara Delano Roosevelt and his wife Eleanor. Perhaps that is one of the reasons why Eleanor decided to relocate after the President's death. Her home **Val-Kill, the Eleanor Roosevelt National Historic Site**, is several miles away and is also open to the public.

Up the road from FDR's house is a mansion that makes his look like a shack. The **Vanderbilt National Historic Site** was the home of Frederick W. Vanderbilt, grandson of the Commodore, and it is nothing short of a palace with a breathtaking marble entry hall, Italian Renaissance furniture, Flemish tapestries and other luxurious trappings. Surrounding the house – which was the work of noted architect Stanford White – are formal Italian gardens and sloping lawns facing the Hudson, where families congregate on sunny weekend days. For another look at Stanford White's distinctive style, head north and west to the **Mills Mansion State Historic Site**, which was built in 1896 and furnished as opulently as the Vanderbilt palazzo. Weather, and a low maintenance fund, however, have taken their toll over the years, and this house has fallen to some degree into disrepair. Major renovations are currently being undertaken.

Up the road on Route 9 is **Rhinebeck**, one of the prettiest towns in the Hudson

Valley and one of the most historic, dating back to 1686. Citizens of the town played major roles in the early days of the Republic, and a number of wealthy industrialists settled nearby a century later. In the 1930s and 1940s, Franklin D. Roosevelt always closed his political campaigns on the front porch of the **Beekman Arms**, the oldest American inn still in operation, dating from 1766. Rhinebeck's two main streets, lined with charming, upscale boutiques, are magnets for shoppers. Some of the town's other streets are even more attractive, featuring impeccably maintained Victorian "gingerbread" houses. Another of its attractions is the **Old Rhinebeck Aerodrome**, a museum of vintage airplanes which puts on air shows of "old-timers." The truly fearless can go up for a ride in an open cockpit biplane.

Above: Rip Van Winkle got lost somewhere in these remote forests. Right: Jimi Hendrix also gave the place a name.

North of Rhinebeck is a handsome estate, **Montgomery Place**, named in honor of a Revolutionary War hero, General Richard Montgomery. This Federal style mansion, completed in 1805, is furnished in period detail.

Farther up the road, on **Route 9G**, is another historic house with its original furnishings, now open to the public. **Clermont State Historic Site** was the home of the distinguished Livingston family, landowners and statesmen, many of whom were named Robert. One of the Roberts was one of the five men who drafted the Declaration of Independence. His patriotic leanings almost brought about the downfall of the Livingstons: In 1777, British soldiers burned the house down. Family and servants escaped, however, and within a few years Clermont was rebuilt. Robert Livingston later served as United States Secretary of Foreign Affairs; and United States Minister to France, in which office he negotiated with Napoleon for the Louisiana Purchase. Also interested in scientific inventions, the Chancellor became involved with Robert Fulton, a partnership that resulted in the production of the first steamship, named *The Clermont*.

About ten miles north is another spectacular house, this one completely different from the others in the area. **Olana**, built in 1872, was the home of Frederic Church, one of the most famous painters of the Hudson River School. Its dramatic setting and architecture, as well as its colors, are clear indications that this was an artist's house. Olana's Moorish arches, towers and pinnacles, clearly reflect an interest in the East developed during Church's two-year sojourn in Persia. The subtle, varied blend of interior colors harmonize with Church's paintings, which are exhibited on the walls, and the furnishings are intricate and worth examining. Set high above the Hudson, the house commands one of the most mesmerizing views of the river.

Thomas Cole, the leading light of the Hudson Valley painters and a teacher of Church, had his studio and house in the nearby village of **Catskill**. Although they're nowhere near as opulent as Church's residence, both buildings can be visited by the public.

CATSKILLS

Originally, the Catskill region was surrounded with an aura of mystery and inspiration. The original dwellers, the Native Americans, believed that the Great Spirit dwelt within the mountains; and the **Catskills**, as a result, became the stuff of magic and legends. Several centuries later, they became the stuff of jokes, as the Catskills became known for the vast resorts in which middle-aged New York couples mingled with others like them in a variety of summer-camp-type activities, to be entertained by stand-up "Borscht Belt" comedians or singers. Those resorts are still around and they are even expanding somewhat after a dip in popularity in

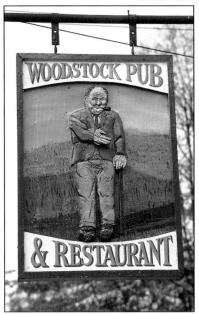

the 1970s. And to many people, they will forever symbolize the region. Others remember the mountains.

The gateway to the Catskills is **Kingston**, a city that was briefly the capital of New York during the Revolutionary War, and which was burned by the British in area skirmishes. Today, Kingston doesn't have much to offer in the way of sights, but it is a fine place to begin a Hudson River tour. **Hudson River Cruises** set sail from the **Rondout Landing** and spin up and down the river, taking in the fine views of the Hudson Valley mansions.

Approximately ten miles away is the artists' community of **Woodstock**, a name known around the world for its association with the famous music festival of 1969. In fact, however, the festival was not held in Woodstock, but in a farmer's field between the towns of Bethel and White Lake; the town of Woodstock pulled out at the last minute, forcing festival organizers to relocate the long-planned event. Woodstock got the publicity nonetheless. Given the historically

North of Shandaken is the small, charming Victorian town of **Lexington**. East is **Hunter Mountain**. The prime spot for skiing in the Catskills, this elevation can be unbelievably crowded in the winter. As the chair lift also operates during the summer, non-skiers prefer to visit then to enjoy the views.

The pretty country town of **Stone Ridge**, southwest of Kingston, is filled with 18th-century houses and natural beauty. Most people come here on their way to **High Falls** and the **DuPuy Canal House**, one of the best restaurants in the area. Further to the south, you'll find the famed resorts. Having originated as boarding houses in the late 19th and early 20th centuries, these blossomed after World War Two into their present massive dimensions, patronized by a predominantly Jewish clientele. Guests here are provided with every imaginable activity, from sports to macrame, as well as more food than they've ever seen before. Although some of the jokes about the compulsive excessiveness of these places may be deserved, they are certainly distinctive regional experiences. The most famous resort of all is The Concord in **Kiamesha Lake,** a self-contained city with 43 tennis courts, the biggest nightclub in the world (2900 seats), three golf courses, skiing, and a dining room serving gargantuan amounts of food.

Nearby in **Monticello** is **Kutsher's**, a more sedate, sports-oriented resort. They still have big portions and planned activities here but visitors do not feel as if they are in the middle of a Fellini movie, as they may at the Concord. Down the road, **The Pines** is a casual, family (meaning overrun by children) place. East of the others in **Ellenville**, the **Nevele** with its art deco decor is considerably more attractive and low-key. And for a completely different ethnic spin, **Villa Roma** in **Callicoon** caters mainly to Italians. The activities and amount of food served are, however, the same.

bohemian nature of the town, it's fitting that its name is associated with this happening. **Byrdcliffe**, an artists' colony founded here in 1902, became a flourishing center for painting, sculpting, weaving, carving and throwing pots. Today, you have to be quite a rich artist to be able to afford Woodstock, but its affluence has allowed the town to preserve its comfortable tidiness. Art galleries alternate with upscale shops and excellent restaurants. It's a great place to visit.

About 20 miles west of Woodstock is an area known locally as the **French Catskills**, which encompasses **Shandaken**, **Mount Tremper**, **Phoenicia**, and **Big Indian**. The name is indicative of its ethnic majority: in this region, French restaurants and inns prevail. Many of these establishments serve wonderful food: try **Auberge des 4 Saisons** in Shandaken, **La Duchesse Anne** in Mount Tremper and **Yvonne's** in Phoenicia.

Above: The Catskills offer climbers something modest to test their skills.

HUDSON VALLEY / CATSKILLS
Access

Amtrak train service extends up the Hudson region, with service to Kingston, Cold Spring and Rhinebeck from New York. There is also a bus service from New York. One of the treats of this region is to explore the side roads and wander at will, renting a car is the best alternative.

HUDSON VALLEY
Accommodation

LUXURY: **The Beekman Arms**, America's oldest inn, U.S. 9 Rhinebeck, New York 12572, Tel: 914/876-7077. **The Bird and Bottle Inn**, U.S. 9 Garrison, New York 10524, Tel: 914/424-3000. **Box Tree Inn**, romantic, with elegant restaurant, in northern Westchester, P.O. Box 477, Route 22 at 116, Purdys, New York 10578, Tel: 914/277-3677. **The Mansakenning Carriage House**, 29 Ackert Hook Road, Rhinebeck, New York 12572, Tel: 914/876-3500.

Mohonk Mountain House, at Lake Mohonk, New Paltz, New York 12561, Tel: 914/255-4500. **Plumbush**, country inn, Route 9D, Cold Spring, New York 10516, Tel: 914/265-3904.

MODERATE: **L'Hostellerie Bressane**, Routes 22 and 23, Hillsdale, New York 12529, Tel: 518/325-3412. **Hudson House Inn**, 2 Main Street, Cold Spring, New York 10516, Tel: 914/265-9355. **Hotel Thayer**, West Point, New York 10996, Tel: 914/446-4731. **Pig Hill Inn**, 73 Main Street, Cold Spring, New York 10516, Tel: 914/265-9247. **Whistle Wood**, 11 Pells Road, Rhinebeck, New York 12572, Tel: 914/876-6838. *BUDGET:* **The Inn at Blue Stores**, Box 99 Star Route, Hudson, New York 12534, Tel: 518/537-4277. **Rhinebeck Village Inn**, P.O. Box 491, Rhinebeck, New York 12572, Tel: 914/876-7000.

Restaurants

LUXURY: **American Bounty, Escoffier, Caterina de Medici Dining Room**, Culinary Institute of America, Route 9, Hyde Park, New York, Tel: 914/471-6608. **The Bird and Bottle Inn**, U.S. 9 Garrison, New York, Tel: 914/424-3000. **The 1776 Tavern at the Beekman Arms**, gourmet New American menu, historic inn, U.S. 9 Rhinebeck, New York, Tel: 914/876-7077. **Le Petit Bistro**, French bistro-food, 8 East Market Street, Rhinebeck, New York, Tel: 914/876-7400. **Plumbush**, continental cuisine, Route 9D, Cold Spring, New York, Tel: 914/265-3904. *MODERATE:* **St. Andrew's Café**, Culinary Institute of America, Route 9, Hyde Park, New York, Tel: 914/471-6608. *BUDGET:* **Foster's Coach House Tavern**, 22 Montgomery Street, Rhinebeck, Tel: 914/876-8052. **Old Fashion**, 83 South Broadway, Nyack, Tel: 914/358-8114. **La Parmigiana**, 37 Montgomery Street, Rhinebeck, Tel: 914/8763228.

Historic Sites

Boscobel, Route 9D, Garrison-on-Hudson, Tel: 914/265-3638. **Clermont State Historic Site**, Route 9G, Germantown, Tel: 518/537-4240. **Mills Mansion State Historic Site**, Old Post Road, Staatsburg, Tel: 914/889-4100. **Olana State Historic Site**, RDZ Hudson 12534, Tel: 914/889-4100. **Springwood**, U.S. 9 Hyde Park, Tel: 914/229-2501.

Val-Kill, the Eleanor Roosevelt National Historic Site, 249 Albany Post Road, Tel: 914/229-9115. **Vanderbilt Mansion National Historic Site**, U.S. 9, Hyde Park, Tel: 914/229-7770. **Historic Hudson Valley**, tour of vintage houses in the region, Tel: 914/631-8200. **Huguenot Historical Society**, New Paltz, Tel: 914/255-1889.

Tourist Information

Putnam County Tourism, 76 Main Street, Cold Spring, New York 10516, Tel: 914/265-3066. **Dutchess County Tourism**, P.O. Box 2025, Hyde Park, New York 12538, Tel: 914/229-0033.

CATSKILLS
Accommodation

MODERATE: **The Concord Resort Hotel**, Kiamesha Lake, New York 12751, Tel: 914/794-4000. **The Pines**, South Fallsburg, New York 12779, Tel: 914/434-6000. **Villa Roma**, Callicoon, New York 12723, Tel: 914/887-4880. *BUDGET:* **Mount Tremper Inn**, Mount Tremper, New York 12457, Tel: 914/688-5329. **Shandaken Inn**, New York 28, Shandaken, New York 12480, Tel: 914/688-5100. **Twin Gables**, 73 Tinker Street, Woodstock, New York 12498, Tel: 914/679-9479.

Restaurants

LUXURY: **DuPuy Canal House**, a restored 1797 landmark, gourmet cuisine, High Falls, New York 213, Tel: 914/687-7700. *MODERATE:* **Auberge des 4 Saisons**, Shandaken, New York 42, Tel: 914/688-2223. **La Duchesse Anne**, 4 Miller Road, Mount Tremper, New York 12457, Tel: 914/688-5260. *BUDGET:* **Yvonne's**, Phoenicia, New York 28, Tel: 914/688-7340.

Tours

Hudson River Cruises, Tel: 914/255-6515.

Tourist Information

Ulster County Public Information, P.O. Box 1800, Kingston, New York 12401, Tel: 914/331-9300 and **Sullivan County Chamber of Commerce**, 26 Landfield Avenue, Monticello, New York 12701, Tel: 914/794-2212.

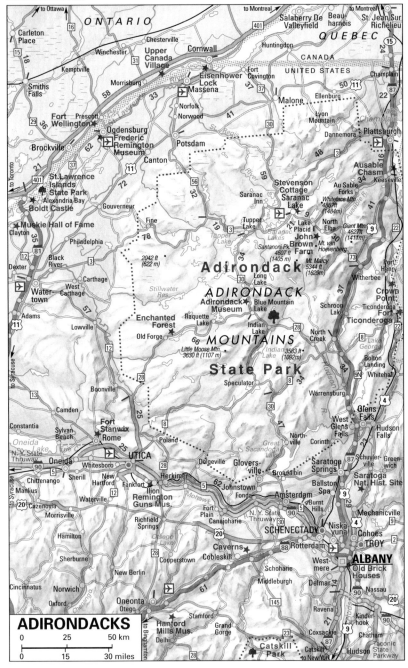

ADIRONDACKS

| 0 | 25 | 50 km |

| 0 | 15 | 30 miles |

CENTRAL NEW YORK STATE

ALBANY
ADIRONDACKS
THE THOUSAND ISLANDS

ALBANY

Contrary to what many out-of-towners believe, New York City is not the state capital of New York. That honor is reserved for **Albany**, a medium-sized city located smack in the middle of New York's eastern side. Although it has its cosmopolitan and cultural aspects, the city has retained much of the sedateness instilled by its founding fathers, the Merchants of the 16th and 17th centuries. With brick houses with stepped gables, or **The Pastures**, a group of restored houses from the 19th century: In the midst of a changing world, and even as it serves as seat of government for one of the largest states in America, Albany has kept a firm grip on its past.

Built between 1867 and 1897, the **State Capitol Building** reflects this deliberate, slow progress in the depiction of the process of evolution, – from microorganisms to mammals – which extends up the main staircase. A notable omission from the sequence is man; at the time the staircase was built, evolution was a hotly contested theory.

The evolution of the city is as clearly visible in its streets as are these images along the staircase, with a certain emphasis on the earlier stages of development. Today home to the **Albany County His-**torical Society**, chock-full of documents of the city's past growth, the **Ten Broeck Mansion** dates from 1764: yet another tangible reminder of days gone by.

But Albany is continuing to grow, and the modern side of things is also well-represented. At the city center, **Empire State Plaza** holds a group of strikingly modernistic buildings of marble and glass. And new heights were reached with the 44-story **State Office Building**, whose observation platform affords a view down the Hudson Valley to the south, the Catskills to the west, Vermont's Green Mountains to the northeast, and, to the north, the wide expanse of the Adirondacks.

ADIRONDACKS

Bordered by Albany to the south and the Canadian border to the north, the 12,000 square miles of woodland known as **Adirondack State Park** comprise the largest park outside of Alaska: six million wilderness acres. Located only a four-hour drive from New York City, the forest attracts approximately nine million visitors yearly yet remains remote, even primeval.

Before the coming of the white man, the Adirondack region was a vast, uninhabited area that the Indians called

225

Couchsachraga, meaning the great and dismal wilderness. Algonquin and Mohawk Indian tribes inhabiting the neighboring **Mohawk River** and **Champlain valleys** used the area solely as a hunting ground. The unfortunates who did settle in the region were referred to derogatorily as *Adirondacks*, an Indian word meaning bark-eaters – in other words, those who lived there were so primitive that they ate tree bark to survive.

The territory was spotted by Europeans in 1535 when Jacques Cartier and his party looked south from Mt. Royal (Montreal). The French explorer Samuel de Champlain is credited with being the first white man to visit the area, and he named the lake which now separates New York and Vermont after himself.

The North Country was of great strategic importance during the 1700s,

Above: The Capitol in Albany, where New York State politicking is done. Right: Most people visit the Adirondacks to feed their eyes on the Fall colors.

through the War of 1812. The first American victory of the Revolution was at Fort Ticonderoga in 1775; a year later, Benedict Arnold led a flotilla of ships in America's first naval battle on Lake Champlain. One of the Revolutionary War's decisive actions took place in the North Country in 1777 when colonial troops and their Indian allies stopped the advance of a British army sweeping south from Canada in two battles at Saratoga.

In the years before the American Civil War, the Adirondacks became the northernmost spur of the "Underground Railroad," the route for escaped slaves coming up from the south. In the town of **North Elba**, near **Lake Placid**, American abolitionist John Brown purchased a farm in 1849 to serve as a refugee community for escaped slaves who had little to fear in the remote woods. Today, **John Brown's Farm** is an historic site where visitors can relive the Adirondack life of the 1850s and actually see the spot where, as the song says, "John Brown's body lies a-moldering in the grave."

It was a Boston minister and lecturer, William H. H. Murray, who first popularized the Adirondacks as a vacation retreat. His 1869 book, *Adventures in the Wilderness*, started the rush to the North Country. "The air which you there inhale is such as can be found only in high mountainous regions, pure, rarified and bracing," he wrote, and his instructions on how to get there and what to bring along were admirably detailed. Soon the mountains became fashionable for city people who wanted to get away from it all. The advent of railroads meant that the region was suddenly accessible to people living in East Coast cities; and the Adirondacks became another playground for America's rich and famous.

Each season in the Adirondacks has special attractions. September and early October ignite mountains and hillsides into a blaze of brightly-colored foliage. Many people make annual autumn pilgrimages, planning carefully so that they arrive in the woods on the day of "peak" color. But the Adirondacks have special beauties all year round. The only time of year it's best to stay away is May and early June, known as "black fly season." The persistent insects have become resistant to all insect repellents and can be incredibly annoying.

Saratoga Springs

Saratoga Springs is the gateway to the North Country and was named *Saragthogue*, meaning "place of swift waters," by the Iroquois. The naturally effervescent water was valued for its curative powers. Saratoga was known as "America's Queen of Spas."

In 1842, the town's first gambling parlor was opened by Ben Schribner. Before long, gambling surpassed the baths as the biggest tourist attraction. In 1864 the first horse-racing course was opened and gambling reached new heights when financier Diamond Jim Brady, a railroad tycoon known for his lavish lifestyle, arrived in town with twenty-seven houseboys in tow and daily changes of jewelry.

Gambling ended in the 1950s, but the town had already seen its golden era tarnish; the Depression took its toll, and the massive hotels with dining rooms that could serve 1000 guests at a time had closed. During the last twenty years, the town has made a comeback, although there are still two distinct seasons in Saratoga: August, a popular month for retreat, and the rest of the year.

During the four-week season at the century-old track, the best thoroughbred horses in America come to race. Hotel prices triple and restaurant prices soar. But the baths and **Performing Arts Center** at **Saratoga State Park** are open throughout the summer. The Performing Arts Center is the summer home of the New York City Ballet and the Philadelphia Orchestra; theatrical performances and concerts feature popular entertainers

Above: Saratoga was conceived for the "well-healed," with spas and a race track. Right: Steamboats still plough the waters of Lake George.

as well. At the **National Museum of Racing**, aficionados can view video clips of famous races, as well as footage of the horses and jockeys who have been enshrined in the museum's Hall of Fame.

Lake George, a beautiful 32-mile long waterway, has been called the "Lake Como of America." A popular natural attraction in the region is **Ausable Chasm**, north of Lake George. First opened to tourists in 1870, this chasm has been cut by the **Ausable River** to a depth of several hundred feet deep and a length of more than a mile and a half. Following the walkways along the chasm brings visitors to the rapids at the end.

A visit to the **Adirondack Museum**, at **Blue Mountain Lake**, offers an insight into life in the Adirondacks during the later nineteenth and early twentieth centuries. Spread over 30 acres, the museum's twenty buildings are filled with displays depicting history and art, including a collection of boats used in the region, from sail canoes to steamboats to the famous Adirondack guide boat.

Lake Placid

Another well-known local site, the town of Lake Placid, hosted the Winter Olympic games in 1932 and again in 1980. The community serves as an official year-round Olympic training center. At nearby **Mount Van Hoevenberg** visitors may ski the same cross-country trails used in the Winter Games. **Whiteface Mountain** is the highest skiing peak in the east and the only Adirondack "high peak" accessible by car. The American Legion felt that one peak should be accessible by car and proposed to dedicate the access road to New York's war dead. Voters upheld the project in a statewide referendum, and President Franklin D. Roosevelt, crippled by polio, dedicated the highway. Standing atop the mountain, he said, "Many persons, due to age or disability, cannot indulge in the luxury of camping or climbing. For millions of people who have not got the facilities for walking up a mountain, we have now got the means for their coming up here on four wheels."

Mount Marcy is probably the most celebrated of the Adirondack's 42 peaks above 4000 feet. It is also known by an Indian name, as Mount *Tahawus*, the "cloud splitter." Near its peak is the source of the Hudson River at **Lake Tear-of-the-Clouds.**

During the late 1800s, influential American families such as the Morgans, Huntingtons, Rockefellers and Vanderbilts built the so-called "Great Camps." These part-time residents did not come to the country to rough it. It was common for them to ferry entire households from New York or Boston to summer in rustic luxury, often reserving several railroad coaches to transport their entourages to the mountains in June, then back to the city in September.

On arriving by private railroad car, estate owners and their guests would be met by servants busily preparing picnic

lunches of poached salmon, caviar and champagne.

Several of the "camps" are today open to the public. Camp Sagamore, now the **Sagamore Institute**, was built by Alfred Vanderbilt in 1897, near **Raquette Lake**. **Topridge**, near Saranac Lake, was the summer home of breakfast food heiress Marjorie Merriweather Post. **The Point**, on **Upper Saranac Lake**, built by William Avery Rockefeller, is today an exclusive inn. The owners give guests genuine Great-Camp ambience; rates are more than $400 a night.

Saranac Lake has been internationally known as a center for curing tuberculosis since Dr. Edward L. Trudeau established a sanitarium in 1885. Author Robert Louis Stevenson came to Saranac Lake during the winter of 1887-8 in a futile attempt to regain his health. Although he once referred to the Adirondacks as "little Switzerland," he did not really enjoy his visit. Describing winter in the region, he wrote, "The mercury in the thermometer curls into the bulb like a

hibernating bear." The cottage where he stayed is now open to the public.

Saranac Lake is also the canoe capital of the Adirondacks from which the **Fulton Chain of Lakes,** filtering into the **St. Lawrence River,** provides a large network of waterways for canoeing, boating, fishing and camping. Indians called the St. Lawrence "the river without end," but French explorer Jacques Cartier renamed it after he first saw it on the saint's birthday. A feat of modern engineering, the huge **St. Lawrence Seaway** opened in 1959, transforming a 602-foot rise between the mouth of the St. Lawrence and the Great Lakes into a navigable trade artery for seagoing ships.

THE THOUSAND ISLANDS

The designation **Thousand Islands** for the region adjoining the Adirondacks is actually a misnomer: it's comprised of

Above: Saddling up for a horseback ride through the forests of the Adirondacks.

more than 1800 islands. Although this American-Canadian border region is calm today, there have been bloody battles in the area, especially during the War of 1812. Today, two-thirds of the islands are Canadian, and bridges make border crossings easy. The area has first-rate fishing. For anglers, the region's most prized fish is the muskellunge, also known as the "muskie." There's even a **Muskie Hall of Fame** in **Clayton**.

One of the most popular ways to experience the spirit of the "Thousand Islands" is to travel through it by boat. Most cruise boats pass **Boldt Castle**, built by German immigrant George C. Boldt in honor of his beloved wife. After arriving in New York he became a successful hotelier who numbered the Waldorf-Astoria among his possessions. He decided to build a six-story, 150-room castle in the Thousand Islands, and the shoreline was dredged to form a heart so he could call his property **Heart Island**. He spent more than $2.5 million before his wife's death in 1904; heart-sick, he left the island, never to return. The partially-completed castle is accessible.

Ogdensburg, founded in 1749, is one of the oldest settlements in upstate New York. It is best known as the childhood home of Western artist Frederic Remington. The town has preserved the home as the **Frederic Remington Museum**, featuring the largest collection of the artist's work, including 14 bronzes, 140 watercolors, 70 oils and a large number of his pen and ink sketches.

When George Meegan, an Englishman who made a seven-year journey on foot throughout America, wrote in his account that "Upstate New York may be America's best-kept secret," he was referring to the North Country of the Adirondacks and the Thousand Islands. Although it attracts millions of visitors each year, the region still maintains the peacefulness that first attracted America's elite more than 100 years ago.

ADIRONDACKS
Access / Local Transportation

AIR: Principal international gateways are New York City (airports are approximately 4 hours south by car from Saratoga Springs) and Montreal (1,5 hours north of Plattsburg).

BUS / RAIL: Greyhound and Adirondack Trailways provide a regional and long-distance bus service. More than a dozen charter operators offer sightseeing tours in summer, fall and winter. Amtrak's Adirondack operates a daily train service between New York and Montreal with stops throughout the North Country.

CAR: Driving in the North Country and Thousand Island region, the main route is the Northway, linking Albany and Montreal. Interstate-81, further to the west, links Syracuse, Watertown and Canada via the Thousand Islands International Bridge.

Accommodation / Restaurants

Many finer accommodations in the Adirondacks are open only during the summer season rates are generally highest in the North Country during the summer. Rates for double accommodation fall into two categories, luxury: $60 and over (sometimes far over), moderate: $40 to $60.

LUXURY: **Adelphi Hotel**, 365 Broadway, Saratoga Springs, Tel: 518/587-4688, renovated Victorian hotel dating to 1877, downtown location, one block from Congress Park. **Adirondack Inn**, 217 Main Street, Lake Placid, Tel: 518/523-2424. Motor inn on Mirror Lake, indoor and outdoor pools, tennis, skiing.

Balsam House Inn and Restaurant, Friends Lake, Atateka Drive, Chestertown, Tel: 518/494-2828, elegantly restored inn overlooking Friends Lake, the restaurant is a regional favorite for French country cuisine.

Canoe Island Lodge, Lake Shore Drive South, Diamond Point, Tel: 518/668-5592. Closed mid-October to mid-May. Main lodge and cottages along Lake George, water sports, tennis. **Gideon Putnam Hotel and Conference Center**, Saratoga State Park, Saratoga Springs, Tel: 518/584-3000, a Victorian grand dame situated on the grounds of Saratoga State Park, within walking distance of Saratoga's Performing Arts Center and the mineral baths.

Hidden Valley Mountainside Resort, Hidden Valley Rd., RR 2, Lake Luzerna, Tel: 518/696-2431, sports, indoor and outdoor pool, beach. Open in winter for skiing.

Lake Placid Manor, Whiteface Inn Road, Lake Placid, Tel: 518/523- 2573. Charming European-style inn with views of Lake Placid and Whiteface Mountain, excellent restaurant.

Lake Placid Hilton, 1 Mirror Lake Drive, Lake Placid, Tel: 518/523-4411, one of the area's biggest hotels, 178 rooms with lake or mountain views, indoor and outdoor pools, fine restaurant. **The Point**, Star Road, Upper Saranac Lake, Tel: 518/891-5674, ultra-luxurious inn costing more than $400 a night per couple. The one-time home of William Avery Rockefeller is operated in the manner of a private home, with eleven lavishly decorated rooms, formal dress for dinner is required, all meals included.

The Sagamore, Lake George, Bolton Landing, 12814, Tel: 518/6449400. A sprawling clapboard inn on a private island, listed on the National Register of Historic Places, lovely formal gardens, original 1920s main building with scattered cottage complexes. Excellent restaurants, marina, health club, indoor and outdoor tennis. Rates are around $250 nightly per person, including breakfast and dinner.

MODERATE: **The Hedges**, Route 28, Blue Mountain Lake, Tel: 518/352-7325, large, rustic Victorian inn with shore cottages, tennis, rental boats and canoes. **Hemlock Hall**, Hemlock Hall Road, Blue Mountain Lake, Tel: 518/352-7706, a main lodge and additional modern cottages set on a wooded shore, good restaurant, tennis, docks with rental boats and canoes.

Hotel Saranac of Paul Smith's College, 101 Main Street, Saranac Lake, Tel: 518/891-2200, operated by college students who work very hard to please, highly regarded restaurant with a broad menu and amenable prices.

BED AND BREAKFAST: Bed and Breakfast Inns have been elevated to a fine art in this region. Information and reservations: **North Country Bed and Breakfast Reservation Service**, Box 238, Lake Placid, Tel: 518 523-9474.

Tourist Information

The **I Love New York Office** in Lake Placid, 90 Main Street, Tel: 518/523-2412, gives information for the North Country, except Saratoga.

Saratoga area information: **Greater Saratoga Chamber of Commerce**, 494 Broadway, Saratoga Springs, Tel: 518/584-3255.

Thousand Islands information: **Thousand Islands International Council**, Box 400, Collins Landing, Alexandria Bay, NY, Tel: 315/482-2520 for collect calls.

Additional information can be obtained from the **Central Adirondack Association**, Tourism Information Center, Old Forge, Tel: 315/369-6983. New York State's **Department of Environmental Conservation**, Albany, New York 12223, publishes excellent trail guides and maps to the Adirondack State Park.

UPSTATE NEW YORK

FINGER LAKES

BUFFALO

NIAGARA FALLS

CHAUTAUQUA COUNTY

FINGER LAKES

The Finger Lakes Region encompasses the center of the state, midway between New York City and Niagara Falls, anchored on the west by Rochester and on the east by **Syracuse**. The area attracts more than seven million visitors a year, although it rarely seems crowded.

It has special appeal for anglers, hunters, boaters, sailors, campers and hikers. Nature is generous with lakes, gorges and waterfalls, and for the weary traveler there are elegant castles and inns, fine wines and dining, first-rate museums, concerts and art galleries.

Wine growing and vineyards are another of the region's many offerings. Not only did retreating glaciers create the Finger Lakes, but they also created ideal conditions for grapes by depositing a shallow layer of topsoil on sloping shale beds. The deep lakes also provide protection from the climate by moderating temperatures along their shores.

It was Iroquois territory once upon a time as the local names still suggest: **Cayuga**, **Canandaigua**, **Keuka**, **Hemlock**, **Honeoye**, **Otisco**, **Owasco**, **Canadice**, **Conesus**, **Skaneateles** and **Seneca**.

Left: Upstate New York and the Finger Lakes provide for rest and relaxation.

Twenty state parks have been arranged in the area. This is a land of dreamers, who founded a religion, invented the camera, started the Woman's Rights Movement, were pioneers in motion pictures and created great schools and universities. Mark Twain wrote most of his classics, including *The Adventures of Huckleberry Finn,* at his summer home in **Elmira**. He particularly loved the **Chemung Valley** area, which he called "the garden of Eden." His study is open to visitors on the campus of **Elmira College**. Elmira is also the "soaring" capital of America and its **National Soaring Museum** has the country's largest display of classic and contemporary motorless sailplanes. Early flyer Glenn H. Curtiss also put **Hammondsport** on the aviation map. In 1908 his *June Bug* flew just under a mile, the longest distance of a pre-announced flight.

Seneca Falls is the home of the American Women's Rights movement and the **National Women's Hall of Fame** is on the site of the first Women's Rights Convention, held in 1848. **Palmyra** was the early home of Joseph Smith, who founded the Mormon Church. Every summer, in late July, Smith and his vision are remembered with the Hill Cumorah Pageant, the oldest religious pageant in the United States.

Corning, to the west of Elmira is famous as the home of **Corning Glass Works** and its Steuben Glass division, which produces fine works of art. Steuben masterpieces have been presented as gifts to foreign heads of state and are in museums around the world. The **Corning Museum of Glass** houses the world's foremost collection of glass. The **Rockwell Museum** boasts the largest collection of American Frontier art east of the Mississippi, with works by Remington, Bierstadt, Russell, Catlin and others. The city's downtown **Market Street** has been restored in its nineteenth century glory and is listed on the National Register of Historic Places.

North is the town of **Watkins Glen** on the southern tip of Seneca Lake. The walled canyon that first opened in 1863 contains nineteen waterfalls in the course of the water's 1.5 mile journey. The name Watkins Glen is also familiar to many as the site of a motor raceway that formerly hosted the Grand Prix. It is still a major racetrack, with racing events going on throughout the summer.

The lakes and the quaint villages around them are wonderful to "browse" through, but one natural gem should not be missed, namely **Letchworth State Park** to the west. Its deep gorge with three magnificent waterfalls has been aptly dubbed the "Grand Canyon of the East." The **Genesee Valley**, a little to the north of the park, was called "beautiful valley" by Seneca Indians.

Local life in the 19th century is documented live at the **Genesee Country Museum** at **Mumford**. A village has been created with houses transported from all over the region. It is "inhabited" by people in period costumes who carry out 19th-century tasks.

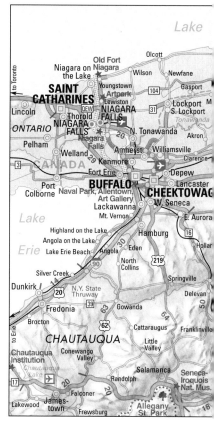

Rochester

New York's third largest city is **Rochester**, home of Eastman Kodak and

Bausch and Lomb. **The International Museum of Photography**, at the **George Eastman House**, has the world's largest collection of photographic art and technology. At her death in 1969, Margaret Woodbury Strong was the largest single Kodak shareholder and she contributed her lifetime collection to a museum.

The city was once known as "Flower City" and **Highland Park** is home to the world's largest collection of very fragrant lilacs. The ten-day Lilac Festival around mid-May is worth seeing.

BUFFALO

Buffalo, the state's second largest city, was once known as a flour-milling capital

NIAGARA -
FINGER LAKES

0   15   30 km

0   15 miles

and nicknamed the "Queen of the Great Lakes." It later got a bad reputation for cold weather and general, post-industrial drabness. The weather cannot be changed, but the city has undergone a process of rejuvenation, including renovation of the downtown area. Free shuttle service on the Metro line takes pedestrians to the car-free inner city.

Spiritually, Buffalo is perhaps most proud of its major league sports teams. During the football season the whole city is usually caught up in football fever. It is a city of taverns, as well as churches, a place with strong and loyal ethnic traditions. It has the largest St. Patrick's Day parade west of New York City, as well as the biggest Pulaski Day Parade, a cele-

bration of Polish heritage, east of Chicago. The city is home to the country's only inland naval park, located at the foot of downtown Main Street on the Buffalo River. The **Naval and Servicemen's Park** features the destroyer **USS Sullivans**, named in honor of the five Sullivan brothers, who died on the same ship during a World War Two naval battle. Their deaths shocked the nation and a movie was later made about the incident.

North of downtown Buffalo is **Allentown**, an area rich in 19th-century homes, boutiques, restaurants and art galleries. The Allentown Art Show, held the second weekend in June, is the country's largest outdoor art show, held in one of the nation's largest historic preservation dis-

tricts. Novelist F. Scott Fitzgerald lived here as a child and Mark Twain lived in the area for two years when he served as a newspaper editor on the *Buffalo Express*. The arts are further celebrated at the world renowned **Albright-Knox Art Gallery** north of Allentown. It is known for its superlative collection of contemporary art as well as a comprehensive general collection.

NIAGARA FALLS

It was a Frenchman, Father Louis Hennepin, who was the first tourist to witness the wonders of mighty **Niagara Falls** north of Buffalo on the Niagara River. He served as a missionary under 17th-century French explorer Robert LaSalle. In his eyewitness account, which was widely read across Europe, he revealed to the world for the first time the "incredible Cataract or Waterfall, which has no equal.

Above: Niagara Falls, where honeymooners contemplate their present and future.

Betwixt the Lake Ontario and Erie, there is a vast and prodigious Cadence of Water the Universe does not afford its Parallel.The Waters which fall from this horrible Precipice do foam and boyl after the most hideous manner imaginable, making an outrageous Noise, more terrible than that of Thunder."

Although Hennepin overestimated the height of the Falls when he first viewed it on a cold December day in 1678, Niagara is impressive. The Falls border the United States and Canada as part of the longest unprotected border in the world. The **American** and **Bridal Veil Falls** are in the United States and the **Horseshoe Falls** are on the Canadian side. Bridges make access across the border easy. The Falls are the birthplace of alternating current and drive the largest hydroelectric plant in the Western World. The water that flows over them drains four of the Great Lakes – Superior, Michigan, Huron and Erie – into the fifth, Lake Ontario, at a rate of 700,000 gallons a second during the summer.

Over ten million visitors a year flock here. They line the promenade opposite the Falls, gape from the deck of boats below, peer out from the caves behind, ogle from a helicopter above – drinking in the vista from every conceivable angle. During the evening colored lights add a magical quality to the scene.

The Falls are definitely romantic and have been a honeymoon destination since 1803 when the first recorded honeymooners arrived. They were newlyweds from Baltimore, Jerome Bonaparte, brother of the French Emperor Napoleon, and his bride, daughter of a wealthy merchant, on a grand tour of the northeast. By 1846, Niagara Falls was a certified tourist attraction and rave reviews began to bring out the daredevils.

In 1859, the great French tightrope-walker Blondin walked across the **Niagara Gorge**, from the American to the Canadian side on a three-inch-thick rope. On his shoulders was his terrified manager and on both shores stood some 100,000 spectators, including the future King Edward VII of England.

Others have challenged the Falls in boats, rubber balls and barrels, many perishing in the attempt. Although the practice has since been outlawed, every now and then a stuntman evades security and tries to go over the Falls and live to tell the tale. Among the profusion of tourist-related shops and things-to-do that cram the city's downtown area, there is even an attraction, called Ride Niagara, designed to replicate the sensation of going over the Falls.

Short of a barrel ride over the Falls, the **Maid of the Mist** boat ride offers the most intense experience of the Falls. In operation more or less continually since 1846, the *Maid* has become as much a symbol of Niagara as the Falls themselves. Just about every visiting celebrity has donned a rubber raincoat and felt the spray on the deck. U.S. President Theodore Roosevelt, one of those cele-

brities and no shrinking violet when it came to pushing the physical to the limit, called the ride "the only way to fully realize the grandeur of the Great Falls of Niagara." One of the three *Maid* boats can be boarded from either the American or Canadian side. The captain expertly guides the boat past the base of the American and Bridal Veil Falls, and almost into the thunderous deluge of the Horseshoe Falls. Spray stings faces and hands and blurs vision. The boat rocks as the engines fight for control in the current. There is a moment on the trip, just a moment, when the world seems to be coming to a watery end. Of course, it is all perfectly safe.

Niagara Falls had its origins some 12,000 years ago, seven miles north of its present location in what is now the village of **Lewiston**, New York. In 1974, **Artpark** was opened in the village on 200 acres overlooking the river. It is the only state park in the United States devoted to the visual and performing arts. A most historic site, this is where Seneca Indians, French, British and Americans fought for control of the strategically important **Niagara River**.

The 35-mile-long river empties into **Lake Ontario** at **Youngstown**, New York. **Old Fort Niagara** has commanded a view of this juncture since 1726. The fort's original stone buildings have been preserved as they were before the American Revolution. On a clear day, not necessarily something that can be counted on at any time of year, Toronto, Canada's biggest city, is visible 30 miles across the lake.

CHAUTAUQUA COUNTY

The last corner of New York State most visitors see is south of Buffalo. **Chautauqua County**, which follows the shores of Lake Erie to the border of Pennsylvania, is a region of rolling hills, vineyards, wineries, Indian reservations, fish-

filled lakes and the area's oldest cultural asset, the world famous **Chautauqua Institution**. It was on the shores of **Chautauqua Lake** in 1874 that John Heyl Vincent, a Methodist minister, and industrialist Lewis Miller began a training center for Sunday school teachers. The tents pitched by the first visitors have given way to comfortable Victorian buildings. The grand dame of them all is the **Athenaeum Hotel**, built in 1881 and wired for electricity by Lewis Miller's son-in-law, Thomas Alva Edison. At one time the Athenaeum was the largest wood frame building in the country. The institution offers an unusual mix of arts, education, religion and recreation during the nine-week summer season. President Theodore Roosevelt called it "the most American place in America." Only at Chautauqua can a visitor fish for record-breaking fish in the morning, attend a lec-

Above: Indian life in New York is generally recalled in the place names and in statues only.

ture by a major speaker, play a round of golf, study music or a foreign language before dinner, and after dinner enjoy a concert in the open-air amphitheater or an opera in **Norton Memorial Hall**. The *genius loci* seems established, for Chautauqua is also home to **Lily Dale**, the world center of the Universal Religion of Modern Spiritualism.

Traveling west from Chautauqua is the **Conewango Valley**, home of a thriving but little-known Amish community, which has not yet been discovered by tour buses and massive invasions of tourists. The people are determined to maintain their old-world lifestyles. They do, however, sell delicious baked goods and hand-made furniture from their homes and at auctions.

Continuing east, on the border of **Allegany State Park**, is **Salamanca**, the only city in the world located on an Indian reservation. The Indian heritage here is explored more carefully at the **Seneca-Iroquois National Museum**, off Route 17, on the reservation.

FINGER LAKES / BUFFALO NIAGARA / CHAUTAUQUA
Access

AIR: There are airports in Rochester and Syracuse for Finger Lakes and in Jamestown for Chautauqua. Greater Buffalo International Airport serves the Buffalo/Niagara Falls area.
RAIL / BUS: **Amtrak** has train stations in Buffalo, Niagara, Rochester and Syracuse. Buses and coaches serve the area, but a rental car is the most flexible mode of transportation for those wishing to explore the area.

FINGER LAKES
Accommodation / Restaurants

LUXURY: **Belhurst Castle**, Box 609, Geneva, Tel: 315/781-0201, elegant twelve-room inn, overlooking Seneca Lake.
Corning Hilton Inn, Denison Parkway East, Corning, Tel: 607/962-5000.
Geneva-on-the-Lake, 1001 Lochland Road, Geneva, Tel: 315/789-7190, historic building overlooking Seneca Lake, suites, gardens, pool.
Holiday Inn-Genesee Plaza, 120 Main Street, Rochester, Tel: 716/546-6400, large, luxurious.
Rose Inn, Auburn Road, Ithaca, Tel: 607/533-4202, small country inn, gourmet dinners.
Sheraton Canandaigua Inn, 770 South Main Street, Canandaigua, Tel: 716/394-7800, busy resort, lakefront location.
Sherwood Inn, 26 West Genesee Street, Skaneateles, Tel: 315/685-3405, in operation since 1807, on Skaneateles Lake, fine food.
MODERATE: **Aurora Inn**, Main Street, Aurora, Tel: 315/364-8842, a 158-year old landmark on Cayuga Lake. **Glen Iris Inn**, Letchworth State Park, Castile, Tel: 716/593-2622, former home of philanthropist William Pryor Letchworth who donated the land for Letchworth State Park.
BED AND BREAKFAST: Reservation through **Cherry Valley Ventures**, Tel: 315/677-9723. Prices $40 to $50 for a double room.
Tourist Information
Finger Lakes Association, 309 Lake St., Penn Yan, Tel: 315/536-7488 or 800/KIT-4-FUN.

BUFFALO / NIAGARA
Accommodation / Restaurants

Accommodation ranges from luxury at $70 and over for a double, to moderate at $50 to $70.
LUXURY: **Buffalo Hilton at the Waterfront**, Church and Terrace Streets, Buffalo, Tel: 716/845-5100, the best rooms overlook the Niagara River and Lake Erie, health club, pool, tennis, squash, jogging. **The Cloister**, 472 Delaware Avenue, Tel: 716/886-0070, Buffalo's best-

known restaurant in the former home of Mark Twain. **Holiday Inn Downtown at the Falls**, 114 Buffalo Street, Niagara Falls, Tel: 716/285-2521, a short walk to the American Falls, indoor pool, family plan. **Days Inn Falls View**, 201 Rainbow Boulevard, Niagara Falls, Tel: 716/285-9321, recently renovated landmark, top floor rooms view the Upper Rapids, fine restaurant.
Hyatt Regency Buffalo, 2 Fountain Plaza, Buffalo, Tel: 716/856-1234, converted office building with a three-story glass atrium. Individually decorated rooms with original works of art, several fine restaurants, pool, sauna, health club.
Niagara Hilton, Third Street and Mall, Niagara Falls, Tel: 716/285-3361, some rooms view the falls, indoor pool and health club, adjoining the tropical Wintergarden.
BED AND BREAKFAST: Reservations for the Niagara Falls/Buffalo area: **Rainbow Hospitality**, 9348 Hennepin Avenue, Niagara Falls, Tel: 716//283-4784. Accommodation varies from historic homes near the falls and an elegant Victorian mansion to a working farm outside of the city. Prices average $40-$45 for two.
Tourist Information
Greater Buffalo Chamber of Commerce, 107 Delaware Avenue, Buffalo, Tel: 716/852-7100.
Niagara Falls Convention and Visitors Bureau, 345 Third Street, Niagara Falls, Tel: 716/278-8010.

CHAUTAUQUA
Accommodation / Restaurants

LUXURY: **Hotel Athenaeum**, Chautauqua Institution, Chautauqua, Tel: 800/862-1881, this Grand Dame, built in 1881, is listed as a National Historic Site. American plan only, breakfast, lunch and dinner included.
MODERATE: **Hotel Lenhart**, Route 17, Bemus Point, Tel: 716/386-2715, old-fashioned, 100-year-old lake-front hotel, breakfast and dinner plan mandatory in summer. **Webb's Resort and Marina**, Route 394, Mayville, Tel: 716/753-2161, marina, bowling alleys and a goat-milk fudge factory with tours and tastings. **The White Inn**, 52 East Main Street, Fredonia, Tel: 716/672-2103, renovated historic hotel in the heart of wine country, highly regarded restaurant.
BED AND BREAKFAST: The **Bed and Breakfast Association of Western New York**, Box 1059, Sinclairville, 14782, handles information and reservations for the Chautauqua area.
Tourist Information
Chautauqua County Vacationlands Association, 2 North Erie Street, Mayville, Tel: 716/753-4303.

Nelles Maps ...the maps that get you going.

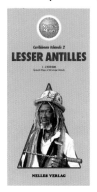

MEXICO

Caribbean Islands 1
BERMUDA, BAHAMAS
GREATER ANTILLES

Caribbean Islands 2
LESSER ANTILLES

HAWAIIAN ISLANDS

NELLES VERLAG

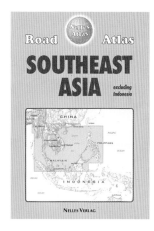

Road Atlas
INDONESIA

NELLES VERLAG

Road Atlas
SOUTHEAST ASIA excluding Indonesia

NELLES VERLAG

Nelles Maps

- Afghanistan
- Australia
- Bangkok
- Burma
- Caribbean Islands 1/
  Bermuda, Bahamas,
  Greater Antilles
- Caribbean Islands 2/
  Lesser Antilles
- China 1/
  North-Eastern China
- China 2/
  Northern China
- China 3/
  Central China
- China 4/
  Southern China
- Crete
- Egypt
- Hawaiian Islands
- Hawaiian Islands 1/ Kauai
- Hawaiian Islands 2/
  Honolulu, Oahu

- Hawaiian Islands 3/
  Maui, Molokai, Lanai
- Hawaiian Islands 4/ Hawaii
- Himalaya
- Hong Kong
- Indian Subcontinent
- India 1/ Northern India
- India 2/ Western India
- India 3/ Eastern India
- India 4/ Southern India
- India 5/ North-Eastern India
- Indonesia
- Indonesia 1/ Sumatra
- Indonesia 2/
  Java + Nusa Tenggara
- Indonesia 3/ Bali
- Indonesia 4/ Kalimantan
- Indonesia 5/ Java + Bali
- Indonesia 6/ Sulawesi

- Indonesia 7/
  Irian Jaya + Maluku
- Jakarta
- Japan
- Kenya
- Korea
- Malaysia
- West Malaysia
- Manila
- Mexico
- Nepal
- New Zealand
- Pakistan
- Philippines
- Singapore
- South East Asia
- Sri Lanka
- Taiwan
- Thailand
- Vietnam, Laos
  Cambodia

GUIDELINES

PREPARATIONS

Climate and Travel Times

New York is best in Spring and Fall when the temperatures are moderate with warm days (bring a rain coat and an umbrella) and cool evenings. During the summer months, the warm weather is often punctuated by unpleasantly hot and damp spells that sometimes erupt into violent storms. July and August are the hottest months with average temperatures hovering around the 25 C° mark. In Winter, which generally only really gets going after New Year, icy winds tend to sweep down New York's canyon-like avenues.

Clothing

New York is fairly unconventional when it comes to leisure-time clothing. However, if on business or patronizing some midtown shops and restaurants, remember that Americans still remain rather formal. A man without a jacket and tie will not get beyond the doorman.

If traveling in Spring or Fall, bring some warm clothing just in case, rain gear and some light to medium clothing. Warm clothing is imperative for winter, whereby New Yorkers tend to overheat their houses, hotels, restaurants and businesses. The opposite is true during the hot summer months, when it is wise to keep a light sweater handy even on the most broiling days: Air-conditioners always seem to be running full blast. Don't be surprised if your nose keeps running throughout your sojourn.

If planning to travel upstate, consider the possibility of hiking or skiing in the Adirondacks, depending on the season, and bring the appropriate clothing.

Customs

Visitors to the USA are allowed to import duty-free: 300 cigarettes, 50 cigars and one quart (0,946 liter) of wine or other alcoholic beverages. All produce, plant materials and wild animals are subject to border inspection by the State Department of Food and Agriculture. Fresh fruits and meats are forbidden entry. Pets must have vaccinations against rabies at least one year prior to entry.

Visa

The recently enacted Visa Waiver Pilot Program, meaning that a visa is no longer necessary, covers the following countries: Andorra, Austria, Denmark, Belgium, Finland, France, Germany, Great Britain, Italy, Japan, Liechtenstein, Luxemburg, Monaco, New Zealand, Norway, The Netherlands, San Marino, Spain, Sweden, Switzerland. You will still need a return ticket to demonstrate your good intentions. For safety's sake, check regulations with the American embassy or consulate nearest you.

ARRIVING AND DEPARTING

As an early warning, if you are arriving from a foreign country and intend to rent a car at the airport, make sure you have some American currency for paying tolls on bridges (US$ 2,50) or thruways. If you have a flight whose departure time coincides with New York City rush hours and you intend to drive out to the airport in question, give yourself ample time!

Arriving by Air

New York City is very accessible, having three airports: Most transatlantic flights land in and take off from the John F. Kennedy International Airport (often referred to as JFK or Kennedy), which lies in southeastern Queens about an hour's drive from central Manhattan; Tel: (718) 656-4520.

LaGuardia in northern Queens is used for inland flights, the Washington and Boston shuttles and private aircraft, Tel: (718) 476-5000.

The third airport is Newark in New Jersey, which boasts a new international terminal, Tel: (201) 961-2000. Most major airlines and a host of lesser ones fly to one of the three airports.

Getting to Manhattan should not be a problem. A toll-free number offers information on all three airports: Tel: (800)-247-7433. A taxi (officially licensed yellow cabs) to midtown Manhattan costs around US$ 35,00 from JFK, US$ 25,00 from LaGuardia. The quickest way to reach Manhattan is a helicopter ride to the 34th street heliport Tel: (800) 645-3494 for reservations). It costs around US$ 61,00. Shared minibuses operate from 7 am to 11 pm and cost around US$ 15,00 and service any location. The JFK Carey Airport Express coach, Tel: (718) 632-0509 costs around US$ 11,00 and services the bus terminals and several major hotels. The cheapest way of getting to the city is by public bus (US$ 1,25) or by catching the free airport shuttle to the Howard Beach/JFK subway station and taking either the A train (US$ 1,25 exact change required!), which runs all the way to Washington Heights, or the JFK express train, which requires a small surcharge, but is a good deal faster and only runs until 57th Street.

Options from LaGuardia include the Carey Airport Express shuttle, which connects the airport with several points in Manhattan (costs US$ 9,00, Tel: (718) 632-0509). Shared minibuses cost around US$ 11,00 and operate from 7 am to 11 pm. The Q33 bus costs US$ 1,25 and carries you to the subway (a further US$ 1,25) where you can catch the 7th, Brooklyn-Queens Crosstown, N, F or E trains. The Q48 runs to the 7th line and to the Long Island Railroad terminal.

Finally, if landing or departing from Newark, call the New Jersey Transit at Tel: (201) 460-8444 or (800) 772-2222 for information about train and bus service to Manhattan, to park-and-ride locations or to the PATH train terminal in Hoboken. A US$ 7,00 ride on the Olympia Trails Airport Express takes you to the World Trade Center, Penn Station or Grand Central Station. Other ways are shared minibus, Tel: (212)757-6840, Tel: (212) 757-6840), or shared limousine Tel: (201) 242-5012 for about US$ 16,00 and US$ 20,00 respectively.

Arriving by Bus or Rail

New York City's single bus terminals is the Port Authority at Eighth Avenue between 40th and 42nd Street, Tel: (212) 564-8484. Tickets can be purchased at the terminal prior to leaving. Buses are a convenient and fairly inexpensive way of traveling through the USA.

New York has two rail stations: Pennsylvannia station stretches between Seventh and Eighth avenues and 31st and 33rd Streets and serves as the departure point for the trains to Long Island among other. The second main station is Grand Central Terminal at Park Avenue and 42nd Street Tel: (212) 532-4900). There are several rail companies: Amtrak, 250 West 34th Street, One Penn Plaza, Suite 1435, Tel: (800) USA-RAIL); Long Island Railroad (LIRR), Tel: (718) 217-LIRR, or at Penn Station Tel: (212) 739-4200. Conrail 's number at Penn Station is (212) 736-6000. The Metro-North Commuter Railroad covers points north and northeast: Tel: (212) 532-4900 (at Grand Central Station).

Arriving by Car

Arriving by car for the first time can be a little confusing in the tangle of expressways that crisscross the city. If coming in from upstate, the New York State Thruway (87) will take you right down to the Triborough Bridge (get into the far right lane!) and to the FDR Drive. Thruways from New England connect with 287 that goes west to 87. The Long Island Expressway (495) heads west all the way to the Midtown Tunnel. The New Jersey Turnpike from the south and north has exits for the Lincoln Tunnel and George Washington Bridge respectively.

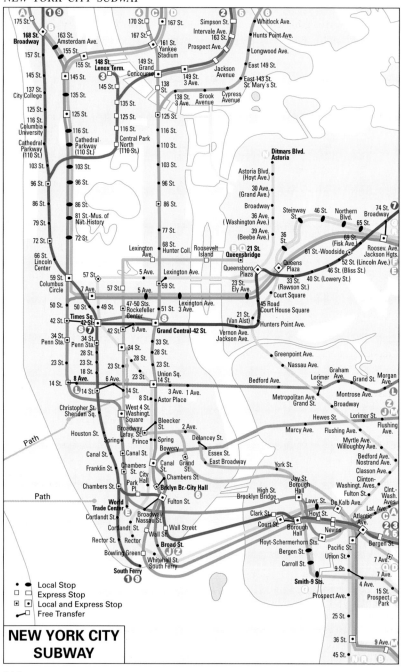

NEW YORK CITY
SUBWAY

Arriving by ship

It's no longer what one sees in the old movies, with hollering porters and celebrities being photographed on gangplanks. The terminal on the Hudson River between 48th and 52nd Streets is about as modern and streamlined as the terminals of JFK airport.

PRACTICAL TIPS

Accomodation

New York has ample accomodations for just about every budget. There are luxury and expensive hotels galore such as the Plaza, the Sheraton, the Waldorf-Astoria, the Marriotts; and then there is the YMCA, which has three addresses in New York: YMCA, McBurney 206 West 24th Street, NY 10011; Tel: (212) 741-9226. YMCA, Vanderbilt Branch, 224 East 47th Street, NY 10017; Tel: (212) 755-2410. YMCA, West Side, 5 West 63rd Street, NY 10023; Tel: (212) 787-4400. Another budget possibility is the American Youth Hostels, which is open to people of all ages and has four- to twelve-person dormitory rooms: 891 Amsterdam Avenue (West 103rd Street), NY 10025; Tel: (212) 932-2300. The New York Convention & Visitors Bureau, Inc. offers information: Two Columbus Circle, New York, NY 10019, Tel: (212) 484-1200, Fax: (212) 245-5943.

Airlines

For tickets in general there is the Airlines Ticket Office, 100 East 42nd Street, Tel: (212) 986-0888. Satellite Airlines Ticket Office, 1 East 59th Street, Tel: (212) 486-9290. Following are the addresses and telephone numbers of some of the major carriers. Any travel agent should be able to assist you in clearing ticket matters, or call information at the airports (see under Arriving).

Air Canada, Tel: (212) 869-1900, (800) 776-3000. **Air India,** Tel: (212)-753-8964. **Air New Zealand**, Tel: (800)-282-1234. **American Airlines**, Tel: (212) 455-6385, (800) 433-7300. **British Airways**, Tel: (800) AIRWAYS, **Continental Airlines**, Tel: (212) 735-1922. **Delta Airlines**, Tel: (212) 704-3025, (800) 221-1212. **Japan Airlines**, Tel: (212) 310-1414, (800) 525-3663. **KLM**, Tel: (800)-374-7747. Tel: (718) 565-3296, reservations (800) 452-2022. **Lufthansa**, Tel: (212)745-0700. **Northwest Airlines**, 299 Park Avenue (49th Street), NY 10017; Tel: (212) 557-4700. **Quantas Air**, Tel: (212)399-3457. **Scandinavian Airlines System (SAS)**, 138-02, Queens Boulevard, Jamaica, NY 11435; Tel: (718) 990-0686, (800) 221-2350. **Swissair**, 608 Fifth Avenue (at 49th Street), New York, NY 10020; Tel: (212) 969-5734, (800) 221-6644. **USAir**, One Penn Plaza, Suite 2028, NY 10019; Tel: (212) 736-3238, (800) 428-4322.

Alcohol

The legal age in the USA is 21, so if you happen to look young, don't forget to bring a legal ID. Driver and passengers are prohibited from drinking alcoholic beverages in a motor vehicle!

Auto Rentals

Several rental agencies run businesses within earshot of the airports. They usually have a bank of phones that only need to be picked up. Shuttles pick up the customer and take him or her to the car park. Try for a package deal and don't hesitate to compare prices and service. When renting the car *make sure the tank is absolutely full*! The gauge might show full, but often two or three gallons still fit that you will have to pay for later.

If not renting at the airport, shop for a good deal using the yellow pages from your hotel or place of residence.

Business hours

There are no official closing times in the USA and especially not in New York.

Any business involved in the service industry sector will try and keep going throughout the night. Banks close at 3 pm, on some days later, but they sometimes have 24-hour drive-in tellers; delis often provide victuals 'round the clock, shops and boutiques will now and then keep on going until 10 pm. In the country, one will find supermarkets that go on through the night selling anything from shoes to tomato paste. Quite a few stores open on Sundays.

Communications

Police, Fire, Ambulance 911
Operator 0
Directory assistance in own area code
. . . . 411
Assistance in other area
(area code) 555-1212
For toll-free number . . (800) 555-1212
Weather . . . . (212) 976-1212
Buses/Subways . . . . (718) 330-1234
Grand Central Station . (212) 532-4900
Main Post Office . . . . (212) 967-8585
Penn Station . . . . (212)7394200
Port Authority . . . . . (212) 564-8484

The American telephone service is privately owned. Phones are found all over the place but, unlike Europe, not in post offices! 0 for operator is the most important number to know. She/he will always be able to give you directions on how to do what. Telephones are used frequently to check up on reservations, check business hours, even to buy things. The 800 numbers are toll-free.

The public phones take quarters, which suffice for a local call. Operator or 800 numbers need no coins. If dialing a long-distance call (1 plus seven numbers or 1 + area code + seven numbers), the operator will automatically report, often as a computer voice, to tell you the toll for the first three minutes. When they are up, the voice will return. It's a little eerie at times. You may notice, however, that various phone companies own various phones. This becomes a bit of a nuisance

if you happen to have a phone card from another phone company, but it is possible to phone from a Nynex phone using, for example, an AT&T card. Just insist, or call the 800 number listed on your card.

On the subject of cards: Phone calls can be charged to a credit card (call the operator, 0, for details) or, better yet, to any number of phone cards issued by US phone companies.

International calls are dialed as follows: 011 + country code + city code + number.

Crime

New York is no joke in this respect. The basic rule is to keep a sharp eye out for criminal activity and don't take unnecessary risks. There are certain neighborhoods that should be avoided, notably the South Bronx, Bedford-Stuyvesant in Brooklyn, Harlem in Manhattan and parts of the Lower East Side especially around Avenues C and D. Manhattan's "bad" neighborhoods tend to lie cheek-by-jowl with the "good" ones. Walking around Columbia University is a perfect example, or around Chinatown. If driving through one of these "bad" areas, it is wise to keep ones car doors locked and windows closed. Carjacking has become a popular sport among criminals. The subway and Central Park should be avoided at night, indeed, even nocturnal constitutionals should be avoided in lonely areas – whereby getting mugged can happen anywhere at any time. By the same token, one should not overreact: Just be careful, leave large sums of money at your hotel but an old habit of New Yorkers is to keep a few bills handy to appease desperate muggers.

Currency

The dollar comes in bills of one, (very rarely two), five, ten, fifty, a hundred, five hundred, etc.... American bills all being the same size and color, make sure you know what unit you paid with and count your change. Cents, of which there are a hundred to the dollar, come in increments of one (called a penny), five (called a nickel) ten (called a dime), twenty-five (called a quarter) and fifty.

Changing money in New York is not as simple as in some countries. Not all banks just do it, and before changing at your hotel (if the service is offered) you may want to shop around for the best rate: **American Express Travel Agencies**, American Express Tower in the Financial Center, Tel: (212) 640-4885. American Express also has offices in Midtown and Downtown. **Canal Foreign Exchange**, 350 Fifth Avenue (33rd-34th Streets), Tel: (212) 279-6150. **Chemical Bank Foreign Currency Exchange**, 970 Eighth Avenue (57th Street), Tel: (212) 935-9935. **Thomas Cook Currency Services Inc.**, Rockefeller Center, 630 Fifth Avenue (50th Street), Tel: (212) 757-6915. **Freeport Money Exchange Inc.**, 49 West 57th Street, Tel: (212) 223-1200. **New York Foreign Exchange**, 61 Broadway, Suite 810, Tel: (212) 248-4700. **People's Foreign Exchange & Travel Inc.**, 500 Fifth Avenue, Tel: (212) 391-5270. **Piano Remittance Corp.**, 645 Fifth Avenue (51st-52nd Streets), Tel: (212) 909-9458. **Harold Reuter & Co.**, 200 Park Avenue (45th Street), Room 332E, Tel: (212) 661-0826. **Ruesch International**, 608 Fifth Avenue, Tel: (212) 977-2700.

With crime being what it is, Travelers' Checks made out in American dollars are highly advisable, as any bank will take them, and they can often be used for payment in shops and restaurants. Plastic money is always appreciated, too. Visa, Mastercard, American Express are all very common. Sometimes there is a small surcharge for credit card payment, especially at gas stations.

Driving around

If in possession of a foreign driver's license, you will need an international permit usually available at your country's national automobile club. Rental agencies by and large accept a European driver's license as adequate dispensation.

In general, Americans are tolerant drivers. The stringent speed limit on the highways (55 miles per hour, 88 kilometers per hour) do make for rather sleepy driving at times. Still, the slow pace out in the provinces should not be underestimated. Changing lanes is frequently done without prior use of blinker, or, apparently, looking in the rear-view mirror.

Driving around in a private car in the city is basically a waste of time and money, especially if you are intending to focus your exploration on Manhattan. Parking spaces are virtually impossible to find during business hours, garages are extremely expensive, and getting towed away is easy and costly. Parking at the curb in Midtown begins at 7pm and ends at 7 or 8 am. Garages in Midtown can cost US$ 25,00 *a night*. You may want to rent a car just to get out to Long Island, visit the other boroughs or to go upstate (see Auto Rentals above).

If you do decide to have a car, keep the following in mind: When crossing most bridges or driving through most tunnels, you will need pay a toll of US$ 2,50. (The Verrazano Narrows Bridge costs US$ 5,00 going to Staten Island, but leaving the island is free, Queensborough Bridge is free). You can purchase rolls of ten tokens at the toll booths for a little less. When approaching a toll station, make sure you get into the proper lane, "full service" if you do not have the exact change.

When parking, make sure you carefully read the little signs that put limits on the space. Parking in garages is a little different, too: You give your car to an attendant who does the work of finding a spot for you. (Small tip expected!)

On some avenues there is a green wave at 35 miles per hour; sticking to it can mean a pleasant cruise all the way down or up Manhattan without once touching the break or the clutch.

Driving in New York City, however, is not fun. Roads and expressways are poorly marked, the exchanges are often complex, requiring the driver to change over several lanes in a few hundred feet (see the Triborough Bridge from Queens to the FDR Drive!). Streets are in poor shape and there is lots of traffic. Pedestrians, cyclists, skateboarders and otherwise mobile individuals consistently ignore red lights, street directions, and traffic. Though it seems a nuisance, sometimes the only way of getting around is by using ones horn. Several radio stations provide traffic news, notably WCBS at 880 AM: every ten minutes "on the eights," (that is at 08, 18, 28, 38, 48, 58 past the hour).

Police are tough but not unfair, and usually they are fairly friendly. They cannot stop you for no apparent reason, though there are here and there exeptions to the rule. Remember, though, there is no point arguing with highway patrols. Your ticket will list the charge and give you a chance to plead guilty, guilty with an explanation or not guilty, whereby the latter two might mean a court case. The best bet is to stick to the law and the limits. Avoid drinking and driving.

Eating

Food is the last of problems in New York. One should try Chinese in Chinatown, Italian in Little Italy or Belmont in the Bronx, some seafood (City Island in the Bronx has a wide range of good, inexpensive places) and some American cooking. The concept of fast food has grown well beyond the leathery meat patty on a bun tasting of cardboard. There are delightful Middle Eastern places selling felafels, Greeks selling gyros, innumerable delis offering overstuffed pastrami sandwiches at any hour of day or night. In restaurants you will often be seated. A bus person brings water and

bread and clears the tables. The waiter or waitress takes care of the rest. Don't forget the 15 percent tip.

Electricity

The USA runs on 110 volts. Nowadays electronic equipment from razors to laptops often have a switch. Look for information in the manual if no switch is obvious on the surface of the gadget. (Some laptops switch automatically.)

Embassies and Consulates

Australia: 630 Fifth Avenue, Tel: (212)245-4000. Canada: 1251 Avenue of the Americas, Tel: (212)586-2400. Great Britain and Hong Kong: 845 Third Avenue, Tel: (212)745-0495. India: 3. East 64th Street (212)879-7800. Ireland: 2234 Massachusetts Avenue, Washington D. C. 20003, Tel: (202)462-3939. New Zealand: 37 Observatory Circle, NW Washington D.C. 20008, Tel: (202)-3284848. Singapore: (Permanent mission), 2 UN Plaza, 25th floor, Tel: (212)826-0840.

Getting Places in Brief

Manhattan, Bronx, Brooklyn and Queens are all covered by the New York Transit Authority.

For driving to Staten Island take either the FDR Drive or the West Side Highway south to the Battery Tunnel, get on the Gowanus Expressway or the Brooklyn Queens Expressway (287) going south to the Verrazano Narrows Bridge. Another way is through New Jersey (use the Holland Tunnel at the western end of Canal Street), head south on 78, then through Bayonne, NJ, to the Bayonne Bridge. Even simpler is catching a subway to South Ferry or Bowling Green, and then using the Staten Island Ferry (50c round-trip) to the Island.

Long Island is best visited by car. Take the Queens Midtown Tunnel that leads straight to the Long Island Expressway (495). Exit 44 goes to Oyster Bay in the north or to the Southern State Parkway in the south and from there to Montauk. If on a budget trip, or if you just want to visit one or two specific places on Long Island and then enjoy a swim, it might be cheaper and just as convenient to pick up an LIRR train at Penn Station.

Getting upstate is a matter of choice and budgets. The bus is cheapest and not unpleasant. Amtrak and Conrail also have good rail service. Renting a car is fairly inexpensive if one snags a special. If heading to Buffalo or Rochester exclusively, however, it might be wise to simply fly, as over 400 miles of New York State Thruway at 55 miles per hour can be the epitome of boredom.

Handicapped

The USA is quite ahead of many counties when it comes to handicapped services. Public places have ramps and adequate toilet facilities. Some tour operators even specialize in excursions for handicapped groups: **Creative Transportation & Tours**, 92-11, Merrick Blvd, Jamaica, NY 11433, Tel: (718) 658-6540. **Enterprise Transit**, E-15 Pleasant Avenue, Paramus, New Jersey 07652, Tel: (201) 845-0200.

Health

Make sure you have travel insurance as health care in the USA is atrociously expensive – albeit excellent, by and large. New York's main health risk is perhaps heat stroke in summer. As mentioned above, too, the tendency to overheat or overcool in Winter and Summer respectively can irritate ones pipes and eyes. Remember the threat of AIDS and be equipped!

For emergencies call 911. Other numbers to be used in the event of illness are: **Doctor's Home Referral Service:** Tel: (718)745-5900. **Doctor's Walk-In**: Tel: (212)683-1010. **Immediate Medical Care:** Tel: (212)496-9620. **American Dental Centers**: Tel: (212)586-3030.

Holidays

January 1, *New Year's Day*. Second Monday in January, *Martin Luther King's Birthday*. Third Monday in February, *President's Day. Good Friday and Easter*. Last Monday in May, *Memorial Day*. July 4, *Independence Day*. First Monday in September, *Labor Day*. Second Monday in October, *Columbus Day*. November 11, *Veterans Day*. Last Thursday in November, *Thanksgiving Day*. December 25, *Christmas Day*.

The Jewish high holidays and especially *St. Patrick's Day* on March 17th tend to shut down the city, inofficially.

Media

There are lots and lots of newspapers in New York. In certain neighborhoods you will find newspapers in Russian, in German, in Polish, in Spanish...

The *Times* of New York is *the* paper of the USA. On Sundays it is so massive you will share it with your neighbors. The *Wall Street Journal* hardly needs an introduction. The *Daily News* and the New York *Post* are in tabloid format. Content is sensational, a lot of inside New York news, gossip, slice and dice. The *Village Voice* has a good reputation for sharp journalism, good cultural reviews. The weekly *New Yorker*, combining articles with very fine cartoons and the rubric "Goings on about Town," is the ideal friend for a trip to the Big Apple. At US$ 1,95 it's quite a deal as well.

The radio dial can be twiddled whichever way for a wide range of music and information. The same goes for the television dial, whereby the most pleasant station is Channel 13, the Public Broadcasting System, which has no advertising and is usually first rate.

Sightseeing

There are numerous companies providing the service on land, water and in the air. Get in touch with the New York Convention & Visitors Bureau (see below).

Taxes

New York has a number of taxes that increase the marked purchase price of items considerably. The sales tax is currently 8.25 percent.

Time

New York time zone is GMT minus 6 hours.

Tipping

Tipping in New York (and in the rest of the USA too to a certain extent) amounts to an extra tax not to be found in the official budget. Though some visitors may be shocked at the 15 to 20 percent usually left waiters, it is wise to keep in mind that the restaurants are allowed to pay them well below the minimum wage precisely because the tip is so high. The tip itself is usually shared with the bus person, who brings bread and water and clears the dishes. A separate tip of about five percent goes to the captain in the fancy places. Taxi drivers also expect a 15 to 20 percent tip. Other unwritten taxes go to the bellhop (a dollar per person with luggage), the doorman (depending on the service rendered but no less than a dollar), and the porters at the airport, who expect a dollar a suitcase and 50 cents for smaller bags.

Tourist Offices

New York Convention & Visitors Bureau, Inc., Two Columbus Circle, New York, NY 10019, Tel: (212) 484-1200, Fax: (212) 245-5943. The Center publishes a shopping guide, a restaurant guide, a hotel guide, and a magazine for New York's visitors and conventioneers. For the Bronx call the Council on the Arts at Tel: (718) 931-9500, for Brooklyn it's Tel: (718) 783-4469; for Queens contact the Queens Boro President's Office at Tel: (718) 520-3823. For Staten Island the number is Tel: (718) 727-1900. For upstate New York contact the Chambers of Commerce in Albany Tel: (518) 434-1214, in Rochester Tel: (716) 454-2220 and in Buffalo Tel: (716) 852-7100.

Traveling in New York

New York's public transportation system is excellent in spite of its reputation as a haven for criminals. It boasts one billion users a year and runs 24 hours a day, whereby it might not be wise to use it during the late-night hours as it could indeed get a little dangerous at that time.

The subway (see map on page 244) has a far-reaching and dense network, and at US$ 1,25 for a token valid for a ride regardless of length, it is quite a deal. There are 25 transfer stations where the traveler can change lines without spending an extra token. Note, too, that there are a couple of lines that run local and express trains (the 4, 5, 6, for example) that allow you to get around at amazing speeds. The token is available in single units or in ten-packs at booths at the entrance of the stations. Bills of over US$ 20,00 will not be taken at the token booths.

New York's bus service also maintains a good network. Bus stops often show the route and schedule of the buses, and the driver has maps for each borough. A single ride in a bus costs US$ 1,25 (the money receiver at the front of the bus takes either subway tokens or change, no dollar bills!

New York has a large fleet (nearly 12,000 at last count) of licensed taxis, whose famous yellow color makes them quite visible. The cost (Summer 1992): US$ 1,50 basic fee, 25¢ for every 1/5 mile; 50¢ surcharge between 8 pm and 6 am. The waiting charge is 20¢ per minute. Just make sure the meter is activated the moment the ride starts. You should always collect a receipt. There is an umbrella number for information concerning cabs in New York: Tel: (212) 830-TAXI. For lost property, call Tel: (212) 840-4734; for complaints Tel: (212) 221-8294. You will have to give the cab's ID number(printed on the receipt).

AUTHORS

Steve Cohen, one of the project editors of this book, is a Durango-based writer and photographer specializing in travel and world-wide adventure. His work appears regularly in major North American newspapers as well as more than 150 publications around the world. He was project editor for *Nelles Guides Florida* and *The Carribean*.

Simon Fisher describes himself as a "freelance, private scholar." He hails from the Catskills originally, but now lives in Upper Bavaria, editing "for fun" and collecting butterflies.

Keith Greenberg lives in Queens, where he has authored 18 children's books, along with the women's self-defense guide *Attitude*. His articles have appeared in *USA Today*, *Cosmopolitan*, and other publications.

Leil Lowndes lives as a full time writer in New York and Italy. She is the author of three books and dozens of magazine articles for major publications.

Anne Midgette, one of the project editors of this book, was born in Oregon, but raised in New York and New Mexico. After studying Classics at Yale, she moved to Munich, Germany, where she works as an editor and writer. She has published in *Opera News* and *Spotlight,* among others.

Marton Radkai was born in New York, but grew up in France and England. He lives near Munich, where he earns his living as a writer, photographer, reporter and editor. He was project editor of the *Nelles Guide Hungary.*

Laurie Werner is a New York-based writer and member of the Society of American Travel Writers for many years. Her work appears in major North American newspapers and magazines including *Ladies Home Journal, Vis-a-vis* and *USA Weekend*. She contributed several articles in the *Nelles Guides Florida* and *The Caribbean.*

Deborah Williams is a former newspaper reporter and editor. She has traveled in the Caribbean for more than twenty years and her work has appeared in a wide variety of books, magazines and newspapers in the United States and Canada. She also wrote for the *Nelles Guide The Caribbean.*

PHOTOGRAPHERS

Archiv für Kunst und Geschichte,
Berlin   14, 16, 17, 18, 19, 21, 22,
          23, 24, 25, 26, 27, 28, 31, 32
Bondzio, Bodo   2, 12/13, 64, 90,
          95, 121, 145, 200
Dombrowski, B. / **Ebert**, Th. / jd   30
Gross, Andreas M. / jd   34, 38/39,
          74, 140, 143
Gruschwitz, Bernd F.   cover
Hartl, Helene   48, 88, 117, 156, 157
Hirner, Gert   1, 87, 91, 139
Ihlenfeldt, Detlef   40/41, 52, 94, 98/99,
          109, 129, 132, 148, 150, 158
Kienas, Falk   236
Kunert, Rainer E.   36, 114, 167
Courtesy of:
New York Convention & Visitors
Bureau   85, 154, 173
Nicolaus, Gisela   58, 60, 84, 186/187
Radkai, Marton   54, 112, 113, 136,
          162/163, 164, 170, 171, 172,
          174, 176, 178, 179, 182, 183, 184,
          188, 192, 194, 196, 201, 202, 206,
          210, 211, 212, 216, 217, 218, 219,
          220, 221, 222, 226, 228, 229, 230,
          232, 238
Seiden, Allan   37, 46, 50, 59, 65, 78,
          79, 80, 82, 100, 108, 130, 166
Skupy, Hans-Horst   44, 62, 63, 104, 105,
          106, 107, 133, 138, 153
Stadler, Hubert   72, 81, 83, 204/205,
          227
Thomas, Martin   10/11, 33, 42, 51, 53,
          66, 67, 70/71, 75, 86, 89, 92, 93,
          110, 116, 120, 124/125, 126, 128,
          134, 135, 142, 144, 146/147,
          151, 160/161
Zielcke, Hildegard   35, 141